MW01198987

A SONGWRITERS JOURNEY:

From The Wonder Years To The Golden Years

BOBBY WHITESIDE
With Robert Delich

American Ghost Media

Santa Monica, CA

Published by
AMERICAN GHOST MEDIA
1305 Pico Blvd
Santa Monica CA 90405

© 2021Bobby Whiteside Inc.
All Rights Reserved

No part of this book may be reproduced, or stored in any retrieval system, or transmitted in any form or by any means, electronic, mechanical, photocopying, recording, or otherwise, without written permission of the publisher. For information regarding permission write to American Ghost Media Attention Permission Department 1305 Pico Blvd, Santa Monica Ca 90405

ISBN:

1st edit: Jan Weeks
2nd, 3rd, 4th and 5th edit: Robert Delich

Book Cover Art: Susan Erwin Prouse
https://www.susanerwin.com

I have a question for you...

Do you have any questions?

No? Well ...here are some things you can ask *me.*

- Did you lock a chicken in your father's car on a hot day?
- What were you doing in New York (when you were 16) hanging around jazz nightclubs?
- Did you really get kicked out of your fraternity, college, and the Chicago Conservatory of music?
- How did you come to work for the mob?
- How did you find yourself able to write for big orchestras without any formal training?
- What brought you to London?
- Tell me about being in Hollywood at Capitol Studios, conducting a 76-piece orchestra for Barbra Streisand as she recorded your arrangements of two of

your songs?

- How did you survive the worst tragedy of your life?

- After you moved to Nashville, how did you handle losing half of your home, your recording studio, and 50 years' worth of music archives in a flood?

- You made it to the golden years. Are you surprised?

- Do you think you'll outlive the battery in your pacemaker?

To answer all these questions and more... turn the page.

DEDICATION

To Brenda

for her unconditional
love and support.

THANK YOU

There are not enough hours in the day to express my gratitude to my amazing friend, Robert Delich. Not only did he convince me to write this book, he spent hundreds of hours looking over my shoulder, correcting my mistakes, and helping the book make sense...a daunting task. I think I owe him a car!

PROLOGUE

My book is not a primer for how to live when you get older. It's the entertaining story of a musician (me) and my turbulent path through the hilarious, but sometimes heart stopping complexities of the music business, to reach the golden years.

I've been a writer all my life. Stories are written with words. Words convey emotion. Words make you laugh and cry, but always remember that your words have consequences. Everything you do, or say in your life has an effect on someone or something. Some stories should never be told, but there are so many that should.

As a writer, I use words to paint visual scenes that come to life in someone else's mind. I've been unencumbered by walls and rules, but armed with an arsenal of words that fuel my desire to relate my version of the world to others.

I've been lucky enough to reap the benefits of a constant flow of creative ideas from all the tales the world spins, which primed my imagination and helped me create articulate thoughts from random words. Despite all the sad, vicious things that exist, and too many people dying from indifference, I have somehow managed to remain an incurable optimist as I attempt to create memorable stories that flow from my heart onto a page.

There is not one second of my journey that I would change. As I look back at the tumultuous times I lived through, I know that someone watched over me. I've had the rare good fortune to live many of my dreams, doing what I love — writing words and creating music.

I have found that life is a play everyone performs in, that exposes undeniable truths. There will be pain you'll never speak about, your heart will be broken, you will laugh, you will be afraid, and you will cry. Eventually, your body may fail, and your mind will have a mind of its own. You may see faces you can't name, and forget endings to stories, but you will never forget the days when you were fearless.

Now I'm living in my Golden Years. It's a critical time. I feel that the world is a tinderbox, breathlessly waiting for the one tiny spark that can fracture our lives forever. Human rights have become a tiresome talking point. Music no longer has a melody. Far too many children are growing up without the safety net of a loving family. Rejection used to make you try harder; now it simply crushes you into the ground.

We don't touch when we dance. We don't talk, we text. We don't have family conversations. We sit at the same table and ignore each other as we punch letters into electronic devices. Our children live in a two-dimensional world hunched over their iPhones.

There is no friendly political discourse. Facebook has given everyone a voice, yet there is still but one microphone. The flag is disrespected and Jesus is not allowed to come to school. It breaks my heart.

But I am still the luckiest guy in the world. Despite the personal tragedies, the tough times, the ups and downs of life and romance, and all the crazy episodes that dotted my life, I managed to survive! I have always shared unconditional love and support with my devoted family, some very close friends and especially my wife, Brenda, my partner, my best friend and my love, whom I couldn't live without.

So now I'm on the other side of the mountain—and this is how I got here. It's been a bumpy ride on a winding path, a life of stories in the music business. Here's the story of my journey from the wonder years to the *Golden Years.*

For a long time I assumed I had an unremarkable childhood. However, as my life unfolded, it became clear to me that many of my early experiences left an indelible impression on the framework of my future thoughts and endeavors. With that in mind...let's start at the beginning.

Chapter 1

May, 1941. World War II raged around the world as Hitler heightened his savage attacks on one country after another. The United States sold war bonds for the first time, unaware that a blinding attack on Pearl Harbor would decimate the armed forces later that year and they would be at war with Japan. The British navy destroyed the fearsome German battleship, the Bismarck, Stalin became premier of the Soviet Union, and a Nazi U-boat scored their first American kill: the USS Robin Moore warship.

At home, the United States formed the Civil Defense Office as Americans worked tirelessly to supply our allies with significant and much needed military supplies. There was a sense of impending doom, as Americans feared that their country would be dragged into the battle at some point.

On the domestic front, Bob Hope performed his first USO show, the movie *Citizen Kane* was released, Cheerios were introduced, and the Yankees played the first night baseball game ever.

In a small town in New Jersey, a fresh breath of spring filled the air as the last winter chill dissipated in the shimmering rays of the warming sun. The robins sang sweet songs as they foraged for nesting materials. A baby rabbit scampered across the yard as bright yellow daffodils magically awakened and smiled up at the blue skies. A pastel display of tulips brightened up the gardens, poking through a thin layer of leftover autumn leaves. During this time of renewal and new life, at 5:43 a.m., another seed sprouted, and I emerged into this amazing world.

(Now, I realize that as a baby boy, I was incapable of conjuring up a cohesive stream of thoughts, but pulling from the stories I have heard through the years, I think the early chapters of my life would read something like this.)

I arrived in this world smiling! Nestled in my mother's arms, I couldn't see her face. The first time I came up for air, her loving looks welcomed me into the world. Then I caught the first glimpse of my father, a serious looking dark-haired man in a grey suit, who seemed disappointed that he didn't have a chance to finish a mystery magazine article he started in the waiting room. When he put his arms around my mother and gently touched my cheek, I knew I'd become part of a loving family.

All I could see of my sister was a curly mop of blonde hair and two blue eyes peering at me curiously over the side of the bed. I think she would have preferred a dog, but she ended up stuck with me!

I left the hospital as an unexceptional baby and performed functions common to newborns. I exhibited absolutely no flashes of brilliance, leaving my parents devoid of any fleeting hope that they might have propagated and produced a future Einstein.

I knew what I wanted, but found it hard to communicate my desires using baby talk. Of course, that turned into a two-way street, as I didn't understand my parent's version of baby talk either. So, we waited until we found common ground with a language that both of us understood: English!

My parents lit up with exuberant smiles when I sat up or rolled over. (My sister might have been right about the dog thing.) In the meantime, I rejected all efforts they made to feed me baby squash.

They named me Robert Bruce Whiteside after studying the family tree and finding a blood connection to Robert Bruce, the Scottish Warrior. When my father snapped a picture of me wearing a kilt, I thought he might have been sorry that I hadn't popped out as another girl.

Now, I know this is from an old joke, but for the longest while I thought my name was "Nono." It takes a long time for a kid to complete all the actions that constitute that bad-boy list, sometimes years!

As I became more adept at getting into mischief, the response was elevated to a stern frown and the use of my two first names. This goes on for the rest of my life, but always remember if they use all three of your names you are really in the deep stuff.

My vocabulary increased...in a surprising way. One night as my sister and I sat in our front room, she was acting like a psycho and doing evil things sisters do to torture their little brothers. Being too young to understand the consequences of an occasional youthful pornographic slip of the tongue, in a momentary lapse of basic childhood wisdom, I angrily and loudly called her an "asshole."

Well, the next minute Darth Vader (looking suspiciously like my father) thundered into the living room with fire blazing from his eyes, smoke pouring from his ears, and I was the recipient of one of the three spankings I can remember. In a futile quest for vengeance, I tried to even the score with my sister. I lied when I told her I was sorry, but I knew I'd have to raise the bar of ruthless reprisals if I expected to survive.

Occasionally when we misbehaved my mother chased us around the house waving a wooden spoon, but we could outrun her. I saw the twinkle in her eyes and never believed she really wanted to catch us.

Both of my parents evolved from interesting backgrounds. My father's father served as a sheriff in Boulder, Colorado, spent some time mining for gold, then purchased a sprawling tract of land and took up farming. My dad came into this world on the family's gold mining site. He shared his adolescence with two brothers, and the family ties that held them together strengthened through the years.

They worked tiring, endless hours to put the oldest (Uncle Bud) through college, and then Bud found employment and helped the next brother (my dad) through college, majoring in Mechanical Engineering. He was only 16 years old. Following that, my dad saved enough money to pay for his younger brother's higher education.

My dad related an occasional anecdote about life in the country. Working long hard days on a farm left them sore and weary, but somehow they found time for fun and mischief. He shared memories about riding bikes off the barn roof, tipping outhouses and cows, and sneaking off to swim in the *bottomless* creek that was only 18 inches deep.

There were many stories full of giving and sacrifice, and how the family always pulled together. I noticed a common thread running through their lives. They prided themselves on walking a path that never compromised their honesty or integrity, and they lived by the belief that a handshake counted as a sacred commitment. They led by example, and I inherited the standards I would hold myself to in my future conduct and dealings with others.

I loved visiting my grandfather's farm in Colorado. On every trip, we paid the obligatory visit to Dad's crazy aunt, a self-professed psychic. She fawned over her pride and joy, a mean ugly parrot named Grady. The crusty old bird, a mottled green mess with a mangy body cratered by the loss of feathers, personified the word *nasty*. That squawker was a nightmare, a sinister apparition. He waddled around on the floor, his beady eyes flashing like lasers searching for a target, until he zeroed in on me. Then that flying rat poked small tears in my clothes as it clawed its way toward my face. Upon reaching his kill zone, that ominous creature dug his talons into my shoulder and stared at me like a hawk looking at a mouse! I wanted to feed Grady a cracker—a firecracker!

One scorching summer day, Dad excused me from the shrouded house and the killer bird. He hadn't learned a thing about leaving me alone with time on my hands. Never having owned a pet, I thought it might be fun to take a chicken home. I opened the passenger side door, and shagged a fat white hen into my father's new Packard with spiffy cloth seat covers. Then I closed the door.

About an hour later my dad came out, took one look at his car and called me by all three names. Really loud! Uh-oh! Hey, I was just a kid. I had no idea that a chicken could crap that much, locked in a hot car with spiffy cloth seat covers.

It should come as no surprise that this constituted grounds for spanking number two, not to mention hours of scrubbing chicken poop off of everything. Every time we rode in the car, my father gave me the evil eye as the family rolled down all the windows. My dad's shiny new Packard smelled like a chicken coop for months.

One other summer, after hours of groveling and begging, Dad deemed me responsible enough to own a real Daisy Red Ryder BB gun. As we wandered around the farm, I blasted away at rusty tin cans and pieces of broken beer bottles. After an hour of aimless shooting, boredom reared its ugly head.

I spotted a big cow across the pasture. Aha! My dad looked distracted as he searched for crystals in the dirt, so I tossed off a quick shot at the heifer. The little devil on my shoulder assured me that cows had thick hides, and she would never even feel it. The devil lied! My BB hit that cow squarely in the butt. She jumped three feet up in the air, let out an earth-shattering HUMMOOWAH, and exploded through the corral fence starting a stampede.

As most of you have probably guessed by now, this incident became known as spanking number three. The furious look on my dad's face led me to believe I'd never be allowed to touch another gun, until I was at least 35.

Chapter 2

Mom didn't share many stories about growing up so I seem to have a shortage of material, but here is what I remember.

My mother grew up in New Jersey, and her family enjoyed copious amounts of money. My grandfather made his fortune by inventing the process to dye the leather that covered all the Lackawanna Railroad train seats. After mom graduated from college, she entered the job market as a schoolteacher.

Grandpa's business disappeared when the railroad wanted to buy his leather patent, and out of stubbornness, he refused to sell it. His false pride prevented him from working for someone else. Poof! Their lavish lifestyle eroded away, and reality set in. My mother, her sister, and two brothers had to chip in and contribute what they could to help their parents meet expenses in their smaller house.

Grandpa pretended to be desperately searching for a job, but my grandmother played detective and followed him one day. She found him sitting on a weather worn, wooden park bench. He'd been spending his days perusing the paper, nipping on whiskey straight from the bottle, barely camouflaged in a brown paper bag.

He never held another job, and he passed away after his liver answered an unavoidable call from the head bourbon angel at the grain alcohol sanctuary in the sky. A few years after lowering Grandpa into his designated spot in the family plot, my parents told me the true story of Grandpa's demise. On that day, I made up my mind that I'd always find a way to take care of my family and do whatever it took to support them.

My father, an innovative genius, landed an engineering job at Bell Labs, the research arm of *AT&T*. He worked with the team that developed the first trans-Atlantic cable, communications into space (Telstar), and he cleverly fashioned a monitoring concept for watts lines and their usage with eight cheap alarm clocks he bought from the dime store.

Unfortunately, he received little credit for his work as his unethical bosses, in their hunger for affirmation and advancement, always took credit for his work. It really upset me when he refused to address it, and I made up my mind that I'd never be anybody's doormat... a defining moment in my life.

During the lean financial years on the farm, dad learned to conserve his money. When he met and married my mother, they were able to purchase the house I grew up in. Shortly after that, he invited my mother's parents to move in with us. My father spent half of his life worrying about others, and as I put him through a million changes with my in and out of school antics, he used the other half to worry about supporting me after I failed in the music business.

Dad dreamed I would graduate from college with an Engineering Degree. I didn't want to! Case closed, or so I thought at the time. In an impulsive moment of condescension, I gave it a brief shot when I first arrived at Northwestern, but more on that later. He should have known I had no mechanical ability by the way I hated standing for hours, only to hand him the wrong tools, when he was working on our furnace. That dilapidated pile of junk gave him more trouble than the smoking mechanical mess in the movie *A Christmas Story.*

Despite the passage of time, I vividly remember certain portions of my childhood. Every other summer we'd vacation in Colorado, to visit the farm and the abundance of relatives that lived in the West. The assembled families made the shoppers on Black Friday look like a small group. They were warm, wonderful country folks, who always greeted us with open arms and stacks of food.

I learned how to ride horses and drive

tractors, and I finally crawled back into my father's good graces after the cow incident. With his dubious blessing, I hunted prairie dogs with a borrowed .22 rifle, even though I hardly ever hit one. It reminded me of playing Whack-a-Mole with a teaspoon.

My infatuation with fishing started at an early age. I started with a small plastic pole and drowned some worms. Then, I moved up to bait casting and spinning rods, and I spent hours throwing lures at a bucket in the yard to help me cast accurately. When we visited my aunt's rustic log cabin in Estes Park, I moved up another level by learning to fly fish with a long pole, a floating line and a lure that looks like a small bug.

Every morning I climbed down the mountain to a sparkling, winding stream to fly fish for the elusive, but numerous speckled brook trout, and managed to land two or three of those feisty little fellows. My aunt fried up my catch, as part of her daily sizable mountain breakfasts.

We enjoyed twilight drives up into the park where enormous herds of deer and elk grazed by the side of the road. I never ceased to be amazed by the majestic Rocky Mountains and the breathtaking beauty of the stunning explosion of colors emanating from the Colorado sunsets.

I spent a couple of miserable years embedded with the Boy Scouts, and worked my way up to a star rating, one quarter-sized cloth merit badge at a time. I discovered I was allergic to every piece of camping equipment in existence, filled with down feathers. In addition, I suffered several asthma attacks, as the smoke from the campfire always seemed to be blowing toward us.

I embarked on my first overnight hike and pitched my pup tent. The scoutmaster advised all the campers to dig a deep rain trench around our tents. In a fit of adolescent laziness, my tent-mate and I blew him off and made about a 2" indentation in the leaves around our army surplus canvas structure.

That night, the Lord answered Indian rain dances all over the country with a downpour of cold water, and Thor lobbed lightning bolts in every direction. Um...we also neglected to use the rubber ground cloths that separated our sleeping bags from the ground.

As an icy Niagara Falls flowed into our tent, I suffered through the most miserable night of my life, frozen, wet, and sneezing. My eyes were watering from those pesky feathers in my sleeping bag, and I violated the God and moral part of the Scout oath with some serious vocabulary.

I painfully wheezed my way through several other pathetic pioneering experiences. I hated scouting! I finally caught a break when my father sputtered out a well-known Archie Bunker phrase, "Waaaaaaait a minute," when one of the other parents informed him that our scoutmaster was gay. So I emerged from the woods, never to wear khaki again. My sons were forced to accept the fact that their scouting fathers' weekends would be minus one.

Some years later: one night in LA, after I guided my oldest son on a tour of *Dan Tana's*, the *Whiskey-a-Go-Go*, the *China Club*, and several other venues, we returned to the hotel. With a cigar in his mouth, a cold beer in his hand, he gleefully observed the bikini babes splashing in the swimming pool. "You know what, Dad? This makes up for all those Scout hikes you missed."

In sixth grade, my mother demanded that I go to dancing school. I don't like to talk about that traumatic period of my life. The boys looked like idiots, stepping on the toes of girls that were six inches taller than they were. The overdressed young ladies exhibited flashing smiles, not because they were happy, but from the disco ball reflecting off the silver braces on their teeth. Dancing school was the beginning of my disdain for dress codes and formal clothing; especially black woolen suits, white shirts, paisley ties, skinny black socks, and shiny slippery-soled Florsheim shoes with laces.

Uncle Jack showed up at our house with a

puppy under his arm. Boy, you should have seen my father's face. Priceless! I thought the poor dog would reside in the basement for the rest of his natural life, but he finally weaseled his way into my father's heart, and became a full-fledged member of the family. The mischievous mutt ended up starring in one of my favorite stories.

I thought of my mom as a loving, sweet lady... very classy and conservative. Once every three months she hosted a bridge club, consisting of twelve overly sophisticated ladies. All gussied up, they'd arrive at our home to play bridge on card tables covered with white tablecloths, situated in our living room.

The pseudo-sophisticated cosmopolitan ladies were perched on padded folding chairs, trying to focus on playing cards while keeping an ear out for juicy gossip. Suddenly, an odor permeated the room that smelled like sulfuric acid mixed with rotten eggs. Twelve prissy ladies dressed in their Sunday best, tried to be discreet, while sneaking glances at each other. The room went silent.

My mother looked down to see the dog peeking out from under one of the tables, with a tablecloth draped over one eye. His demeanor, tainted by a deer-in-the-headlights look and an expression that oozed guilt, left no doubt as to who did it! He beat an inglorious retreat to the basement to evade scathing looks from the ladies, not to mention the "wait until later" look that shot from my mother's squinted eyes. Every woman in the room silently thanked the Lord that the dog did it.

On a sad note, my grandmother's mind was failing and we had to place her in a nursing home. I often visited her, but when she began to call me Charlie (my mother's brother's name), Mom told me I could stop going to see her.

Some years later, I mentioned it to my uncle, Charlie. I informed him that Grandma ended up calling me Charlie, so I discontinued my visits. He nodded somberly. Then I said, "So she died really pissed off at you!" Glad my family had a sense of humor!

Other than taking mandatory piano lessons and being forced to play mellophone in the school band, my early years were normal for the times. The mellophone was the instrument they gave you, when all the others were taken. It resembled a French horn, but was played with the same fingering techniques as a trumpet.

We covered miles on our bikes, saved each other from imaginary Indians by wearing white cowboy hats, and relentlessly firing our cap pistols. As pioneers, we forged paths and discovered secret places in the dense woods, built impregnable forts and tree houses, and sometimes skipped the make believe and simply hung out. We spent endless hours on the slides and swings at the playground. Visiting friends set the stage for us to indulge in wild make-believe adventures pretending to be cops and robbers. Adding to our endlessly available means of entertainment were games of marbles, pickup sticks, hide and seek and hopscotch. I rarely found myself bored, and my brain actually developed in three dimensions. I consider myself lucky that iPhones hadn't been invented yet. Sadly, our grandchildren will never get to experience a simple uncomplicated childhood, unencumbered by fears of kidnapping and threats from some increasingly dangerous members of society. Unfortunately, today these circumstances force parents to keep a short leash on their kids, and a GPS in their backpacks.

The formative years helped me set the foundation for my future life. I wanted to live in a world full of family values, ambition, compassion, honesty, and love. I was bound and determined to commit to the same incredible amount of integrity that my father and his father lived by.

At the time, I didn't realize how extensively those hated piano and mellophone lessons would influence my career in the years to come.

Chapter 3

Oh, crap! Not dodgeball again! When you are a sophomore in high school, weigh 136 pounds, and one of the last guys to be picked for any team in gym; you have but one function in dodgeball. You are a target!

This sport taught me one of life's most valuable lessons. If you see it coming at you, DUCK, STUPID! Just saying! If nothing else, you learn how to keep a low profile, something you might find helpful later in life.

Today, our kids are given the option not to play dodgeball because they might suffer severe, but unsubstantiated trauma. Instead, they are allowed to put puzzles together, or play games on their iPhones, safely stashed in their delegated "safe spaces." Therapists and crisis counselors will be available. So sad!

Don't get me started on not keeping score! The *modern* politically correct parents and faculty feel they must make it a priority to see no one's feelings get hurt. So they give the pathetic little sissies a trophy anyway! And these kids are going to grow up and run the country? Hah!

Then there's the problem of rapidly emerging

addiction to electronics. As George Carlin once said about kids and their "bromances" with technology, "The next generation of kids is going to be an ass with fingers."

I struggled socially in high school. Not being smart enough to be an authentic nerd, or cool enough to be one of the guys, I spent a lot of time nesting in nerd purgatory. This, however, had its advantages. In biology, I partnered with a high school Einstein, named Dennis Richie, the gentleman who went on to invent Linux. A timid girl, who wore the same black and red sweater every day and blankly stared at me through horn-rimmed Coke-bottle thick glasses, bailed me out in algebra.

We didn't call it bullying in those days. The Internet didn't exist, so other kids couldn't ruin your world anonymously. My friends and I in nerd purgatory were summarily ignored, pushed aside, occasionally punched in the arm, and recipients of occasional disparaging words.

After cracking both my wrists in basketball, failing at football, and being an inconsequential team member on soccer and baseball teams, I realized I was a useless cog in the wheel of athletic endeavors.

It was my misfortune to have a pole-vaulting accident that dislocated every vertebra in my back. I had no idea how this injury would change my path of life at a later date.

Residing at the bottom of the barrel of organized sports, I became an equipment manager, sometimes known as a water boy, for the football team. This demeaning job came with a couple of perks. I had sideline seats at every game, and it opted me out of wearing scratchy marching band uniforms!

I could have passively suffered through a really miserable time in high school, but I flashed back to that doormat thing and decided to forge my own way. The actual time frame of some of this story is a little foggy, so forgive me if I skip around a bit.

What could be as cool as being in a car club with a fancy jacket in high school? The popular guys formed two clubs called the Mustangs (bright red jackets), and the Vikings (vivid green and blue jackets). Everyone admired their new threads, but I didn't think they knew squat about fixing cars. They must have misplaced my application, as I didn't get invited to join either one. I remained unjacketed, ignored, and unacknowledged in my plain tan windbreaker.

To amuse myself, I pedaled my prized English racing bike across town to watch the champion boxer, Floyd Patterson, as he trained for his next fight. I always found him to be friendly and approachable. One day he taught me how to throw a punch. Big stuff for a kid!

On my way to see Floyd, I'd glided by a mammoth weathered red barn and saw a group of men working on cars. My curiosity got the best of me, so I stopped for a look. The sight of a collection of beautifully customized show cars, dragsters, and pristine restored classics intrigued me. The barn seemed to be set up to do everything automotive. I entered into a neighborly atmosphere, where numerous older men worked on automobiles in various stages of completion.

They invited me to attend meetings, and tap into their comprehensive knowledge of automobiles. "The Squires" were a bona fide car club, made up of consummate pros and one of the most respected custom auto clubs in New Jersey. The group competed in the dragsters they built, and won trophies for their unique, glittering custom-built autos and the brilliantly refurbished classics, at car shows.

Life became significantly more interesting for me the day I appeared at school wearing my bright red Squires jacket. Now *that* was a jacket! It was a new experience to be the recipient of envious looks, even though they were only directed at my meaningful apparel, and I metaphorically thumbed my nose at the self-anointed high school elite.

My parents turned me loose in my sixteenth

summer, and I journeyed to my uncle's home in Colorado. There, you could earn a driver's license at 16. My fearless cousin laughed off the grey hair resulting from her skillful lessons, as she taught me how to operate a car on country roads covered with slippery sand. (I utilized these skills many years later driving on the icy streets during Arctic Chicago winters.)

My uncle introduced me to Bob and Tom, two local country boys. Bob owned several beautiful horses and I learned to ride bareback, my knees clasping the horse's neck like an Indian. Boy, did that take balance.

A black stallion with a violent disposition reared and snorted every time someone came near him. He restlessly paced back and forth in an L shaped corral, and did everything in his power to avoid us. After we caught him, I climbed on his back to race from one end of the enclosure to the other. Halfway down the pole fence, the corral made a sharp 90-degree shift to the right. That vicious horse tried to scrape me off on the corner fence post as he slammed around the turn. If I timed it right, he ended up with bruised ribs. If I timed it wrong, a football sized bruise appeared, like magic, on my thigh.

One of his favorite equine misdeeds involved wading into the muddy farm pond and rolling in the water when I least expected it. It took both my friends to haul me out from under that flailing horse before I drowned.

Bob established himself as a skilled bronco-riding, barrel-racing rodeo competitor. He lacked the funds to purchase a farm trailer, so he constructed rickety elevated wooden sides for the bed of his pickup, and he was able to squeeze two of the animals into the enclosure.

One night, after they loaded the black stallion into the enclosure, I stood on the ground next to the truck holding his reins, waiting for them to prod the other horse up the ramp. A lightning bolt blasted a hole in a nearby parking lot and scared the stallion half to death.

Panicked, he exploded into action. He reared up on his hind legs and rolled over the side and crashed to the ground, barely missing me. Controlling a 1000-pound panicked horse would have been a chore for the Hulk, and I only weighed a scrawny 140 pounds. He reared, and I dangled four feet off the ground. Hooves flashed on either side of me. I had nightmarish thoughts of being trampled to death.

Fortunately, when he came back down, two men grabbed him before he could jump again. My shaky knees gave out and I stumbled over to sit on a barrel, counting my blessings.

On an occasional dusty afternoon, the three of us trolled through the burly tumbleweeds in the pastures, hunting for jackrabbits in Bob's '48 Ford. One guy drove; the other two carried rifles, each perched on a running board of the old car.

On one of our hunting expeditions, we spotted an elusive maniacal jackrabbit and fired simultaneously. There was nothing but a whirling dust cloud where we marked that bouncing animal, and we proudly believed we blew it to bits.

All of a sudden that damn rabbit came hopping out of the swirling haze, skipping around like a drunken Bugs Bunny. That elusive little bugger had more dance moves than Michael Jackson.

I returned from Colorado to New Jersey in the fall a crack shot, and a reasonably proficient driver, two distinctly different new skills. I thanked Bob for the shooting lessons, and my cousin for her patience. It would be some years till I had the time to target shoot, but only a short period of time before I could cruise the neighborhood and vanquish the turnpike.

Nine months remained before I could legally drive in New Jersey. I started on a quest to find transportation. Miraculously I found the means for my future mobility! My prize; a 1940 Ford coupe, a rusted wreck that had been sitting in my neighbor's yard for about ten years, that I bought for $30.

After my father weathered the initial shock of his first look at the lean, mean, junk machine, he helped me tow it to the back of our driveway. He retreated into the house, shaking his head. (You are going to feel sorry for my father by the end of this book. I never did turn out to be the model son he hoped for.)

I started at the beginning, working under the hood. I did a massive amount of work and replaced many parts of the motor. My part time job at an auto parts store got me a nice discount.

I switched on the ignition, ground the starter for a couple of minutes, and made some adjustments to the carburetor. I'll be damned if that old flat head motor didn't start up.

Then, I tackled the toughest part, spending hours sanding the paint down to bare metal and filling the rust spots and dents with fiberglass and body putty. I attempted to replace the kingpins that held the front tires on, but needed to call for help from the Squires after a leaf spring in the front suspension exploded and almost took my head off. I carefully primed the old relic and spray-painted it a flaky bronze color. Not bad for an initial investment of $30!

The Ford wasn't quite ready for the road yet. I blew out 17 candles and headed into the next phase of my life with a spanking new driver's license in my wallet. Until the beast was up and running, my dad gave me his little washed out ugly green Austin. It looked like a baby hump-backed '47 Packard. I hated that color, so I sanded it down and painted it maroon. Much to my dismay, it turned the same color as Barbie's convertible.

I cringed every time I drove my repugnant pink jalopy down the road, trailing blue smoke. At least twice a week I'd leave school at the end of the day and find it on the sidewalk—or just plain missing. The football players picked it up and stuck it wherever they wanted. I was relieved when I launched my freshly painted Ford onto the road.

My bronze bomber had one small glitch: a tooth missing from one of the transmission gears, which was not necessarily a bad thing. When I shifted the car into first gear, floored the gas pedal and spun the wheels, my ancient clunker jumped into second all by itself. This made it accelerate faster than other cars of the same vintage caliber as I didn't have to waste a second engaging the clutch to shift. It was surprisingly quick for a gnarly old car.

After I racked up some east coast highway miles, I made an appearance at the drag races in Vineland, New Jersey. Surprise! I won a couple of trophies in the old car class. I couldn't take them home because my parents assumed that I'd spent the day at the beach. Being the only one who knew the secret of the transmission, it didn't surprise me when the competing drivers thought I might be cheating. Other racers could challenge the win, and make you disassemble your car, to see if you added any illegal accessories to make it run faster. I refused to let anyone touch my bronze baby, so my career in drag racing ground to a quick halt.

A quirky, but brilliant, chemistry teacher named Doc Lukens had become a legend with the students. He continually blew things up and inadvertently set small smoky blazes in his classroom. The fire department responded to at least one call a month and the school evacuated many times because of Doc. His reputation reached new heights the day he made an abundance of a mixture that smelled like rotten eggs and seeped into the ventilation system. Inspired by Doc, I embarked on my next adventure—this time in munitions.

Doc taught us how to make flash powder. We placed a small amount on an asbestos sheet and set a match to it, resulting in an immediate pyro reaction.

I, and two of my lab cohorts, felt that we could improve on his formula and make superior gunpowder. I vaguely remember a concoction of powdered aluminum, magnesium oxide, and saltpeter (all available at hardware and drug stores), but I'm probably missing something—which is a good thing.

We formulated an incendiary batch at my friend Kenny's house, and he produced a small empty .410 shotgun shell. We poured some of our gunpowder in the shell, added some cardboard packing and covered it up with electrical tape. After a visit to the hobby store we returned with some Jetex fuse. I cut a small hole in our baby bomb with my old scout knife and inserted the end of our makeshift igniter. We lit that sucker in his backyard, and it exploded with a reasonably loud bang. Were we satisfied? Nooooo!

Always on the quest for bigger and better, we speculated about how enormous the explosion might be if we used a large empty 10-gauge shotgun shell. We found one, packed it *full* of powder, taped it shut, and inserted the end of a 20-inch fuse into a tiny hole in the side of the shell. In the middle of a spontaneous moment of bad judgment, I suggested, "Why waste it? Let's set it in Nancy Jacobs' backyard."

We wore hoodies and dark clothing as we set out on our nighttime stealth mission through the woods. Ducking from tree to tree, we navigated to the thickets behind Nancy's house without being detected. We set our carefully crafted masterpiece on an old cedar shingle to keep it dry. Kenny wrapped the fuse halfway down a cigarette, lit the smoke, took a couple of sinful puffs, and placed it next to our explosive device, giving us time to escape before the cigarette burned down enough to light it. Pulsing with excitement, we beat a disorganized retreat four blocks back to my house. We waited to see if anything would happen.

Boy, did it ever! When a cherry bomb goes off it goes bang. When our cataclysmic weapon detonated, it boomed. A massive percussive "whump" rattled windows!

We were slapping each other on the back and bumping fists when we heard the fire engines. We neglected to take into account the fact that Nancy lived two blocks from the CIBA Pharmaceutical Company. The fire department thought the plant exploded. There were cops and firefighters all over the place looking for the site of the detonation. Then, the FBI showed up.

I lived in fear for the next week. I thought we were in the clear, until Kenny ratted us out to his mother. I missed going to jail by a nanosecond. My mother spent a substantial amount of time at school, and I worried about my father stacking my clothes out in front of the house.

A few days later, we convened for a post-event meeting in Kenny's bedroom and he proudly held up a remaining jar of our contraband powder. We were discussing how to get rid of it when Kenny lit a cigarette. The jar flared up in my hand. I ended up in the hospital with second-degree burns, but I got even with the little snitch. I threw the flaming bottle out of his window and set fire to his roof.

I dumped the mellophone, switched to

trumpet, and found out I was a natural. My parents were extremely happy with this progression of events, until I walked into the house with my first guitar, after an impulsive purchase. I sensed that my father felt the evil spirits of Little Richard and Elvis entering our own staunchly conservative, traditional Scotch Presbyterian house. He recognized the devil when he saw it.

"What the hell are you going to do with that?" he grumbled.

"Learn to play it!" His pitiful sigh weighs on my memory.

I figured I'd land more chicks on the beach playing "Michael Row Your Boat Ashore" on my guitar than I would by playing "The Star Spangled Banner" on my trumpet. Also, it didn't hurt if you got sand in your guitar, just in your bathing suit.

So, I invested in several instructional manuals and started to learn some chords, fueled by the sound of soft breaking waves and visions of bikinis and bonfires in my head.

Chapter 4

When I met Hank Jaeger, my life jumped to a new plateau. Hank resembled James Dean, and his ambivalence toward the high school hierarchy was similar to mine. Hank owned an enviable sparkling green and white '55 Chevy convertible. We became best friends immediately. We both procured fake IDs that enabled us to trek to the bowling alley in Staten Island, toss back some cold beers, and heave rental bowling balls into the gutters of those worn-out lanes.

We dated an assortment of cute girls from out of town and shared spine-tingling thrills with our dates, on the challenging roller coaster rides at Olympic Park. It became a Friday night tradition to go watch the drag races from the parking lot at the White Castle on Route 22.

My father loaned me his spotless forest-green '49 Cadillac to go on a double date with Hank. We neglected to tell him we were going to the drive-in. We shared a perfect evening until I backed out of my parking space with the speaker still in the window.

My father never truly believed that someone had broken into the car, but I think he let me skate on the premise of reasonable doubt.

Hank and I killed time by simply driving around. It became a tradition to share Sunday dinners at each other's houses. It was a rather formal affair at mine, and a wonderful warm family time at Hank's.

Some weekends we'd motor down to Normandy Beach or Seaside Heights, wade in the ocean, and sneak peeks at the bikini chicks through our mirrored sunglasses. We caught some sun lying on the beach, and tested our skills on the games in the arcades on the boardwalk.

On one of our exploratory excursions into ocean-side life, I discovered *Murphy's Sea Bay Inn*, a seedy bar located in Normandy Beach. At night, the place featured an innocuous old relic who played the organ. His aging face was creased by wrinkles on top of wrinkles, his bloodshot eyes missed very little when they were open, and a tousled thatch of greying hair stood up every which way. He looked like a character from *Casablanca* as he lovingly stroked the keys, nodding in time to the music. The Lucky Strike that dangled from his mirthless nicotine-stained lips added another layer to his mystique.

The bar, filled to capacity with a crowd of beach people in various stages of intoxication, drew me in like a fly to a picnic lunch. I sat with the old musician and played trumpet, and they offered me a job performing on weekends. My first bar gig! Trumpet and organ! You can't make this stuff up, folks.

I met a dapper little guy at the bar who looked like a pocket-sized version of Errol Flynn. He wore his shirt knotted under his chest. A tiny mustache sat on his upper lip, and his smile captivated the blonde bartender. He was married to an attractive well-muscled lady named Roberta, who brought to mind a picture of my favorite female wrestler.

She was a tremendous asset for Dick. Almost every night he would drink his limit, stand up and start to fall over. She slung him over her shoulder in a fireman's carry and took him to their home, a half block from the bar.

Dick worked as a freelance sports writer for *Field and Stream* and other outdoor magazines. He offered me a job teaching water skiing on Saturdays and Sundays. Seventeen years old, and things were definitely looking up. I took both jobs, and Dick graciously informed me that I could stay with them on weekends, if I didn't mind sleeping in a jungle hammock on the screened-in porch.

Living a dream life rocked: playing music, fishing, boating, crabbing, and eating my fill of succulent lobsters and shrimp—every kid's fantasy. I loved being on and in the water. I became enamored with the idyllic lifestyle at Normandy Beach, even though I knew I'd be leaving this paradise in the fall. I had to hand it to my parents. As long as I avoided trouble, they left me free to go anywhere, whenever I wanted. This was probably easier on my father's heart. (It was that "out of sight, out of mind" thing.)

I finally found something I excelled at. I practiced my trumpet for hours and began performing at a level of proficiency that amazed my parents. I sat in the first chair in the orchestra and became one of the best trumpet players in the state of New Jersey. However, playing "The Trumpeter's Lullaby" with a full orchestra and chorus in the spring concert, bought me just about as much high school cool factor as a laxative at a Bran Flakes convention. My sight-reading sucked, but if I heard it, I could play it.

In my sophomore year I was asked to join a surprisingly sophisticated dance band made up of young musicians. We played country clubs, proms, formal dances, coming-out parties, and concert halls; a remarkable learning experience. The guitar player attracted the girls. The trumpet players attracted their mothers. (Note to self: practice your guitar!)

This band was my introduction to learning the classic songs of those times, as we played in front of voluminous crowds. The other trumpet player held the first chair in the New Jersey State Orchestra, so I had to put in long hours of practice to keep up with him.

We delivered sonorous versions of songs by Stan Kenton, Harry James, Woody Herman, Tommy Dorsey, Les Brown and many of the popular big bands of the times. We were as accomplished as any other professional big band around. Audiences were stunned by how well we played, considering how young we were.

Then, I began my New York era. I climbed on the train every chance I could, to go into the Big Apple. With my phony ID in hand, I frequented Birdland, Basin Street East, the Metropole, the Half Note, and the Village Vanguard, inhaling every bit of big band music, Dixieland, and vintage jazz that I could listen to. I reveled in performances by Duke Ellington, Stan Kenton, Harry James, Dizzy Gillespie, John Coltrane, Oscar Peterson and so many more.

One night, as I listened to music in Birdland, a wise guy shot a well-known Italian mobster. Not wanting to be caught with my fake ID, I startled the kitchen crew, as I blew out the back door into the alley to miss the police that were coming in the front door. However, for the most part, my New York excursions were trouble free, and I took delight in the intense feelings of euphoria from all that music, music, and more music!

I finally turned 18. All that high school stuff was out of the way and I prepared myself to launch my next scholastic adventure at

Northwestern University in the fall. After I discovered talking to girls on the telephone, my high school grades took a rather steep dive. Since my sister was already attending Northwestern, she begged them to accept me; she always did get her way.

I wanted to earn as much money as I could during that last summer, so I worked construction Monday through Friday, eight to four, and took on some shifts as a short order cook, Monday through Thursday from seven to midnight. On Friday, after I cleaned off the mud from my construction job, I jumped in my car and headed for the beach, where I played trumpet at Murphy's and taught water skiing with Dick Borden for two glorious days of never-ending craziness. I rented a small room in a garage, 75 yards from the ocean and a short walk to the bay.

Working with Dick on the ski boat brought a never-ending series of tumultuous episodes. I slalomed in the ocean in five-foot waves, but mostly we stuck to skiing in the bay.

Occasionally, Dick made it through the night without passing out. We took the boat out on the water, went as fast as we could, and made a sharp turn causing it to stand on its side. We cleaned the barnacles off the bottom by buzzing the metal channel markers. Of course, that wasn't dangerous or anything. In the morning when the ocean was calm we'd paddle out in a rubber raft and fish for sharks. (My dad is spinning! I can feel it!)

There were parties on the beach, and the bonfires and bikinis I dreamed about became a reality. I finally knew a few songs, so I played and sang by the fire, a small but auspicious beginning to my vocal career.

The lifeguards were insane. They concocted a baseball game where the bases were six-packs. As you reached each base you drank a beer. The games normally lasted two innings, max. They rode in a gnarly old Studebaker coupe. One night, after excessive beer-chugging during a three-inning ballgame, they decided to turn it into a convertible.

Someone produced a blowtorch and they carved off the roof, making it a permanent topless wreck. It was amusing to see them cocooned in the car on a rainy day, dressed in yellow full-weather gear. When they stopped and opened the door, water seeped out onto the street. Those lifeguards absolutely knew how to party.

For a couple of bucks, an older guy supplied us with cardboard quart containers of Schaefer light beer on tap that we'd drink on the beach. I can still taste the forbidden, fresh, cool flavor of that bubbling amber nectar; a gift from the teenage gods!

All my friends water-skied at a professional

level. One of my sun-worshiping buddies owned a metallic blue ski boat that topped out at about 55 mph. He called me one day, said he had a hot date, and needed a spotter in the boat so they could water ski. I drove to the dock and we headed out. They grooved through the water for a while. Then it became my turn. His date climbed in the front seat next to him. I pulled my water skis on, jumped over the side, grabbed the tow rope and we took off around the bay.

The couple started necking and failed to keep an eye on me. I skied by something cutting the water that looked out of place, and suddenly recognized the fin of a large shark. I tried to get my buddy's attention. I screamed and hollered, slipped off to the side to try to catch up with the boat, jiggled and whipped the towrope, but no dice. He was deeply engrossed in the architecture of her bikini top or lack of it.

Just as I thought I'd have to change my bathing suit, he took a cursory glance over his shoulder and saw me in panic mode. I pointed out another shark fin. Was he cool about it? Hell, no!

He slammed the boat into a screaming turn and headed straight for shore. He whipped me around and I crashed into the beach at God knows how many miles per hour. I came out of the skis, did three awkward front flips in the sand, and thumped to a crashing halt, thanks to a big piece of driftwood. I looked like I'd been dragged face first through a privacy hedge. The resulting scratches, bruises, and sprains lasted for weeks, not to mention the time it took for the skin to grow back. I felt lucky I hadn't broken any bones.

That afternoon, the coast guard sent a patrol out on the water and shot five hammerhead sharks. My buddy and I had some words, but he soothed my wounds with an endless supply of Schaefer beer. I hated to see that summer end, but it was probably a good thing. If I had been a cat, I would have been hanging by one life.

My '40 Ford finally bit the dust and I bought a royal blue '48 Ford convertible with a white top, from Hank's brother. I felt like I'd won the lotto. The car had one problem. Shortly after I bought it, the clip that held the distributor cap to the front of the engine broke off. The distributor is the car part that triggers the spark plugs and makes the engine run. The cap flapped loose, breaking the electric contact, the damned car groaned to a stop, and there I was, stranded. In a cloud of disgust I had the car towed home. I quickly diagnosed the problem, and I went shopping for a new clip.

Well, no one had one in stock and no one knew where to get one. Yankee ingenuity set in and I figured out I could hook the cap back on using a rubber band. Unfortunately, my quick fix only lasted for a limited amount of miles. Then, the band melted and the car would stop. I filled the glove compartment with rubber bands and continued on my travels.

One night I took a casual drive with an especially attractive date. The most recent rubber band gave up the ghost. She looked at me and said, "Not this old trick."

"It's okay. I'll fix it," I replied.

I pulled a rubber band out of the glove box and headed for the front of the car. I don't know whether she was happy or sad, but I did hear her mumble; "Now I've seen everything."

I recorded my very first song in 1959: "Misty Skies," a commercially acceptable duet song that I had written, and performed with a girl named Trudy. We recorded on one track, (mono) which was the only technology available at the time. I learned my first valuable music business lesson from this production that I'll tell you about later.

Then I headed for college.

Chapter 5

August 1959! Northwestern University! I caught my first glimpse of the beautifully wooded campus, honeycombed with perfectly maintained old classic stone buildings, interspersed with some sleek modern ones. I couldn't believe the size of this place. I pulled up in front of my dorm after negotiating my way past a long line of double-parked cars in the process of being unloaded. My new nesting place sat on the shores of Lake Michigan.

It had taken me awhile to find my dorm; trying to follow one of those crappy maps they send you. At first glance, it looked like a penal institution.

My room assignment read 321. Elevator? No way! So I dragged my stuff up three flights of stairs, and tried to put it in some semblance of order. When I returned to my car, I found my first in a long line of campus parking tickets on my windshield. Ouch! Welcome to Northwestern University, home of the Nazi campus police.

Then I met my snooty roommate, "Thurston The Third." He might as well have worn a prep school button on his wine-colored blazer, and the instant friction that filled the air, boded ill for our future time together. As the quarter progressed I learned that "Thurston The Third" had a penchant for playing loud music, being obnoxious, and peppering me with stupid questions when I was trying to study. I hoped his parents had a life insurance policy on him as I dreamed about killing him. He didn't like me either, but that's the only thing we agreed on.

The tasteless over-cooked food in the cafeteria made me long for a canned army meal, although I did develop a taste for the oily scrambled eggs. If I wanted to eat mush, I'd order it. I preferred my meat to look like meat and my fish not to taste fishy; so hot dogs, potato chips and pretzels became staples in my food program. Cold cans of baked beans were a delicacy.

To atone for some of my previous sins, I reluctantly heeded my father's pleas and enrolled in the school of Electrical Engineering, burdening myself with physics, calculus, mechanics, and English. (An Electronic Engineering Degree? A seal would have had a better chance at getting a loan in Phoenix, Arizona.)I enjoyed English, but did not want to become another Nikola Tesla.

Due to Thurston's negative influence on my brain, and my demeanor, I staked out a comfortable spot in the library. I studied there as much as possible, more for the peace and quiet, than the ambience and the solemn pursuit of academic success.

For me, studying physics, calculus, and mechanics was like putting a mouse through a buzz saw. I never worried about my IQ before, but I began to doubt that I had one after I tried to comprehend the contents of those textbooks.

Then came the usual rush of parties for freshmen. Fraternity houses searched for pledges to run up and down stairs for no reason, be hazed, and say, "Yes, sir."

I had enough of that kowtowing crap in high school, but belonging to a fraternity seemed to be a social necessity, if you wanted a chance to score a date with a prissy Northwestern girl. Don't ask me how or why, but I pledged one of the most prestigious fraternities on campus. I quickly grew to hate Greek Life. However, I figured it might possibly be worth it when I garnered the attention of a cute cuddly coed.

To further complicate matters, due to all the hours I worked that summer, my immune system was hovering at minus two, and I came down with mono. When the night nurse slept through her shift, I spent a couple of episodic evenings in the infirmary, involving perky coeds and contraband beer. Then they shipped me back to New Jersey, and my life went on hold.

Since it was so late in the quarter, they graded me and I flunked my classes, based on the work that I hadn't been able to do. I spent several weeks at home recovering and when I got my strength back, I headed out on my first foray into New York to try to sell my song, "Misty Skies."

This is where the first valuable lesson in the music business came in. Every radio station in the country played "The Mountain's High," Dick and DeeDee's monster hit song, almost nonstop. Their producer wanted them to record my song. Feeling that Trudy and I could be stars, I rashly turned him down.

I made my first stupid move. What could have been a smash for them, turned out to be a dud for me. No deal, no contract, no money (that would have been a lot) and Trudy and I never left rock and roll anonymity.

Later in life, when I became entrenched in the music business, I never held back a song. If someone had the urge to record it, I'd hand deliver it and send chocolates and flowers.

I spent countless hours practicing my guitar. In January I went back to Evanston as a Business major, leaving my father with another shattered dream. I had a new lease on life; while my subjects were anything but easy it was night and day compared to Engineering. I felt I could supplement my musical knowledge by taking a few theory courses along the way.

Back at Northwestern I picked up my fledgling fraternity activity where I left off, but the girl I dated moved on. I borrowed a shiny red '55 Thunderbird convertible from my pledge advisor to take a young lady to dinner, and the brakes went out. I panicked for a minute, but due to my experience with race cars I downshifted the roadster to a stop, avoiding an accident. The guy I borrowed it from blamed me instead of his worn-out hydraulic system.

I faced the beginning of the end. The fraternity kicked me out for conduct unbecoming an esteemed member. The last straw; the young woman I casually dated seemed to be the president's girlfriend—or so he thought. Alas! Again, no jacket!

One turbulent night, the situation between "Thurston The Third" and me came to a head. Due to an involuntary, long overdue urge, I attacked him. I can't say I completely kicked his ass, but the next day his parents showed up and moved him out.

I finished out the quarter, a solitary man blissfully alone in my peaceful room, and I passed all my courses. I practiced guitar, tried to learn all the songs I could and continued writing. Fortunately, I made some new friends in and out of the fraternity system. In a school of thousands, I found there were an abundance of nice coeds to take out, who weren't hung up on Greek letters. All in all, life started to look up.

I finished out the year, completed my schoolwork, and by then I'd achieved a fair-to-middling proficiency on guitar. Furthermore, I composed a smattering of new songs, and writing became a tad easier. I recorded several of my new tunes at a studio in Evanston and headed back to New Jersey for the summer. I still practiced trumpet, but it slowly took a back seat to my other activities.

I decided to get my feet wet in the "real" music business, so I took exploratory trips into New York, to try to expose my new songs to the record industry. In those days I handed a tape of my song to an engineer, who fed it to a turntable that physically cut it onto a record disk. I watched the cutting needle etch grooves and ended up with a large vinyl record of the song that could be played on a record player. These "dubs" cost 15 bucks apiece, a lot of money at that time, so I couldn't afford to make too many. In theory, I'd play this disk for a record label A&R (artist and repertoire) man, or a publisher, to see if I could get them interested enough to publish or record my material. I performed the vocals on the records and I sounded remarkably similar to Ricky Nelson. There was one song I liked, so I decided to start by pitching it.

The trade magazines referred to the music business in New York as *Tin Pan Alley*. Two buildings, 1650 Broadway, and the Brill Building, were the epicenter of activity. They reminded me of beehives, with one office piled on top of another, housing dozens of music executives, songwriters, and producers. I started my new journey at 1650 Broadway.

I struck gold, not by selling anything, but by meeting a wonderful man named Gerry Teiffer. He granted me my first significant appointment. I had no idea the depth of the friendship that would develop between us.

Gerry headed up an international music publishing company. Throughout his career he took the helm of many major organizations, and finally landed in Nashville as an expert witness in a Beatles copyright infringement lawsuit.

He recorded as a professional whistler, called everybody "Podna," and graciously accepted the love and respect of his peers. Any time I met with Gerry, he brought a smile to my face. He immediately became my mentor. He felt my song had merit so he placed a few calls for me.

He set me up a meeting with United Artists. I walked into the front office and a gravelly voice said, "Whaddaya want?"

No one sat at the reception desk, so I poked my head into this guy's office and told him Gerry Teiffer sent me.

He snapped, "Gimme the dub."

I handed it to him and he placed it on his turntable. He listened to about half of the song, made a contemptuous face, ripped the vinyl off the record player, and tossed it at me. "My

49

turntable runs slow. Your song suffers from it. Get out!"

And there it was, my first introduction to rejection, an inauspicious start to my publishing career.

My second meeting: Harry Meyerson at Decca Records. He couldn't have been nicer. That completed my initiation into the turbulent world of music. Thumbs down, thumbs up...an interesting balance.

He kept my dub and offered to play it for a few people.

At $15 bucks apiece, I only made one at a time, so I ran to the studio in the basement and had another one cut, before my next meeting. I didn't sell any music on that trip, but I started to build up my base of contacts in the industry.

On my next trip, I met Vera Hodes, another publishing executive. She shared an office with Don Costa, the brilliant arranger who worked with artists ranging from Frank Sinatra to Paul Anka. Bert Burns, the producer of a hit record named "Hang on Sloopy," also shared space with the group. They were kind enough to offer me the use of an empty cubicle, and their conference room when I was in town, as a place to hang my hat and use the telephone.

Watching Don Costa work always turned into a remarkable experience. Don, the sovereign head of the conference table, held court with music sheets strewn all around the room. At the centerpiece of the chaos sat a bottle of Jack Daniels. Lost in a world of music, he created magic for hours at a time.

He invited me to the original recording session of Sandi Stewart singing "Coloring Book," performing live at Bell Sound Studios with a 70-piece orchestra. Multi-track recording hadn't been developed yet, so the singer and the orchestra had to get it right at the same time, with no redos or fixes. They completed the record in four takes. Unbelievable!

At one point Don stopped conducting, pointed at a viola player and told him to tune his D string. What an ear.

That day, I realized I'd been blessed with a unique gift. I could hear all the individual parts of the orchestra in my head. Later in my career, as I wrote orchestral scores, I found that I could miraculously visualize each instrument in the orchestra, and it all fit together with amazing clarity, but I'm getting ahead of myself here.

Bert Burns offered me a recording contract, but unfortunately he passed away before we could finalize the deal. I felt like a jinx as I headed back to school.

The six-year span of my spotty scholastic attendance record at Northwestern drove my father crazy. I thought he might take up drinking due to my numerous drop ins and outs, but he was resilient and stuck to his one highball a month party plan. He strongly felt that after I failed in life, he was going to have to support me, so he needed to stay sober.

I returned to Northwestern for my sophomore year, to nothing unusual. I lived off campus in a room on the second floor of a historic house, with an icebox, an outside entrance, and no beer police. Freedom!

One night, musicians were jamming in the lobby of a dorm and I sat in on guitar and sang. People seemed entertained by the music, and I realized it was time to formulate a plan to put a band together.

My parents graciously covered my tuition, but I felt the need to help out. It came to my attention that the sorority houses served food that tasted like food, so I landed a job at the Theta House, working in the kitchen and waiting on tables. This turned into a double bonus. Not only did I have the opportunity to expand my social relationships, I finally ingested some decent food.

One of the first female friends I made called herself Ann Margret. When we were cutting class to go have coffee at the college hangout, I never dreamed she would skyrocket to stardom. Northwestern proved to be a springboard for emerging talent. I felt like I'd landed in the midst of creative inspiration.

Chapter 6

Some close friends asked me if I wanted to take a ride to hear some country music. I agreed, but never asked where we were going. As we drove to the bar, the neighborhood began to deteriorate and we ended up at Montrose and Broadway, the center of the "hillbilly ghetto" of Chicago. We entered a vintage country conclave, scarred by broken bottles, busted-chair fights, tattooed women, and angry drunken country boys just looking for fun, which they thankfully found in the music. Many of the people who lived in this area, migrated from Appalachia in search of a better life. Disenchanted by the rejection of a society that did not understand them or want them around, they were forced to accept low-paying miserable jobs. Their desire to succeed seemed inconsequential, so many of them found solace drinking bottles of rotgut whiskey and listening to country songs.

The venue of choice for the night turned out to be the *Club Jubilee*. Almost afraid to leave my car, I crossed the pot-holed parking lot and ventured through the door into a rough, seedy bar, smelling of sweat and stale beer. At the time, I didn't realize where this fun-seeking jaunt to a surprisingly uncivilized part of town would lead me in my career.

The joint vibrated with music as the band launched into song after song. My eyes were drawn to the lead singer/guitar player, an imposing football player-sized guy with wavy long black hair, a big grin, and eyes that took in everything around him. Boy, could he ever play guitar! He strummed every genre of music, from Chet Atkins to rock and roll. His long fingers made his guitar take on a personality of its own when he played classic country songs. He sang with a distinctive country-rock voice and you could tell he had a lot of miles on him. He went by the name Big Bill Schaeffer. Under his real name, Bill Berryhill, he previously traveled the country as a stump preacher and Friday night tent evangelist. I wouldn't say he was one of the fallen; I'll just say he changed careers.

A talented rhythm guitar player, another burly country boy named Jimmy Nichols, looked like someone's serious father, sang like Johnny Cash, and knew at least 5,000 songs. The drummer, a small curly headed dynamo named Little Al sat next to the bass player, a quiet backwoods boy named Jack.

I talked to Bill on a band break and he invited me to sit in. As I performed, something came alive in me and I realized I was destined to play music. After taking a good look around, I hoped I wouldn't get mugged or killed doing it, as I explored this new and exciting world. Bill assured me that musicians were treated like gods in that neighborhood, as many people were very poor and music was the only entertainment in their tough lives.

I took him at his word, but before I went back to the Jubilee I bought a .25 automatic that I carried religiously. We returned to the Club Jubilee every weekend. I played and sang, and Bill asked me if I would like him to give me some guitar lessons.

I knew I needed to be a better guitar player if I expected to compete in the business, so I dropped out of Northwestern for a quarter. I won't even tell you what my father said. I think it rhymed with bun-of-a-stitch.

I quit my job at the sorority house and landed a similar job at an Italian restaurant. I practiced guitar every morning for three hours, then washed dishes at the restaurant at lunchtime. After lunch, I drove back to my room and practiced for another three hours.

As I washed dishes during the dinner hour, I scotch-taped pages of lyric sheets on the wall and memorized them while I worked. After my shift ended, I went to the club, took an early lesson from Bill, and played with the band anytime they'd let me. I did this seven days a week for three months.

I branched out, started to sit in at all the other bars in the neighborhood, and with my trusty .25 automatic in my pocket, I stayed out of trouble.

The self-titled hillbillies were consumed by two hobbies: drinking and fighting. At least once a month someone ended up getting thrown through the plate glass window at the front of the Jubilee. They finally boarded up the bottom half, which kept the fighters from crashing onto the sidewalk in a shower of deadly shards. It certainly cut back the ambulance bills.

The alert bouncers earned their money, as peace rarely came to Montrose Avenue. I learned to keep my head down, but anytime a disturbance started to head my way, several locals would jump in to put a layer between trouble and me.

Talk about seeing the whole world go by! I witnessed wild unleashed emotions like tragedy, rage, fury, assaults, hostilities, abuse, sorrow, pity, and tension—and that was just on Friday night. Saturday night: more of the same, but things seemed to cool off on Sunday (that "day of rest" thing).

One night, I asked Bill why he played that ugly-ass–pink solid body Fender guitar. He smiled knowingly. "Son, someday you'll know why."

The Jubilee featured a huge circular bar. I sat about four feet from the bandstand, so I could be close to the music. One night, as I watched the band, the degenerates on each side of me engaged in a violent argument. The drunk to my left smashed a bottle on the bar and reached across my chest with the broken glass remnants in his hand, threatening to cut the guy on my right. I inhaled, trying to make myself as skinny a target as possible.

Schaeffer very calmly unstrapped that guitar, wound it up and smacked the guy holding the broken bottle, right on the top of his head, knocking him out cold. They were in the middle of a song so he strapped the guitar back on and continued to play. The damned pink thing stayed in tune. At the end of the set Bill winked at me and grinned. "That's why I play that ugly-ass pink, solid body guitar, son."

Some of my friends from Northwestern drifted down to the wild country to hear me perform. One guy, a squirrelly idiot and unpredictable when he drank, played a mean saxophone. He asked me if he could come down and sit in. I said yes with reservations, as drinking might push him over the edge and make him do something stupid. He showed up, downed a few cocktails, and I warned him the club was packed with serious, potentially dangerous, people so he needed to behave himself.

Mr. Saxophone, in a somewhat inebriated state, tossed caution to the wind, and decided he would give everyone a thrill by strutting on top of the bar while he played. I bowed my head and prayed that God would keep him from being terminally stupid.

My silent prayer went unanswered as he bent over and wagged his butt in a lady's face. Her boyfriend stuck a switchblade knife in his rear end, sending him to the hospital for stitches. Tough crowd!

The club closed at five a.m. on Saturday. In a spontaneous last-minute decision, a waitress and I decided to go down to Montrose Avenue beach and watch the sun come up. By the light of a full moon, we found a well-hidden paradise, a deserted stretch of soft white sand with a weathered grey block building located in the center of the property. A worn eight-foot cyclone fence protected the beach, and feeling no pain, we clumsily scaled the rusty wire barrier after a few flailing, cartoon-like attempts. We weaved our way down toward the soothing sound of the water and sat on a blanket, anticipating a glorious sunrise.

We were jolted from our reverie by an off-key bugler, playing Reveille. Every window in that block building filled up with unshaven faces, whistling loudly and yelling obscene comments. It seemed the Budweiser buzz prevailed over common sense and eyesight, and we had clambered into the middle of a National Guard training weekend on an abandoned military base.

We vacated our blanket and dashed for the fence in a wobbly sprint, one slapstick comedy Three-Stooges-style climb away from a couple of stumbling half-asleep weekend-warrior MPs. We watched the sun come up hiding in my car.

I heard about an orange Chet Atkins guitar for sale for 150 dollars. I bought it and went to take it home. I found a young southern couple using the guitar case as their baby's crib. I felt a bit guilty for taking the kid's nesting place, but only for a minute. I took my new purchase and went home to practice some more. I didn't know it at the time, but this turned into one of the best investments I ever made when I sold that guitar a few years ago for 10,000 dollars.

Every musician who lived in that neighborhood and played the local clubs, had a nose for trouble. One Friday night I played at a country saloon, performing on a bandstand located in the middle of another huge circular bar. Morgan, the lead guitar player, whispered, "Bobby, put your guitar away quick."

I always paid attention to these guys when working on their turf, so I swiftly unstrapped my guitar and placed it in its hard shell case. Within two minutes, the club exploded into a melee that made western-movie bar brawls look like a girl's gym class. The entire place erupted, and the situation turned into a nightmare.

Morgan said, "Follow me!"

We jumped off the bar on top of two guys fighting on the floor, using them as a springboard to bolt through the front door. I didn't worry about my guitar. I knew it sat safely in its protective case, but for a couple of anxious moments, I worried about myself. The cops charged in, busted some heads and quashed the violent battle.

One other night, I played in a club called the Silver Dome, located directly under the elevated train tracks. The door opened, a sinister-looking man walked in, and shot a patron out of his chair directly in front of the bandstand. His eyes met ours with a serial-killer look as he backed from the club to disappear into the crime-filled darkness of Wilson Avenue. In those days, no matter what happened, you never stopped playing until the bartender told you to stop, a common though unproven belief that the music would cover up the sound of the disturbance, and help keep it from escalating.

We continued our song, but we played a hell of a lot louder and faster than we ever had before, nervously glancing at one another. When the police arrived, of course we said, "We didn't see nothin'!"

At the end of the night, the club gave us a sizable bonus, but you can bet your life I never played in that place again.

I used that line, "We didn't see nothin'," quite a few times further down the road when I was performing on downtown Rush Street, in nightclubs run by the mob.

Bill Schaeffer opened up my eyes to a world I never knew existed. Bill, an intensely profound resident of another place and time, told a million stories about his tempestuous life as a traveling bible-thumping preacher and a career music man. Spending time with him is something I'll never forget.

My designated three-month hillbilly music education program came to an end, and I knew I'd reached a satisfactory proficiency on guitar, thanks to Bill. In fact, the picking I learned over that three months probably ended up being a large percentage of my guitar playing ability for years. I also managed to memorize a significant repertoire of songs.

My father breathed a sigh of relief and put his Prozac back in the medicine cabinet when he finally believed I'd returned to school. He fervently hoped this silly music thing had come to an end.

Back to school! Studies during the week and music in hillbilly heaven on the weekends! I started to accumulate a small pile of equipment; a powerful guitar amplifier, a couple of microphones, and a PA set. After an extensive search for musicians, I put my first band together.

I found Richard, a brilliant guitar player, playing banjo at the Velvet Swing, a '20's themed bar on the northside of Chicago. Someone referred me to a reliable drummer named Rick, and we hired Jack, the soft-spoken bass player from the Jubilee. I played rhythm guitar and sang lead, and we started playing small jobs on and off campus.

The band rehearsed for long hours and started to gel. Richard constantly threw temper tantrums and Jack hit the bottle, but we were ready to invade the world of fraternity parties.

As the school year ground to an end, I decided to stay in Chicago for the summer, so I rented a room at another fraternity house. The members were a diverse group of guys that knew how to throw a party. They pledged me and wanted me to join, but I was over the fraternity thing. In order to keep me around, they leased me a small apartment in the basement of their house where the cook lived in the past. Another outside entrance hidden from the beer police secured my privacy. I had my own secret party lounge man cave right in the heart of the campus.

My sister persisted in trying to fix me up with her sorority sisters. She didn't understand why *my* taste in coeds seemed to be light years away from hers. One day, in the throes of frustration she challenged me. "Why don't you bring someone you like over for dinner, so I can see what you consider to be a good-looking woman?"

I had wanted to take out a lovely lady named Jacqueline Jean Mayer so I took her. The following day, my sister called me. "I don't think she's that cute." We agreed to disagree.

A few years later my phone rang and my sister said, "OK, you win."

"What are you talking about?"

"Jaqueline Jean Mayer has just been crowned Miss America!"

Better late than never. I think she finally got it.

Northwestern assigned me to a new advisor. His name: Stewart Henderson Britt, a dapper, white-haired older gentleman with a handlebar mustache. Stewart was a nationally renowned marketing expert, who authored the state-of-the-art textbook for college marketing classes. He and I became friends. He headed part of a group that focused on psychological warfare in World War II, so we shared many eye-opening conversations. I changed my major to Marketing, after I earned my only college A in his course, and the knowledge I gained helped my advertising career significantly, later in life.

Northwestern had another remarkable professor named McGovern. He looked like W.C.

Fields, with a protuberant nose better suited for Grandma the Clown. He looked like a homeless man, but his intelligence belied his appearance. He consulted for the government and established himself as one of the preeminent authorities on the Middle East. Substantive, but incredibly entertaining, his lectures were always profanity-laced surprises.

He continually filled the auditorium with students eager to hear his unique unpredictable narratives. The girls in his class decided to get up and walk out the next time he used bad language. The following day, he launched into a historical diatribe, which ended when he said, "So they put all the whores on a boat."

All the girls got up and started to leave.

He said, "You don't have to hurry, girls, the boat doesn't leave for two hours."

And then I did it again!

Chapter 7

Answering the need to expand my musical horizons, I dropped out of college, to enroll in two fundamental courses at the Chicago Conservatory of Music. Another earthquake rocked my house and as my dad pounded on the walls, the dog ran for the basement.

Continuing my search for practical studio experience, I also produced more records, and did a smattering of arranging on the side for an assortment of small record companies.

I sorely lacked technical music knowledge, so I signed up for a music theory class. However, hearing all the parts in my head and being able to write them down, somewhat compensated for what I lacked in formal training. I decided to take voice lessons to strengthen my vocal cords.

My theory teacher, a distinguished older white-haired gentleman named Mr. Stroop, challenged the class to take a lead melody and create an appropriate harmony. Boredom overwhelmed me after the first two assignments, so I decided to let creativity lead my musical thoughts. Mr. Stroop perused my music, frowned, and then a thoughtful look appeared on his face.

After observing his reaction I thought, "Uh-oh!"

He called me into his office. "Who are you and what do you do?"

I told him my story; how I was currently doing some writing, performing, and arranging.

He said, "I want you to quit my class."

My heart dropped into my shoes. "Oh no," I thought. "I can't get kicked out of the Conservatory of Music." I threw him a pleading look. "Why?"

He said, "You are doing everything wrong and I am starting to like it. If you continue in my course I will ruin the free-spirited creativity you're gifted with." Wow!

In the ensuing discussion, he asked me why I signed up for classes at the Conservatory. I told him I needed to broaden my knowledge of orchestration and writing transposed scores.

Every instrument is tuned to a different key relative to the actual key the song is written in. Instruments in an orchestral score need to be "transposed." If the piano part is written in the key of C on the score, you have to write the trumpet part in the key of D, the French horn in the key of F, the English horn in the key of E flat and so on and so forth. It's similar to writing a book in five languages.

Mr. Stroop handed me manuals on transpositions and notation, and kicked me out. His parting words rang in my ears. "Memorize these books and keep doing what you do. I'm confident that you'll be successful and I feel it's going to be sooner than you think."

It looked like an insurmountable mountain of work! I had acres of new subject matter to study, and I expected to spend long hours learning it.

My singing teacher, a woman in her late 40s, resembled a stern high school librarian, and dressed like Hillary Clinton. I never heard singing coming from behind her locked studio door when I arrived, and when it came time for my lesson she always looked rumpled and flushed. I thought she might have a thing going with the cocky cavalier dude that had the lesson before mine.

She pushed me to sing songs like "Moon River" and "Strangers in the Night," and repeatedly asked me to take her out drinking to a music club to hear me perform. Can you say, "Cougar"?

I bailed out of the voice lessons and curled up in my apartment with Professor Stroop's books. I realized how important it had become to learn this treasure trove of information, make it or break it, part of musical composition that I needed to master.

Down the road I had to be prepared to compose music to film. This created a whole new set of challenges. Some composers were brilliant at screening films and writing music that smoothly enhanced the changing scenes, off the top of their heads. Being light years away from that particular skill set, I had to learn film scoring by rudimentary, mathematical techniques, a complicated process.

The hardest commercial I ever worked on was a 7-Up "Bubbles" commercial containing seven different time changes in 29 seconds. Every song has a time signature. In modern music, rock and roll is mostly 4/4 time (four beats per measure). Jazz can be 5/8, classical music can be 6/8 and so on. When I composed the 7-Up track, in order to accommodate the scene changes, I had to start in 4/4, change to 2/4, go to 3/8, then flip to 7/8 back to 6/8, and so on.

Fortunately, I had one of the industry's foremost drummers, Earl Palmer, playing on the session. A veteran of the famous "Wrecking Crew," he made those difficult transitions as smooth as silk. I'd explain how we did it, but I don't want to bore you to death.

School again! My father was becoming immune to the whole thing, but there were deep creases in his forehead I had never seen before. I kept up with my studies and my band turned out to be one of the most popular bands on campus. I still managed to take a road trip to enjoy a well-needed dose of hillbilly heaven on an occasional weekend.

My competition, a band named "Mr. Lonely and the Teardrops," featured a skinny Elvis type singer. His jet-black hair tumbled over his narrow shoulders. He looked like a rock star, had a strong commercial voice, and an impressive flashy light show. I fronted a funky honky-tonk rock and roll party band, just as wild and uninhibited as a musical ensemble could be. The fraternities and sororities had a choice of class or crash. Both bands worked often. I played at the drunken toga-parties and he performed at the classy, dress-up dances.

As a bandleader, I learned to "read the room." I started to get a feel for what kind of music the crowd looked for; when to wind them up, and when to slow them down. We have all been at parties where the bandleader plays music that is disappointing, or inappropriate for the occasion. When people weren't dancing I felt like I wasn't doing my job, unless we were asked to play background music behind a dinner or some serious occasion. Surprisingly, we *did* have a repertoire of soft music.

I continued writing and recording songs and building up my studio hours. I found music to be a vocation where you never stopped learning, but when you love something, it's not a job; it's your life.

I met a man named Paul Glass who owned a record company and Allstate Distributors (the company that distributed records for Atlantic, Chess and many others, throughout the Chicago area). I recorded my first song on his label, Destination Records, which became my first flop, but it was a start. I had so many balls in the air it made me dizzy. Then my life changed again.

During a casual walk on campus, I caught a brief glimpse of a brown-haired pixie as she drove by in a green MG sports car. She had me at drive by. I found it to be a daunting task to track down one coed in a group of 7,000 students. My tenacity paid off and I located Jill, a theatre major and a talented actress. It took some doing as she was "kind of" seeing someone, but she agreed to meet me for coffee.

The more time we spent together, the more I grew to care about her. She felt the same way and we shared warm, wonderful times. Homecoming rolled around and she wanted me to meet her family. We never discussed our parents at any length, so I didn't know much about them, other than she worshipped her father and they shared deep family commitments and love.

Then she dropped the bomb. She told me she never mentioned her father, as he ran General Artists Corporation, the biggest talent-booking agency in the country. Being a theatre major, all her fellow thespians would have continually badgered her for an introduction to her dad.

I knew my future lay in the music business, but she had become an important part of my life. I realized I needed to be very careful to keep my professional career aspirations away from my personal relationship with Jill. I met her family, and her father reminded me of Gerry Teiffer, another remarkable compassionate human being.

Her dad, an imposing but modest man, put his family first despite his deep involvement in the business. At one time he helmed RCA, and amassed a multitude of entertainment and creative successes. We grew very close. His two best friends were Perry Como and Jackie Gleason.

While Jill was still in high school, she and her brother Larry were in the middle of doing homework when her father brought home a tape of a recording artist he wanted them to listen to. He considered signing the artist and wanted to know how young people would react to the music. They went crazy over the singer so Jill's father went to sign him to a management contract. Colonel Tom Parker beat him to the punch, but her dad succeeded in signing Elvis Presley to record on RCA.

On school breaks, we traveled east to Jill's elegant but comfortable house in Westport, Connecticut. Thousands of LPs filled the shelves on one complete wall of his den, and pictures of stars hung in prominent places. I hoped to have a room like that of my own someday.

We accompanied Jill's father to dinner at the Stork Club in New York, the night he signed the actress, Sandi Dennis. He made reservations at the Copacabana, where we viewed an impressive performance by Bobby Darin. At another time, I had the pleasure of meeting Perry Como, a relaxed mellow gentleman, as smooth as his voice.

Jill's father scoped out my band at a fraternity dance, but we never talked about my business in relation to his. One day he called me into his study and asked me what he could do for me: get me a recording contract; put me on *Shindig,* the pop TV show; get me bookings?

I thanked him profusely, but told him I didn't feel ready to handle a major career yet. I told him I had no desire to be a one-shot wonder, and there were many mountains for me to climb before I felt I was proficient enough to perform at his professional level. I refused to take advantage of my relationship with his daughter, whom I was crazy about. I told him that if and when I felt ready, I'd like the opportunity to meet with him. He seemed surprised at my answer, but he sat back in his chair, smiled at me, nodded and said, "I hope you marry my daughter." Knowing him will always be a special part of my life.

Jill and I remained joined at the hip for a long time, so you'll hear more about her further on in the story.

One night, her brother came into town. He asked me to take him to some Chicago venues. We toured a few of the most popular music clubs, and ended the evening in an illegal after-hours gambling joint in Villa Park. I noticed there were an inordinate number of gamblers wearing oversized Hawaiian shirts capable of concealing weapons, and my "Spidey sense" began to tingle. "Let's get out of here," I whispered. As we pulled out of the parking lot, the FBI launched a full-scale raid on the place. At least my world was never dull.

While I walked the tightrope of life, I tried to keep my balance, and find my way to the other side. I busted through barriers, snuck under (and over) fences, and had so much fun it should have been illegal.

My band continually went through personnel changes. I replaced Rick the drummer with a guy named Norby King, a somewhat unhinged fellow, but a fine musician. As a result of a childhood accident, he ended up with a glass eye. He performed a spectacular finale to his drum solos as he threw it into the air and caught it in his mouth. Ewwww! Dinner with Norby always turned into a memorable time, when his eye magically appeared in your salad, or at the bottom of your bowl of soup. Funny at the time!

Jack drank too much, and Richard could not seem to temper his moody disposition. I removed Richard, found another bass player, played my own lead guitar and added my close friend Eddie

Rusk on saxophone. The responsibilities of being a bandleader could be a royal pain in the ass, but fortunately the band continued to improve.

I focused on my writing, but in those days the lyrics to hit songs were bland and banal. I wanted to raise the creative bar and write something classy and meaningful. I wrote serious songs for myself, as the radio audience seemed to only respond to simplistic doo-wop records. Then, I had a creative breakthrough.

Every writer inadvertently experiences at least one notable writing lesson. The first time I truly began to comprehend the content of a great song, occurred when a prolific writer came into town to do a seminar. He pointed to a table and said,

"What would you write about that?"

I thought about it and noted how strongly it was built, and how it added character to the room, etc. My ideas were all about the table.

The writer said, "You must look at that table as a conduit to life; what kind of man built it, who sat at it, and how many sad stories had been told around it? What were the families like that owned it? How many secrets had that old table heard, and what were they?"

Aha! It all snapped into place. I'd been spinning my wheels writing about situations and objects without taking them to a deeper level, opening them up to the unexpected, projecting pain, or finding touches of humor that others missed.

Suddenly, I emerged into a whole new level of writing. I could virtually feel my brain expanding. I couldn't wait to apply my new skills.

Paul Glass hired me to produce several groups for his USA-Destination label. The first band, the Exceptions, featured Peter Cetera on vocals and bass. We recorded a trendy, catchy commercial song, but pop radio wasn't ready for them yet.

Peter left the group to become a member of the music group soon to be named "Chicago," and the Exceptions broke up. Jimmy Guercio, the talented producer who put Chicago together, owned a magnificent ranch in the mountains of Colorado. Before the band released its first album, they lived in a compound on the property. They rehearsed and churned out commercial songs for months. When they were finally ready to start performing and recording, they were incredibly prepared for their impending success.

Chapter 8

When I produced a band, I recorded the basic band mono (on one track) the only available technology at the time. Following that initial step, the group overdubbed all the extra parts. When I performed an overdub, I added another part by recording the original mono track and the overdub at the same time, making a composite to a second mono one-track tape machine. The downside of this process: we lost fidelity with every added part. Today, new technology gives musicians an unlimited number of tracks, so they no longer have to go through that complicated process of adding more instruments in order to enhance a production.

Recording rock and roll bands in the early '60's took serious work and hours of preparation. From the 70s on, the studios set up their own drum kits, ready and waiting to be played. The microphones were set in place, so all I had to do to get a super sound was turn them on.

The non-professional groups dragged their own instruments into the studio, and the drums had usually been sitting in someone's garage, or car trunk full of moisture. When they were played, it sounded like someone pounding on cardboard boxes. I had to resort to a variety of tricks to improve the sound; duct taping the drummers wallet to the snare to stop the rattle, and putting a blanket in the bass drum to prevent it from thumping, I had to convince the bass player to change the worn out strings that had been on his bass for five years.

I allowed for the fact that a lot of these musicians found themselves out of their element in the studio. They were in the habit of slamming away in big halls and had little or no recording experience. I *quickly* learned to place a small microphone *inside* the acoustic guitar to keep the drums from splashing into the guitar sound.

A few years later, someone came up with the idea of separating the drums by putting them in a different room called a drum booth. Removing the drums from the room improved the clarity of the record, since the loud percussive noise had been covering up a lot of the individual sounds of the other instruments.

Sometimes I brought in a professional musician, when a band member lacked the skill necessary to play a certain part, or found it hard to keep time in the studio environment. It could be a challenge! I continued soaking up as much knowledge as I could. I recorded several more groups, and cut two more records of my own, but that elusive brass ring, the hit record, continued to evade me.

Meanwhile, back at Northwestern, I spent as much time as I could with Jill, and put some effort into my scholastic endeavors. I met an affable fellow named John Kelley, and he invited me to dinner at *Sigma Chi,* his fraternity. I thought about it and finally convinced myself to go, even though I had pretty much written off the whole fraternity system.

The Sigma Chi members were reputed to be notorious hell raisers. (Think of the movie *Animal House.*) They often found themselves on probation for their frenetic and demented parties, so I thought it might be a good fit for me.

At Sigma Chi, I met an intriguing guy named Chet Rondinella who became a lifelong friend, as did John Kelley. Chet's career is a book in itself. Among other things, he's been a consultant, an entrepreneur, managed chains of restaurants that he conceptualized, pioneered a phone company, strip-mined in a river, and who knows what's next?

John Kelley entered the Navy straight out of college. He flew 100 missions over Vietnam as a Phantom Jet navigator, and retired from the service with a high security clearance and a sensitive government job. He returned home, and established several successful businesses in the civilian world. I feel very lucky to have these two loyal, solid friends in my life today.

I'm going to do something unusual here. I'm turning the book over to Chet. He sets up the next chapter of this story, *The Sigma Chi Era—my last gasp at collegiate life*, in a way I think you'll enjoy.

Chapter 9

Recollections from Chet Rondinella

Bobby Whiteside! I distinctly remember the first time I heard that name. It was 1961, and most of the leaves had fallen from the trees on the Northwestern University campus, in Evanston, just north of Chicago. The first brush of snow was just beginning to waft across the sidewalks. I was a newly arrived junior transfer student from Notre Dame University and was getting the feel of the NU campus, and its culture. In a convoluted twist of fate (a story best left for another time) I had pledged the Sigma Chi Fraternity, and gone through its intense hazing to become a full-fledged "brother," a hazing practice now banned in today's politically correct and pampered college society.

Sigma Chi at Northwestern was considered by most to be the animal house on campus. And, indeed, it was filled with brawny football players, Neanderthal-like wrestlers, and a tall basketball player with flaming red hair. About half the house was on athletic scholarships. There was also a smattering of bright, suave "face men" who filled out the ranks.

The common bond of brotherhood in the house was a rampant irreverent attitude about most things in life. The Sigs were consistently ranked 27 out of 28 academically, and when the postings came out each quarter, there always was indignation that someone had beaten them out for bottom place. The house was, by day and by night, a noisy, chaotic melee of red-ass comments, adolescent pranks, tall stories, and feats of strength and daring. It definitely wasn't a place conducive to serious study, and it was clearly and often stated that academics were an individual matter, not a house responsibility. The collective grade point average of the group was a testimony to the success of that mission statement.

The irreverence carried forward to fraternity rituals as well. Where most Sigma Chi chapters across the country treated their chapter rooms with dignity, and usually held ritualistic fraternity meetings where a coat and tie were usually the required dress code, the Omega Chapter at Northwestern used its chapter room on the third floor as an exercise and weight room for the jocks.

It also served as a storage space for miscellaneous things such as a motor scooter, the Sigma Chi owner of which was being sought by the Evanston Police Department because of the near complete destruction of two of its motorcycles that had given chase to the little scooter and its two fraternity brother riders. The cops collided with each other when one tried to make the same turn into a parking lot as the scooter had made; while the other police motorcycle rammed straight into it at high speed.

Broken motorcycle parts were strewn all over the street as a rather large crowd of unsympathetic male Northwestern students gathered. The two police officers were scratched up a bit, but only their egos were seriously hurt as the crowd jeered at them in retaliation for the high handedness that the police department continuously doled out to NU students. The motor scooter stayed hidden under a big carpet on the side of the chapter room for quite a while. I distinctly remember the two brothers worriedly running into the house through the front door carrying the scooter and dashing up three flights of stairs with it in hand.

At chapter meetings on Monday nights, business was conducted amidst laughing, taunting, and general mayhem. Many of the jocks used the meeting to pump iron and the clanging sound of weights being moved and hitting the floor filled the air. Among the jackets and ties, there was an occasional bathrobe, shorts, or a grey jock t-shirt. Somehow, amidst all that chaos, they actually managed to take care of fraternity responsibilities.

I think it was my second chapter meeting where, being a new guy, I sat quietly in a back row of benches watching the cacophony of nonsense unfold. It always was quite entertaining, and one *could only shake one's head and laugh at some of the bizarre antics displayed and ribald comments made.*

It was in that chapter meeting that somebody announced, "Whiteside has de-pledged again." The room instantly became silent as boisterous voices and the clashing of weights were stilled. A serious, focused tone filled the air. Someone commented that that was the second house he pulled out from. Another said, "No, I think it's the third."

Someone else said, "I think he got kicked out of the first one."

A quiet and earnest discussion then ensured to determine if anybody in the Sig house knew him. One brother, John Kelly, said, "Yeah, I do."

Someone asked, "Do you think you could get him over here?"

John said he thought he could. Further discussion determined that Bobby Whiteside should be invited to the house for a Wednesday dinner (we always used Wednesday dinners to entertain guests; I never did know why).

I sat in my back bench-row seat absolutely amazed that the group had become so silent and focused. I remember thinking, "This guy Whiteside must really be something to capture the attention of these animals." Wednesday dinner came around, and we were all seated in our basement dining room ready to chow down.

You always held your plate on the table with

one hand, because if you released your grip, your plate would immediately be whisked away by the board jobbers who worked in the dining room. The Sigs were very parochial about money matters, and had long ago determined that if money had to be paid to board jobbers, they should be Sigma Chi brother board jobbers. Most other fraternities and sororities hired outsiders to perform mealtime chores. Unfortunately, all the Sigma Chi board jobbers were jocks with attitudes and a strong motivation to get the meal over with as quickly as possible, so you really had to guard your plate if you wanted to finish your meal.

Dinner was just being served when John Kelly walked into the dining room and announced, "Brothers, I want you to meet Bobby Whiteside."

Everybody in the room looked up and gave Bobby welcoming applause with a few added whistles of appreciation. I sat staring, fork in one hand and plate in the other, stunned at the vision of the guy standing next to John. I don't know what I had expected, but it certainly wasn't a skinny, scrawny guy with long hair who looked like he was coming off of a long weekend. Bobby just stood there in a slouched stance and said hi to everybody. I remember thinking to myself, "That's Bobby Whiteside?"

The long and short of it was that Bobby and I ultimately became good friends, and drinking buddies, a friendship that has lasted a lifetime. The *two of us couldn't have been more different in look and disposition. My theory about how the friendship evolved is that we were both nocturnal.*

By 11:00 pm, 50 guys were fast asleep in the house. Bobby and I were wide-awake and looking for adventure. Since Chicago had four a.m. liquor licenses, we'd cruise the rough hillbilly bars in the northeast side of Chicago, better known as the Wilson Avenue District. I knew it well because I had sold Gallo wine to liquor stores in that area one summer.

Bobby was always looking for new talent to manage, so we would go to places that showcased newcomers. He also sat in and played guitar and sang with any band that would let him. Knowing the area, I always kept an eye out for the mean drunk from some hollow in a southern state, who would stick a knife in your back without saying a word just because he didn't like the way you looked. At least in the black areas on the south side and west side of Chicago (where I also had sold wine), a mean drunk in a local bar would make a lot of verbal noise before he came at you with a broken bottle.

John Kelly was our pledge trainer that year so he had the power to assign pledges to active brothers who served as pledge fathers, general guides who looked after the wellbeing and development of a new pledge. For some inexplicable reason, John assigned Bobby to a 230-pound, ill-

tempered lineman on Northwestern's football team.

I distinctly remember the moment John introduced Bobby to his new pledge father, Fred. Fred roomed across the hall from me and usually kept his door open while he studied at his desk, wearing a tattered blue bathrobe.

John walked in with Bobby in tow and said, "Fred, meet your new pledge son, Bobby Whiteside."

Fred slowly half turned around in his chair, gave Bobby a long hard up-and-down, head-to-toe stare, and in a deep, hoarse voice said, "Boy, we're going to have to build up your body." Fred turned back to reading a classic comic book to prepare for an English test.

A week or so later, he arrived at Bobby's basement apartment just south of Evanston with a set of old barbells he had filched from somewhere, and a wrinkled piece of paper that contained a handwritten daily exercise plan. He was obviously serious about Bobby building up his body, but the only time I ever saw Bobby touch those weights was when he gave them a push with his foot to roll them out of the way for a forthcoming party. They literally rusted away in his living room.

Bobby once called me at my family's flat in Cicero, Illinois. It was Christmas vacation, and Bobby had to fly back to Chicago from New Jersey to play a gig during the holiday week. He wanted to get together. I talked to my dad who asked who

Bobby was. I told him he was a fraternity brother from Northwestern. My dad said, "Any friend of yours is always welcome here, Chet." I told Bobby to catch a cab at O'Hare Airport when he arrived, and drive directly to our Cicero address.

The next day, in the early evening, the doorbell rang. I turned on the front porch light and ran down the stairs to greet Bobby. There he was, standing outside the glass front door, shivering in the cold, with an old beat-up suitcase in one hand and a guitar case in the other. He was wearing a terry cloth bathrobe over his street clothes. I invited him in and asked, "What's with the robe?"

*He just replied, "Hey, man, it's fu...fu...fu****g cold and I didn't bring a coat."*

I laughed and sent him ahead of me up the stairs. My dad was waiting at the landing above to greet him. They exchanged pleasantries and as I followed Bobby past my dad into our flat, my dad whispered into my ear, "Where the hell did you find this son-of-a-bitch?"

We later sat in the kitchen where Bobby downed three large plates of spaghetti and uncountable glasses of Gallo red wine, always a good thing to do to make a favorable impression in an Italian household. My dad found him to be thoroughly entertaining and bright.

Later we retired to the TV room where Bobby had left his luggage. My dad pointed to the guitar case and asked, "Do you know how to play that thing?" Bobby replied,

"Yeah, man, I can play it."

My dad replied, "Play!"

Bobby knelt and opened the guitar case on the carpeted floor. As the upper lid swung open, a loaded automatic pistol fell onto the floor. My dad just looked over at me, closed his eyes, and shook his head in mock disgust.

Bobby then proceeded to give us a terrific 25 minute mini-concert. His songs immediately won my dad over again. For the rest of the time he was alive, my dad always asked how my friend, Bobby Whiteside, was doing.

So, from its first mention in that ubiquitous fraternity chapter room at Northwestern University, the name Bobby Whiteside has had a special meaning in my life, that of an old and trusted friend who is smart, both intellectually and street-wise. A lot has changed over the years, but not Bobby. The Sigma Chi House is now a model of academic excellence and meritorious community service.

I visited it some years ago and found that the average height of a brother there has diminished by about five inches. Gone are the jocks and the irreverent atmosphere of the place. I came away a bit sad, but quickly recovered when I talked to Bobby on the phone about my experience there.

Bobby has remained the true spirit of that old group of guys with his funny, quick-witted,

observations of people and things, his professional focus on his craft, and the success he has achieved in his industry. However, it is his impish grin, soft sarcastic laugh, and his ever-present playful irreverence about most things in life, that makes me feel all is not lost and that there is still hope for most of us.
-Chet-

Most of the Northwestern students fondly perceived Sigma Chi as their own version of the fraternity in John Belushi's uproarious movie, *Animal House*. The administration viewed the house as the dark side of Greek Life .

I felt that this might be my last chance to enjoy the fun part of the collegiate system, before I committed to the impending challenge of the professional music career that waited in the wings. I looked at this rowdy group of great guys living on the edge of bad taste and frivolity, who possessed a cavalier attitude toward everything. I decided to jump into the deep end for a swim. I needed one last fling, temporarily devoid of my self-imposed structured music education, filled with spontaneous thoughts and crazy antics. At the time, I didn't realize what lay below the surface of this ocean of nonsense and levity, and the surprising depth of some of the experiences I shared, while I was embedded with the brotherhood of Sigma Chi.

Political correctness, forbidden at the Sig House, included the use of nicknames. The guys called Chet "Wop," due to his Italian lineage. Stamison earned the name "Greekie" for a similar reason, and it went on to 'Big Dago," and "Little Dago" (Because the name "Big Dago" had already been taken). Some of the other pseudonyms were: "Squatty Body" (a beefy football lineman), "Stew the Jew" (the treasurer of the house), "Honker" for um... obvious reasons, 'Turkey Tom" (the scholar), and a host of others. They were proud of their disrespectful monikers. They wanted one for me, but found it difficult to demean a white, Anglo-Saxon Presbyterian from New Jersey, so they simply called me, "Whites." The use of these completely irreverent nicknames sometimes lead to misunderstandings, as many of our parents found these names to be offensive, which was of course, the whole point!

Chet 's dad, Patrick, an impressive man, took pride in his lineage: 100% vintage Italian aristocracy. He lived in Cicero, Illinois; the home of many mobsters, strip joints, and illegal gambling clubs. He was noticed immediately; a swarthy, but handsome man with piercing eyes and long jet-black hair, who wore an expensive black cashmere overcoat and a white silk scarf. If he snapped his fingers, you might find a horse's head in your bed. Pat, Gallo Wine's trouble-shooter, covered the dangerous south side of

Chicago, and we often kidded Chet about his dad's white Thunderbird having bulletproof windows.

Immediately after Chet transferred to Northwestern, his dad arrived at the fraternity house to pick him up for their weekly dinner. One of the hulking "jocks" stopped throwing a couch at another ball player long enough to shuffle to the bottom of the stairwell and yell at the top of his lungs,

"Hey, Wop! Your Dad's here."

Then his flip-flops slapped the floor as he meandered back to the den to resume the furniture fight. Chet arrived downstairs to find his father's face the color of an heirloom tomato.

"Chet, how dare you let those guys disrespect you like that? Those were fighting words in Cicero."

He proceeded to get madder and madder.

It took some fast-talking, but Chet made his father understand the harmlessness of our purported lack of political correctness and social graces, before he torched the fraternity house.

After Pat got to know us, he grew to care about the brothers. He became an integral part of our social lives. A contingent of guys from the fraternity ended up at his apartment in Cicero on Friday nights, where they drank smooth vintage Chianti from crystal wine glasses. He served bountiful portions of his awesome spaghetti, made from scratch from his grandmother's

Sicilian recipe. We argued about race, religion, politics, and every other controversial subject that we could think of. Some of my fondest memories came from those round-table discussions in Pat's cozy kitchen. There were many diverse opinions, and sometimes the conversation became heated. However,unlike today, at the end of the night the sacred bond of friendship prevailed. I spent long hours visiting with Pat after Chet went to grad school and into the service. Despite my inauspicious armed bathrobe appearance at his household, we became family. I miss him.

Chapter 10

The Sigma Chi freshman pledge class contained a wide array of ostensibly diverse guys, who continually added new chapters to the never-ending book of outrageous antics.

Andy, the first pledge that comes to mind, held the title of the world's strongest teenager.

The dining room at the Sig House had a low ceiling. One of the hulking football players glared at Andy, the strongman. "Let me see you press one of your pledge brothers."

Instead of picking up Speedy, the little guy, he picked up a 6-foot tall dude by his shoulder and his thigh, and proceeded to lift him up over his shoulders like a barbell. There was a slight problem. Every time he pressed his arms all the way up, he smashed him into the ceiling tiles. I winced, and hoped it wasn't a preview of things to come.

Ah, but it was! The pledge class, in a creative moment during a discussion on new and improved ways to meet women, decided to rent a couple of motel rooms out by the airport, and extend an invitation to some ladies from the stewardess training program. The party got so rowdy that the owner of the motel appeared on site to shut it down. The world's strongest teenager, fueled by a couple of pitchers of beer, tore the door off the motel suite and smacked the guy over the head with it. Stu the Jew (the treasurer) purged the fraternity funds for bail money.

A previous pledge group of young free thinkers were told to procure a Christmas tree. They produced a magnificent tree, placed it in a stand and carefully decorated it. It was one of the most perfectly shaped trees ever seen at the fraternity. As some of the guys were zoning out on the twinkling lights, a couple of active members stormed into the room, grabbed the tree and rushed it up four flights of stairs to the chapter room, leaving a trail of broken ornaments and crushed tinsel ground into the carpet. They piled blankets on top of the tree and stashed it next to the scooter. It seems the FBI was going from door-to-door, checking Christmas trees. Unbeknownst to the pledge advisors, the young men scaled the sacred pine tree at the *Bahai Temple* and topped it. The fraternity was scared to death their Greek clubhouse would be turned into a parking lot.

The house contained enough intelligent guys to make up for the jocks who found it hard to study, due to the time-consuming pressures of their athletic scholarships, so we avoided academic probation. However, social probation was an entirely different story.

Sigma Chi threw legendary parties. Toga! Toga! Toga! John Belushi would have approved. My band played all the alcohol-sodden soirees. Picture a room full of swirling drunks wearing sheets, flip flops, and frilly pillowcases, and you'll understand why the parties were notorious.

Sororities loved our parties. The university powers-that-be, *really* hated them. Due to our probationary status, we hid them miles away from campus in a barn or some other venue, out of the prying eyes of the campus police. Jill joined me at all the festivities. While I was on the bandstand, the fraternity members kept her red plastic cup filled with adult beverages. I presented her with my pledge pin, but due to my rocky scholastic record, I didn't have the grade point average to become a full member. I had to wait to go for the big kahuna and pin her with my elusive Sigma Chi Cross.

John Kelley took matters into his own hands. He invited Jill to a candlelit dinner at the house. After a nice supper, John symbolically pinned Jill to the whole Sigma Chi Fraternity with his own Sigma Chi Cross. Then the entire group of roughnecks sang, "The Sweetheart of Sigma Chi." I don't think this had ever happened before. It surprised me that this scruffy group of guys could be so sentimental, though they would never admit how rough edges could hide a heart.

After that, at every dance, each of the fraternity members approached Jill to dance with their pin-mate. It was a wonderful tribute to the character of the men who offered me a chance to become a fraternity brother, and I knew I'd made the right choice to be part of it.

And then, the ultimate bash! Chet, the unofficial party planner, suggested that we throw a Hawaiian luau the day after the other students left to go home for Christmas break. This looked to be the granddaddy of all his great ideas. He turned the Sigma Chi house into an incredible Hawaiian garden. He constructed a waterfall, flowing into a river that ran all the way through the living room, down the hall and out the back door (we assumed), appropriately named, "Wop River."

Following a long-standing tradition, our social director concocted our special Hawaiian punch. After fall break, everyone brought back partial bottles of alcohol that their parents hadn't finished while celebrating autumn. They dumped all that liquor in a garbage can, and topped off the toxic-looking mess with a bottle of 7-Up and a pineapple. After the second drink, no one cared what it tasted like.

Now we come to the downside of "Wop River." No one ever asked Chet where it ended up. The fraternity next door came back from vacation to find four feet of water in their basement. His masterpiece had long since been dismantled, so the great flood had the university plumbers scratching their heads, and it remained a mystery for years.

Chet, the sommelier of the fraternity, earned his title after everyone found out his dad had been involved in the wine business. Squatty Body (Rich) looked at Chet one day and curled his lip in disdain.

"Wine is a sissy drink. How do you drink that crap?"

Chet told him that he would gladly supply the wine and he could judge for himself. They embarked on their wine tasting and I went off to play a gig. I returned to the house at five in the morning to hear a strange noise emanating from the shower room. I peeked in to see Squatty Body sitting on the floor, leaning against the moldy tile wall of the stall with all his clothes on and his wallet firmly lodged in his pocket. He rocked back and forth, holding a half-empty gallon bottle of Gallo wine in his chubby hands. He continued to sip as he sang out of tune and talked to himself. The water was on full blast and running cold.

I sensed the motion of someone behind me. I turned around to see Chet. He stared at Rich with a satisfied smile.

"Sissy-drink, huh?"

In a slurry voice the chubby drunk said, "Cheers, mate," flipped Wop off, and went back to his song.

The following day, as I walked down the hall by Squatty Body's room, the door flew open. Standing there, an apparition: a perfect poster child for a sign captioned "This is your body on wine." He put his fingers to his lips. "Shh! The sound of your sandals slapping on the floor is making my head pound."

He never lived that one down. I think that is where the expression, "*Sheeeeeit no*", came from; his immediate answer every time someone asked him if he wanted a glass of wine. Chet added one more level to his already burgeoning legendary status.

After the chaos and the frivolity ends, when I look back on the free spiritedness of fraternity life, I discovered what we truly shared. Hiding under the fun and the light-hearted lifestyle, existed a thread of seriousness, and a bond that developed between the young men who were members of this group. This life-long fellowship based on: deep convictions, a resoundingly strong spirit, lending strength to others, and acknowledging life's responsibilities; resulted from associating with the Sigma Chi brotherhood.

When you scraped the icing off, you discovered the metaphorical cake, the real stuff! It amazes me that after 55 years I still have three close friends that were brothers in Sigma Chi. Chet lives in California, Pete Shellenbach lives in Chicago, and John Kelley lives in South Carolina. We stay in touch, see each other when we can, and know that this gift of friendship emerged from the fraternity we were lucky enough to be members of at that particular time in our lives.

I spent many of my younger years not really being a part of many meaningful groups, and that made belonging to Sigma Chi particularly sweet. I cannot name one member of our Sigma Chi Chapter who has not gone on to be extremely successful. We purged a lot of excess energy, which helped us focus on the future. When one can look back at wildly fun times, and still look ahead to a solid productive existence, that's part of having it all.

Due to my untimely ejection from Northwestern (which I will tell you about later), I was unable to be initiated as a full brother, although they always treated me as one.

Several years ago, I got a call from Pete Schellenbach, asking me if I could be in Chicago on a certain weekend. I said I probably could and I asked him why. Through Pete's efforts, the Sigma Chi International Headquarters passed a resolution, enabling me to be initiated into Sigma Chi as a full brother. John Kelley and Chet flew into the Windy City for the ceremony. Of all the awards and honors I've received, this will always be the most touching. 55 years later I finally pinned my own Sigma Chi cross on my lifetime sweetheart, Brenda.

Chapter 11

In 1965, the music business rocked my world when my record, "Say It Softly," went top ten on WLS and WCFL; two major pop radio stations in Chicago. My life would never be the same. The record, a big ballad, mirrored the "Wall of Sound" created by the renowned music producer, Phil Spector. His magical productions consisted of layers of vibrant string instruments drowned in mountains of echo. It sounded like a haunting, voluminous orchestra playing in a high domed, cave-like cathedral.

I shared exciting times with my friends whose records hit the airwaves at the same time as mine: The Cryin' Shames with "Sugar and Spice"; the Buckinghams singing "Kind of a Drag"; the American Breed with "Bend Me, Shape Me"; The Rivieras lauding the "Warm California Sun"; and a host of other local Chicago groups.

Some of the DJ's from the radio stations, asked me to make appearances at record hops to promote my record, which turned into a journey down the rabbit hole. The DJ's were unique. One of them hated kids, so he'd hide out on his breaks and wouldn't sign autographs. A couple of the others were totally over-the-top crazy.

It felt strange to show up at these gatherings of giggling girls, climb up on the stage, and pretend to sing to my record when they played it over the PA. Then, the DJ and I did what we were there for; sat at a table and signed autographs.

The next few months were peppered with tempestuous experiences, some funny and some not. I'd have to write another book to tell you all of those stories, but let me share a couple of them.

My worst excursion into the world of pop music occurred when I made an appearance at a state fair on an enormous farm in Indiana. It seems the headlining act (I won't mention any names), molested the farmer's son.

The DJ grabbed me, threw me into his car, and we escaped by frantically driving through the cornfields, with the rabid property owner and his inebriated friends in hot pursuit. I had a flashback to some of the hangings I saw in my old history textbooks.

After a wild chase, we tore through a fence and blasted down the highway toward Chicago, with barbed wire stuck in the grille of the DJ's Mercedes. The tabloids would have killed for that story!

Dawn was nearly breaking, and I hadn't gone to bed until six a.m. At seven a.m., my doorbell rang persistently. In a bleary haze, I almost fell on the floor climbing out of bed. I staggered to the door where my half-closed eyes tried to focus on a five-piece British punk rock and roll band, standing in my alley with goofy smiles plastered on their faces. The lead singer, a portly female named Penelope, was garbed in trendy thrift shop attire and white go-go boots. She sported frizzy red hair, looked like she'd been hit by lightning, and when she smiled I couldn't help but be distracted by a wide space between her two front teeth.

I asked them how I could help them. They told me one of my DJ "friends" said I would listen to their tape, and would be most receptive if they woke me up really early in the morning. That son-of–a-bitch!! I was only half-conscious, but I waved them into my apartment and reluctantly screened their tape. They really sucked! I kicked them out. I dialed my DJ friend at home, woke him up and asked him, "What the hell was that?"

He said, "What did you think of Penelope?"

I said I thought she looked like a tiny little teapot, short and stout. Then, I painted his phone with expletives and went back to bed where I dreamed of ways to extract revenge. Later that day, I sent him a vase full of fragrant flowers laced with black pepper and a triple dose of jalapeño pepper dust. I signed the card…"Love, Penelope." He never woke me up again!

I continued to produce records. I wrote the follow-up song to the Riveras' "California Sun," and ended up singing the lead, as their singer had a slight cold. I wrote, produced, and/or arranged for: The Family, The Exceptions, The Flock, The One Eyed Jacks, and a host of other Chicago groups. There were many other local groups on the scene, but only a handful of them advanced to the top. Those national number one hit records were almost impossible to come by.

The music business faced the British Invasion, led by the Rolling Stones and The Beatles. The sound of commercial rock music changed drastically. Motown and Chess were tearing up the R&B radio stations, and songs in general were beginning to demonstrate substantially improved and more eloquent lyrics. I doubled my efforts to change with the times, knowing it would be vital to my continuing success in the future.

I had the chance to open the show for the Dick Clark *Caravan of Stars* tour at the Civic Opera House in Chicago. I shared the bill with the Four Seasons, The Righteous Brothers, Brian Hyland, Gene Pitney, The Shangri-Las, The Zombies, Del Shannon and 15 other major artists. After surviving a panic attack, I went out on that massive stage to sing for a colossal, enthusiastic crowd. Fortunately, my performance was well received by a swooning swarm of groupies. I felt I'd reached some new fans, and I saw a significant spike in my record sales.

Then, on a different front, life changed direction again. An old philosopher said that sometimes you are holding on to love so tightly that it doesn't have the space to breath, and sometimes you're not holding on to it tightly enough. A talented producer/artist named Richard Landis wrote a beautiful song named "Natural Causes." He wrote, "People change and love can die by natural causes too."

Jill and I inadvertently drifted apart. It was just what it was when all is not enough; nothing contentious, merely two people at a fork in the road about to travel on separate paths. I knew I'd miss her warm heart and the affection we shared. It felt strange not having her in my life, and I deeply regretted losing my relationship with her father. Bittersweet! All the same, I had to move on and focus on what was to come.

My musical life became so frenetic that my grades were plummeting. I convinced my English teacher that I suffered from a rare, very serious disease, which made it hard for me to make it to all my classes. She appeared sympathetic and showed up at my apartment with some chicken soup. Oh, boy!

Two days later, the Northwestern paper featured me, and my emerging music career in a headlining article. Man, was my English teacher pissed! The writing was on the wall.

I accepted an offer to do a show in Hatfield,

North Dakota. (I don't know where that is either) One of my Sigma Chi friends, Dave Moore, hailed from North Dakota. Only 19 years old, he'd been flying ambulance rescue missions around the Dakotas since his middle teens. He pulled hunters and trappers out of the wilderness and flew them back to civilization, so I felt he was competent enough to ferry me to North Dakota. Piece of cake! So I thought.

Chet gave me a little background on Dave. He debated on the high school team that won a national championship. While staying at their hotel in New York, he became bored out of his mind. Being an avid electronics nut, and dangerous with a screwdriver, Dave acquired a small transmitter. With it he found a way to drop a wire antenna out the window, hacked into the police radio bands, and started directing the police cars to go to crazy places. The FBI frowned upon his conduct and dropped a wall on his head! My kind of guy!

When Dave offered to fly me up to North Dakota, I acquiesced to another one in a long line of questionable decisions that spotted my life's trail. I faced three final exams on that Monday, but Dave assured me I could be back at Northwestern by Sunday (failing, of course, to take into account the ever–looming Murphy's Law).

Sight unseen, we rented a single engine plane out of a small airport to embark on our four-hour flight. I wish I'd known then what I know now about flimsy aircraft.

My first sighting of our tiny rent-a-plane was horrifying. I crept up to the Lilliputian death machine and reluctantly squirmed up into the cockpit. A premonition of disaster, not to mention a case of creeping claustrophobia swept over me. Knowing I had an extra-large flask of Jack Daniels tucked away in my guitar case gave me courage.

As we left the ground the wind buffeted the plane with a vengeance. I realized then and there that this would not be a smooth commercial flight, or a smooth anything for that matter. We popped up and down, up and down, while we were just taking off. How the hell does a plane bounce off of an air pocket? Within minutes, we were flying in a cloudbank at 10,000 feet where we couldn't see up, couldn't see down, and couldn't see spit!

It stayed that way for four hours. Now, you have to understand, in those days GPS wasn't available, so we had to home in on a radio beacon generated from the destination airport, when we were approaching the area. Finding the airport seemed like an insurmountable problem. Dave sat slouched in his pilot's seat, maps and charts perched on his lap, making calculations with a compass, and rocking back and forth. I wondered what the hell he was doing.

"Dave, I understand the charts and the compass, but why are you rocking back and forth?"

He shrugged and said, "I always do that when I am nervous."

I asked him what the chances were of colliding with another plane, since there was zero visibility and the plane wasn't equipped with radar. He shrugged again and said, "I don't know."

I started to drink! Once I was lubricated enough to override common sense and life-ending thoughts, the flight was actually boring. Um... except for the short time when Dave grabbed a plastic bag and told me to take over so he could answer a quick call of nature. It's kind of hard to do that when the plane is going into a dive.

I considered it a small miracle when he finally located the beacon that should have led us to the Hatfield airport. We broke out of the clouds to see...nothing! Not one thing that resembled an airport!

Dave recalculated. "It's got to be here somewhere." He began to fly back and forth, searching for the airport.

I spied a dilapidated barn at the end of a cow pasture, where a faded pink windsock flapped in the breeze. I pointed it out to Dave.

"Hmm, that's got to be it. There's no runway. I guess we'll have to land in the pasture."

"Um... Dave, the field is covered with water."

He did one of his signature shrugs. "I know!"

Then, he landed that aluminum coffin,

crosswind, in two inches of water in the cornfield.

I checked all my appendages, took a deep breath, took my pulse to make sure my racing heart hadn't exploded, and gulped down another shot of Jack! I've never been so glad to get my feet on the ground... I mean, in the water.

Dave taxied up to the ramshackle building to see... not a human being in sight. Great! Here we were on a deserted field in the middle of God's country, looking for signs of civilization. In the distance, we heard an old car rattling and gasping as it drove up the road toward the building. It turned out to be an antiquated two-door Cadillac Fleetwood, splotched with mottled grey spray paint, rust, and deep-purple primer.

A wizened old guy, who looked like a bootlegger straight from the casting call for the backwoods movie *Deliverance*, pulled up to the plane. He gingerly eased off his torn seat covers and his joints crackled like bubble wrap when he stood up. He wore scruffy work boots, a faded denim shirt, and an old straw hat that would have looked better on a scarecrow. His skinny legs were encased in an old pair of Wrangler blue jeans that were almost white. They must have been washed at least two hundred times (but not lately). We wondered if he had driven his old rum-running vehicle down from his whiskey still in the mountains, to pick us up at the *airport.*

He stuck out his hand.

111

"Gladtameetcha! Your motel is right over yonder."

His loose false teeth added a whistle to his dialogue.

He pointed to a crumbling run-down structure that looked like the motel in *Psycho*, with a burned-out sign hanging sideways by a single wire that someone had attached to one corner. The sign said, "Vacancy!" No kidding!

I glanced at Dave, he shrugged and we threw our bags in the trunk of the beater, next to a flat spare tire and some rusty wrenches. I placed my guitar carefully on his rear seat, trying to avoid the oil stains and the protruding metal springs. Then we joined him on the front bench seat and drove over to check in.

We walked into our room and our shoes left tracks in the dust on the floor. The first thing that met our eyes was the fading red-flocked wallpaper peeling off in chunks. The room was damp, the mattresses were bowed in the center, and I was afraid to touch the grungy yellow pillow! The straight-backed, hand-hewn wood chairs and the faded black carpeting were pre-Civil War. The linoleum-covered desk smelled like the remnant of a fire sale. They should have paid us to stay there. Red and black...my favorite colors, just not necessarily side-by-side in a dusky motel room.

Our geriatric guide expressed his desire to show us the venue I was playing at. We dropped our stuff on the floor, thought about cockroaches, put it up on the bed, and climbed back into his antique pride and joy.

We drove for several miles and pulled up to a huge single-story concrete block building that looked like the Alamo. He pursed his lips and mumbled, "We're here!"

I dubiously looked at the place, and asked him why there was no sign on the building.

He guffawed and rasped, "Every time we put up a sign, a mob of rabid Baptists storm the place, start a brawl, and tear it down 'cause it has an image of liquor on it." Then he lit up his corncob pipe and leaned against his car.

I looked at Dave, he shrugged, and we went inside to see a huge room. I wondered where they'd get a crowd to fill it? Then I remembered Bill Schaeffer talking about the power of music in a rural area. I rehearsed with the band for a couple of hours and we went back to our moldy cave.

When we returned to do my show, trucks and cars were stacked on top of each other, and the place was slammed. I finished the show in front of a well-oiled, enthusiastic crowd and we gathered up our belongings and started to go back to the Bates Motel.

As we went to leave, we were confronted by several preening rednecks. One of them felt his girlfriend was paying too much attention to me. After a brief, but insignificant altercation, our ancient guide drove us back to our motel. A line of broken down, oil-burning pickup trucks followed us, and circled the motel for a couple of hours.

I winced as I remembered what the Indians had done to Custer. Of course, Dave and I weren't completely defenseless due to the fact that both of us were armed. Though we weren't looking for a shootout in Hatfield, the farmer boys finally got tired, ran low on gas, and pointed their sputtering pickup trucks toward home.

Our bare feet hit the black carpet bright and early, and we were ready to jump in our flimsy winged chariot and speed back to Chicago. Remember that Murphy's Law thing? Grey clouds covered the sky, making it too overcast to take off. I spent the day trying to study, and Dave checked the sky every five minutes.

As twilight (or grey light) rolled around, I had to face reality. I was screwed! Sleep abandoned me as I tossed and turned, praying for sunshine, so we could leave at first light. I fervently wished we'd be lucky enough to see sunbeams when we awoke, and I might be able to get back for my afternoon finals.

Morning brought another desolate day.

Bored out of my mind by the endless wait, I noticed a raggedy, unkempt golf course across the road that obviously hadn't been maintained for months. The greens were cratered by missing divots, weeds ruled the fairways, the sand traps were dirt traps, and the water hazard; a half-filled millpond covered by green slimy algae that looked like the result of a science project gone wrong.

I didn't play golf, but inactivity forced me to rent a cheap set of golf clubs from the one-eyed, gin-scented groundskeeper wearing a soiled wife-beater. I bounced the ball off an occasional tree, shot into the pond, dug grooves in the mud traps, and hiked through the rough, constantly searching for that damned little white sphere for a couple of hours.

I perked up when I spotted Dave racing across the golf course, loaded down like a packhorse with our luggage. One leg of my sweat pants stuck out of my bag, flapping in the wind.

He shouted, "There's a hole in the clouds! There's a hole in the clouds!"

I looked up and I couldn't see anything but grey. He pointed up and exclaimed, "Right there!"

I looked and looked and finally saw it, this itsy-bitsy teeny-weeny dot of blue in the middle of that ominous sky.

I abandoned the golf clubs on the seventh hole, and we ran for the plane. He started the engine and we took off with no warm-up and no flight check. I kept my fingers, my legs, and my toes crossed and entertained a fleeting hope that God wasn't ready for me yet.

Up, up, and away we went, buffeted by the wind, our vision sporadically limited due to some wispy low-hanging clouds. We went... straight up!

Miraculously Dave found that little blue hole and he set our aircraft on a course back to Chicago.

Upon arrival, I rolled out of that flying deathtrap and kissed the runway like it was a Super Bowl trophy. Needless to say, I missed all three finals. Back on campus, I went to my professors to plead my case. It should be no surprise to you that I bombed in English. (My teacher still hadn't forgiven me for the soup thing.) My statistics teacher, one of those geniuses from India whom you could never understand, wouldn't give an inch. I wasn't sure he *understood* me.

I actually *flunked* Advertising, the worst of all possible scenarios. This seemed ironic as I ended up writing and producing thousands of commercials, and returned to Northwestern to deliver lectures on advertising to grad students.

I went to see Stewart, my advisor, to see if he could salvage any way for me to proceed down the path toward my degree. We talked at length, and he said, "You know what you need?"

I shook my head, wondering what the right answer really was.

"You need to get the hell out of here and do what you were meant to do."

I shuddered as I thought of my father. His worst nightmare! I had been kicked out of Northwestern in my senior year. Done! Finished! Stewart told me to come see him in a year if I still wanted to finish school. I never went back.

Chapter 12

Several months before Dave and I embarked on our nightmare flight to North Dakota, I moved into an apartment one-half block from the beach, on the north side of Chicago with John Kelley. Our little apartment building sat in the midst of tall multi-room dwellings housing Loyola coeds, stewardesses, singers, and secretaries. We hung out at the beach whenever we could steal time away from our busy schedules. John seemed like an ideal roommate.

A friend of Chet's wanted to show off a litter of Basset Hounds. I went with him to see the puppies with no intention of buying. Once I saw the doe eyes and floppy ears on one little irresistible tiny ball of fur, I brought him home. We named him JB (one in the future line of liquor referenced dog names). We started trying to train the little guy.

John had his eye on a perky coed from Northwestern, and after a long arduous pursuit, she agreed to meet him at our apartment for a drink. Naturally, she loved JB. John mixed two martinis and he and his date sat on our lumpy couch in the living room, and played with the puppy. We had no table or any convenient place to set the drinks, so John and his date placed them and the cuddly pup on the floor.

The afternoon wore on, romance filled the air and they started to get friendly. Suddenly there was a slurping noise they tried to ignore. JB crawled out from under the couch, after managing to polish off John's martini, olive and all.

He lay on his back with all four feet up in the air and proceeded to make whining noises and snore drunkenly. Talk about a mood breaker!

JB had taken his first step toward becoming a *doggyholic.* He would climb on the couch holding his leash in his mouth, then walk *us* down to the cozy little neighborhood bar on the corner. The bartender served him a Bud Light in his own personalized ashtray. When he attempted to run home, he stepped on his ear, did a front flip, and embarrassed himself in front of the stuck-up poodle that lived in the big brownstone next door.

JB continued to polish his chick magnet skills. While we were down on the beach, he'd meander close to a group of bikini babes sitting on a blanket to check them out. If he liked what he saw, he turned around and dug sand so it splattered all over them and their beach bags. At that point, John and I felt the need to saunter over, apologize to the ladies, and start a conversation. JB was almost as good as a guitar for attracting girls. Better maybe!

John, a closet adrenaline junky, became

friends with the Hedlund brothers, world champion small hydroplane boat racers. John caught boat fever, bought his own little hydroplane and competed on the water every weekend. He took JB along and the hound became the mascot of the flotilla.

Then, one Saturday morning I received the worst phone call ever. While John prepared his boat for a race, JB wandered out toward the street. A drunk driver swerved toward the curb and hit JB on purpose, killing him. I tried to reassure John it had been an accident, but nothing made him feel anything except remorse. John thought of me as a forgiving friend, sensitive to the issue, until he called a few days later. I picked up the phone and said,

"What do you want, dog killer?"

It was a bad attempt at humor in the midst of a tragedy, but that's how we dealt with things at the time. RIP at the great doggie bar in the sky, JB.

On another funny note, one night a musician friend of mine consumed more than his quota of Jim Beam. He picked up an aging homely girl, extremely late in the evening; living proof that the girls really *do* get better looking at closing time.

He tentatively knocked on my door and asked me if he could borrow a blanket to use when he took her down to the beach. I gave him a ratty old blue bed covering, then I dropped off to dreamland. My dreams were disturbed by scuffing noises originating in the kitchen, but I thought it must be my imagination, so I rolled over and went back to sleep.

At about 5:30 a.m., I woke up to get a glass of water and tried to push the kitchen door open. It seemed blocked so I hooked my fingers on the door and pulled it open the other way. There lay my friend and Miss Agricultural Digest shacked up under my kitchen table, and the entire kitchen floor was covered with a two-inch layer of sand.

My flip-flop flew off my foot when I kicked him in the ribs to wake him up. "You want to explain this?"

He told me he was down on the beach getting frisky when a cop poked a flashlight in his face and said, "What are you doing?"

"Okay 'till you came along."

The cop had absolutely no sense of humor and gave him ten minutes to get off the beach.

He made a drunken promise to this barroom babe that he would provide romance in the sand, and being a man of his word he went down to the basement of our building and borrowed the coal shovel. They weaved their way back to my apartment 14 times carrying 14 blanket-loads of sand up from the beach, and dumped them onto my tiny kitchen floor.

In a fit of disgust, I stuck them into a cab and sent them back to the darkness from whence they had come. I still had sand in that kitchen six months later. I never loaned out another blanket.

I threw myself into my music career with all the energy I could muster. Eddie Rusk, my new roommate and lifelong friend, played sax and keyboards, and Bobby Delich held down the drum chair. We started to work full time, in nightclubs on the north side of Chicago. I continued producing and arranging records as opportunities presented themselves, and recorded a few more of my own songs. Unfortunately, success seemed to be on hiatus for the time being.

The band spent time performing on the road. The "Starlight Lounge" in Rockford, Illinois became one of our favorite venues. During the day it showcased a large wood-burning grill off to one side of the bar. We bought hamburgers and steaks and cooked them ourselves. Then we filled our plates from a long table covered with side dishes. It was a great concept. No re-cooks! If we screwed up our meat, it was our fault. They covered it up at night to allow for more seating.

The place drew over 1,000 people every weekend evening, a lively fun-seeking crowd of drinkers, dancers and music lovers. Bobby Delich, an accomplished musician and a ray of sunshine, found humor in every situation. He also played trumpet and the bass player, Wayne, performed magic. I played guitar, bass, trumpet, trombone, and a tiny bit of drums on one song. Eddie added the reeds and keyboard.

We were now a rock "show group," and our repertoire covered every type of music, spanning genres from Ricky Nelson and Neil Diamond to hard rock, Dixieland, and Frank Sinatra ballads. If you requested it, we could probably cover it.

We broke the monotony of being on the road by playing hide and seek with our new mid-sized mascot, my playful 45-pound, over-friendly part Doberman/Labrador mix named VO (our favorite cocktail at the time). He loved everybody.

He could also be our watchdog. He bit a motel owner who came into our room supposedly checking for drugs, something none of us ever indulged in. Although, every time we stopped drinking a liquor store closed somewhere.

For some reason, our bass player found it difficult to land a date. He finally brought a not-so-nice lady back to our motel one night, and it looked like he would finally, um...fulfill his dreams. In the middle of his attempted conquest, Delich opened his door and threw a bucket of ice water into the room. It took all of us to keep Wayne from throttling Bobby D.

Wayne responded with a stream of oaths and some loud threats! It ruined his date, not to mention her hairdo, and the dye on her shoes washed off in rivulets. It took some convincing to get him to stay with the band. He finally agreed, but he put us on "Be nice to Wayne" notice.

Back in Chicago, we started a long run at the "Cubby Bear Lounge" (then called the Cub's Lounge), an older, well-known watering hole across from the Cubs ballpark. We found it to be another cavernous, semi-seedy bar with an occasional rough crowd, but on game days it was packed with lubricated baseball fans. It still sits near the ballpark, serving adult beverages to die hard Cubs fans.

Here we met and added another notable individual to our ever-growing list, a superb blues guitar player named Larry. I enjoyed spending time with him, but he had a mercurial disposition that made him one of those guys you needed to evaluate before you hung out. He was one of the toughest human beings I ever met, and he never backed away from a fight. You didn't want to be around Larry if you found him in a bad mood.

His main squeeze, a waitress at the Cubby Bear, a pretty lady with a Connie Francis 1956 style bouffant hairdo, wore a sexy little outfit when she was working at the club. Larry was crazy about her. One night some drunken truck drivers made the mistake of yelling, "Send the *ho* over here!"

Larry headed for their table like a cat to an upended can of tuna fish, and the bartender sighed and picked up the phone. I looked on with apprehension. "Calling the police?"

"No, an ambulance."

Larry decided he'd take karate. A group of bar owners shuddered at the thought. Larry earned a first-degree black belt. One night, I sat at a club up on Lincoln Avenue on the north side of Chicago. Larry played with his eyes shut, lost in a tasty guitar solo. As I enjoyed the music, some intoxicated idiot threw a beer bottle at him, which smashed on the wall directly beside his head. Larry's eyes shot open, and he very calmly put down his guitar.

The bandstand ran behind a long bar. The average crowd at this joint consisted of people who had been in jail, bulky construction workers, and folks who were probably about to go to jail.

Larry started at one end of the bar, grabbed the first customer by his shirtfront and said, "Did you throw that bottle?"

The guy turned white and shook his head. Larry went down that bar asking the same question to the rest of the men, one stool at a time. Finally one large construction worker said, "Yeah! What are you gonna do about it?"

I winced! Wrong answer! The guy pulled a knife. Larry disarmed him in about two seconds, beat him to a pulp, and for the grand finale he smacked him over the head with a table. There were also some rumors about someone kicking out all the windows and setting fire to the guy's car, but everyone in the club had scattered by then.

While playing at the Cubby Bear, we noticed a couple of thuggish looking guys in dark suits leaning against the far wall. They looked like the type of muscle that worked for the mobster, Bugsy Siegel. They came into the club several times, and scoped us out over the period of a week. One Sunday night they approached me, and one of them said, "The boss wants to meetcha."

I asked him, "Who's the boss?"

He leered at me and said in his best James Cagney voice, "Joe." Well, who was I not to accept this *formal* invitation?

I climbed into the back seat of a black sedan and my silent escorts drove me downtown to Rush Street, the sizzling hotbed of nightclub entertainment in Chicago, to meet "Joe." They parked in front of the Maryland Hotel and escorted me to a two-room suite on the first floor. The front room resembled a living room, and there were four extremely big guys who looked like bouncers (polite for gangster), playing cards, watching TV, and drinking beer.

The second room was a lush wood-paneled office. An intimidating Oriental man sat in a leather chair behind a giant mahogany desk. Memories of *The Godfather* ran through my brain, and I assumed I had just met Joe. One of my bodyguards pointed to a chair and I sat down, glad to be off of my shaky knees.

The two "talent scouts" walked out and closed the door. Joe stared at me sending shivers down my back. He finally said, "I want your band to come play on Rush Street at a show lounge."

Joe did not look like the kind of chap who would negotiate, so deciding that I wanted all my arms and legs intact, I asked, "When?"

"Two weeks."

"I'm not in the union."

"Come here tomorrow at two, bring your guitar, and see Mario."

I went back to the club and told the guys we were having a change of scenery. We were about to venture into uncharted waters. I took my guitar downtown the following day, and met "Mario." In those days, to join the union you were required to audition, so I had no idea how this would go.

We were ushered into a conference room at the union building, where two unsmiling officials sat at a long, intimidating conference table. Mario nodded at me and said, "Play!"

I played two chords and he said, "That's enough."

"Don't you want me to play a song?"

He scowled at me and growled, "I said that's enough!"

He shot a vicious look at the union officials and told me to put my guitar away, and poof! I was in the union. It must have been those two exceptional chords I played.

I attended another meeting with Joe and he informed me we would be the second band on the bill with the featured act that I'll call, "Richie and the T's." He showed me a picture of the band. Wow! Just wow! These guys stepped out of the old *Peppermint Lounge* in New York, but instead of wearing wild-colored tuxedos, they were dressed in pajama-like medieval costumes. Richie, the lead singer was smaller than the other band members, but he had a substantial head of hair.

I thought, "This is going to be interesting."

We moved our equipment down to Tony's Show Lounge on the corner of Rush and Walton, a short elevator ride down one level below the sidewalk. We began to set up for our big opening.

Ironically, the club was located in the basement of the building that housed Universal Studios, where I spent hundreds of hours of my future life recording music. Oh yeah! Welcome to Rush Street.

Chapter 13

One could compare moving from the Cubs Lounge down to Rush Street, to transitioning from a suburb to the glitter, the traffic, and the excitement of New York City.

The "Street" displayed an undeniable aura of desperation—people trolling bars and strip clubs, searching for a break from their mundane lives. It had become an oasis for the lonely, the disco dancers, the thrill seekers and the music lovers who pushed their way down the sidewalks, moving from venue to venue.

Inside the trendy drinking establishments, you could hardly miss the hunger in the weary eyes of aging, married businessmen, gazing longingly at tables of twittering secretaries. A stockbroker stood at the bar sipping a double martini, discussing social issues with a college student who was chugging a beer, sitting on a chrome barstool.

Out on the street, a lady of the night whispered promises of a brief erotic encounter from the darkness of a doorway. So, there on a corner in this neon fantasy world sat our new abode, Tony's Show Lounge.

You could call Tony's a classy joint and a bona fide nightclub. First walking into the club with a cave-like cabaret entrance; attention drawn to a massive antique bar and vivid maroon carpeting. The tables were unusually large. Smoky glass globes sat in the middle of white tablecloths, and soft velvet chairs were spaced comfortably apart. A polished dance floor located in front of an oversized bandstand, glowed from spotlights strategically placed in tracks on the ceiling, to create countless dramatic effects. Nice setup! We moved our equipment to the rear of the stage to leave room for Richie and the T's.

Tony, a suave Italian-looking host, wore a shiny sharkskin suit. The spotlights reflected off his glistening black hair. Microphone in hand, he walked onto the dance floor, pandered to the ladies, and told a few slightly suggestive jokes. Tony warmed up the crowd before he introduced the T's.

The spectators were extremely well dressed. Imposing Italian men in custom tailored suits, escorted platinum blonde "nieces" in fur coats, low-cut dresses, and designer shoes. The remainder of the crowd seemed diverse, and the demographic changed every night.

The place resonated with a completely new vibe. I liked it! I didn't think I'd have to worry about anyone getting in a fight in this place. (How wrong you can be!) Tony did his shtick and introduced Richie.

Your first look at Richie and the T's made you blink your eyes a few times. Here were these stereotypical rockers, dressed like Robin Hood. They wore cloth boots, hospital-green tights the length of pedal pushers, and fitted shirts, scalloped at the hem in a pattern that looked suspiciously like valances from Windsor Castle. The band had their hair styled like Elvis Presley (pompadour hairdos), but not Richie. He looked like he stuck his finger into an electric socket to get his hair blown up. Small guy, big humongous hair! Why not? It worked for The Four Seasons!

Richie was an ebullient rocker—not a singer, but a rocker. They made lots of noise, the sax player wailed away, and they played thumping loud rock and roll. Richie put on a great show, and the crowd danced, drank, and loved it. It made me rethink my powder blue tux jacket. We performed after they finished their show and Joe stood in the corner, smiling.

The manager/maître d' of the club, a gracious, soft-spoken oriental man named Cecil, seemed to have everyone's respect. He supervised the club and everyone who worked there, including the waitresses, who could be a handful (no pun intended) at times. For some reason, everyone seemed to do whatever Cecil asked with very little resistance. I found out why later.

The bartender, built like a sumo wrestler

without the tummy, had arms as big as my thighs. His name tag read "Chang," and he smiled and laughed at everything.

Joe told us it was mandatory to rehearse every Tuesday afternoon. They rolled back the cigarette machine at the rear of the club, and behind it we glimpsed what looked like a conference room that resembled a cave, surrounded by solid rock. Men I pretended not to recognize held clandestine meetings in the vault. We were required to rehearse at full volume to foil audio surveillance, and of course, we didn't see nothin'.

You never knew what was going to happen at Tony's. One night, Eddie, put down his sax and walked over to the bar. A deranged fellow stuck a gun in his ribs and said, "I've been looking for you."

Eddie thought quickly. He pointed across the room. "You must mean that other guy over there."

When the gunman averted his glance, the bartender jumped over the bar and clocked him.

On another night, four drunken football players came rolling out of the elevator, carrying on and cursing loudly, and they attempted to straight-arm their way past Cecil into the club. Cecil very politely said, "Gentleman, you cannot come in here. You have had too much to drink."

One of the guys started to shove Cecil and called him an ethnic slur.

If I hadn't been watching, I never would have

believed the chaos that followed. Our mild mannered club manager turned into Bruce Lee. In ten seconds, three of those guys were beaten, bruised, and lying on the floor. Cecil looked at the only guy who still stood upright, who stared at him open mouthed, trying to figure out what happened.

Cecil very calmly said, "The only reason you are still standing is so you can take out the trash." He hadn't even mussed up his hair. The guy dragged his buddies into the elevator, Cecil pressed the up button, and that ended the episode.

At my startled look, Chang started to laugh. "Oh, you don't know about Cecil? He was the head martial arts instructor, Japanese army in World War II."

One night I arrived at the club early to share a drink with Chang and catch Richie's set. Cecil approached me with a worried expression. "Mr. Bobby, we have a problem."

Richie's drummer hadn't shown up and the club was packed to the rafters. Bobby, my drummer, wasn't due to arrive for 45 minutes, so Cecil told me to play drums for the T's.

I pounded on the drums for about 45 seconds on one tune in my band's show, but a drummer I was *not*.

Cecil said, "Go! Go!"

I couldn't say no. I didn't want to risk getting

on his bad side, but I thought, "This is going to be a disaster."

I reluctantly dragged myself up on the bandstand and sat down, surrounded by an intimidating array of calfskin heads on a mind-boggling set of drums.

"Richie and the T's" played loud and long. I tried to keep a beat with my right foot on the bass drum, pound away on the snare with my left hand, crunch the hi-hat with my left foot (about every other beat), and added an occasional tom-tom and cymbal smash to keep things interesting. Boy, did I suck! The guitar player looked like he wanted to kill me, but I mouthed, "I'm all you got."

What a nightmare. I felt my foot might fall off when the nerves in my toes erupted in pain, then my right ankle froze up. I developed blisters on my fingers from the slippery sticks and one on my butt from trying to keep from falling off the wobbly drum stool. My last drop of energy oozed from my body, and my heart almost jumped out of my chest as I gasped for breath. After what felt like an eternity, the set finally ended. I've never been so thankful to see something conclude in my whole life. I never even got a thank you.

Cecil probably kept The T's from killing me, and praise God, their drummer showed up for the next show. I wouldn't have lived through a second set. I limped for a week. I kissed my guitar goodnight and prayed for heaven to send lightning to strike me dead if I ever had to do that again. Cecil snickered, but I wasn't about to call him on it. No health insurance!

One night after work, we inhaled a super-sized breakfast at a greasy spoon around the corner from the club. The cops came in and rousted us for possessing drugs. Surprised, we could only look at each other. We did *not* do drugs, although I'm sure we would have failed breathalyzers. Chicago's finest told us they found some pills in the booth behind ours that had been full of female impersonators from a club down the block.

I smelled a setup. Bobby and I were sitting in the back of the paddy wagon and Bobby exclaimed, "Well, at least Eddie got away."

Door opened! They pushed Eddie in with us and we drove to the police station. What a joke. They hauled us out of the paddy wagon and sat us around a table in their "break" room where we anxiously awaited the next development.

A cop came in and told us to get up, place our hands on the wall and spread 'em. It was reminiscent of a scene from an old gangster movie. The officer came up behind Bobby and said, "What's your name?"

Bobby spun around, stuck out his hand and said, "Bob Delich! What's yours, man?"

I thought the top of the cop's head was going to come off. I began to think that we were going to proceed directly to jail!

I needed to use the washroom and the cop pointed and said, "Down the hall on your left."

Some security! I could have walked out the front door. That's when we definitely smelled a rat. Sure enough, Big John, the ominous hulking bouncer that worked for Joe, showed up and said he paid our bail. He told us we'd have to work for two weeks without pay to reimburse Tony's for the money.

We later learned that business at the club had been slow. They didn't want to lose us, but needed to cut down on expenses for a couple of weeks to please the "oversight committee." And of course, the cops were on the pad. Welcome to Chicago, folks!

A delightful, lovely girl had been coming into the club. We started talking and eventually shared a couple of casual dates. One night, Chang whispered to me, "Do you know that is (senior family member's) daughter?" (The names are omitted to protect the health of the author).

It got worse that night, when a mountain of a mob enforcer walked up to the bandstand. He stood down on the dance floor and I stood up on the bandstand that sat 18 inches higher, and the top of his head was even with mine.

He put his nose two inches from my face, stared into my eyes with a threatening look, and in a raspy rumbling whisper said, "(Blank) don't want his daughter datin' no musicians. *Capiche?*"

"*Yessir!*"

My knees stopped shaking about a half an hour after he shot me one last vicious look as he shuffled off, shaking the bandstand with every thundering step he took. I've seen scowlers before, but this guy terrified me. After that I always vetted my dates for any nefarious relatives.

I dated a beautiful blonde waitress named Jane for a few months. This created some problems for Cecil. When my friends from Northwestern came to see the show, Jane scoped out the group for anyone I could have dated, or I might show a future interest in.

Jane turned out to be a devious innovator with a jealous streak. When she discovered a person of interest to me, she casually spilled a drink on the past or prospective offender. If the girl happened to be wearing a white sweater, she'd "accidentally" dump a pink Cosmo or a glass of red wine all over her. She had a unique ability to find an appropriately colored drink, to inflict a maximum amount of damage to whatever outfit the target was wearing.

Cecil told me to inform him when my friends were coming in, so he could put them at a table in the farthest station away from the one she worked at that night. I stopped paying dry cleaning bills and dating her at about the same time.

Chapter 14

Joe ran at least a half-dozen clubs within a three-block radius. After a run at the Show Lounge, we were booked into The Whiskey A Go-Go, more of a rock and roll bar, where Joe thought he could take advantage of the publicity I'd received from my hit record. This clamorous party club featured wildly gyrating go-go dancers, flashing strobe lights, and a high-end clientele who loved to shake off their inhibitions and dance. Always crowded to the roof, the club received regular visits from the fire department. We were perfect for that place. Rush Street, the mecca of music entertainment in Chicago, no longer intimidated us. We were on the mountain to stay as long as we wanted to be there.

There seemed to be a small nucleus of guys, who continually started fights and stirred up trouble in the clubs. Unfortunately, several of the worst culprits were related to the "bosses." This made handling the problem a bit delicate at times. A phrase often stated at these scenes of civil unrest; "Do you know who I am?" Eventually, some sizable no-nonsense muscle arrived and escorted the offenders out of the club.

We played ballads and Sinatra songs at the Scotch Mist, wild rock at the Losers, show music at the Happy Medium, dance music at the Rush Up, then went back to the Show Lounge for another stint. Richie went to Las Vegas, and now we were playing on the bill with the Dukes of Dixieland. What fun! Everyone in that group was an accomplished New Orleans-style player.

We met Barrett Deems, their hyper, geriatric drummer. Life on the road had taken its toll on his appearance. Eyes ringed with dark circles, stared at us from a face wrinkled by a lifestyle of fast food and too many days on the road. A raspy cough interrupted his stories and his fingers were tainted mustard yellow from smoking too many unfiltered cigarettes. Barrett was older than dirt, cussed like a sailor, and funnier than *Two-and-a Half-Men*. He was known for his unique signature one-handed drum roll. He played drums on the table with his silverware every time we went out to eat. This drove the servers and the people at several surrounding tables crazy. He was prone to spew out hilarious personal anecdotes laced with profanity that kept us in stitches. We gave him a special place on our list of favorite memorable characters.

We played a fun four weeks opposite the energetic show group: The Treniers, a fancy tuxedo clad, raucous entertaining band of soul brothers straight out of Vegas. They sang, they danced, they had FUN; it was infectious. They were hilarious, superb musicians, great dancers and had become favorites of Frank Sinatra, Dean Martin, Jerry Lewis, and Sammy Davis Jr. They also rocked the Ed Sullivan show a couple of times. You can find vintage videos of the Treniers on YouTube that I know you will enjoy, especially the one with Dean Martin.

My memory is a bit hazy on this but, Bobby Delich reminded me we also backed up the soul group, The Flamingos. Their hit, "I Only Have Eyes For You," had topped the charts for many weeks.

The last act we shared the stage with turned out to be Johnny Winter, the talented albino blues guitar player. His sensitivity to light rendered him almost blind, so he wore wrap-around dark sunglasses all the time. He reminded me of some of the great Chess players as he poured out his soul into the music.

We'd run the gamut at Tony's, sharing the stage with Richie's pounding rock and roll, vintage Dixieland from the Dukes, Vegas Show Lounge music from the Treniers, 50s do-wop with the Flamingos, and finishing up with one of the best up and coming blues guitar players in the country. The time had come for us to bow out and move on to other places.

So our Rush Street era ended. The "family"

wanted to put us under contract and send us to the "Thunderbird Lounge" in Las Vegas. I'd seen some of those "lifetime" contracts, and wanted no part of that kind of commitment, so with great reluctance we made our exit. We left with an unblemished reputation and on friendly terms with everyone, even Joe. I produced demo tapes for him on several artists that he wanted to send to Vegas, and he seemed pleased. Better than the alternative.

I made friends with many of the "street" people; the bartenders, entertainers and music aficionados, whom I continued to run into for many subsequent years, when I went down to Rush Street to listen to music.

The band needed some time off, and Eddie and I were offered the opportunity to perform with a Beatles/Rolling Stones cover band at the Metropole in New York. That historic old place, one of the few remaining jazz night clubs on the East Coast, brought back memories of listening to music before I turned 18, thanks to my phony ID.

New York passed an ordinance that said if you paid one cover charge, you could stay for both shows. This killed the clubs, as they needed the cover charges from both performances to meet expenses and pay the musicians. The Metropole's solution; bring in a grunge rock band (us) and have the musicians turn up their amplifiers to crushing ear-splitting levels. In theory, the raucous music would drive all the jazz lovers out, and the club could let in a new crowd for the second show and collect another entrance fee.

A long stage ran behind the bar at the Metropole. The musicians found it too narrow for more than one musician to sit, so the entire band stretched out in a straight line. A problem emerged when you sat 25 musicians on that stage; the guys at the end had a hard time hearing the guys in the middle, so it sounded a little disjointed at times. We didn't care. There were only five of us, and we played so loud we couldn't hear anything anyway.

Eddie worked with the band when we played opposite Gene Krupa, but he needed to return to Chicago to complete some summer school classes.

The rest of us continued to work as the break band for Stan Kenton, Dizzy Gillespie, Woody Herman, and Buddy Rich. Buddy came off as a notorious grouch, but the rest of the musicians were open and friendly.

All of a sudden, our band outdrew the big bands. Rusty, the older gal who ran the place, put a go-go dancer in front of our unconventional noisy group, and we blew the jazz bands right out the door.

Some years later I ran into a couple of musicians from Stan Kenton's original big band. They told me they held me personally responsible for killing jazz in one of the few remaining premier nightclubs left in the Big Apple.

Most nights, after performing at the "Met," I wandered to the Village on the Lower East Side of Manhattan. Greenwich Village, well known as an artistic community, catered to flower children, musicians, poets, tie-dyed t-shirt makers, avant-garde jewelry designers, and average everyday hippies. Each individual owned a guitar, a drum, a flute, another instrument, or a poetry book. I honored the unwritten dress code. I either wore a black turtleneck or a tie-dyed t-shirt, possibly a frayed sweater, torn bell bottom jeans with flower patterns sewn on them, and sandals. There were no buzz cuts in sight. The villagers sported long unruly hair, mostly dark, but sometimes purple. You might see a smattering of beards, colorful beaded necklaces, and hand-woven wristbands.

I sang folk songs at the Gate of Horn. When I finished singing, I left with some mellow, free-spirited beatniks to play music, or read poetry in some obscure shadowy coffee house. We'd meet other small groups of people, then move to a wine bar and talk about politics and the evils of modern society.

As the night progressed, I'd end up in someone's crash pad, filled with people playing flutes and bongo drums. I sang protest songs and sipped cheap wine. When the festivities wound down, I dropped off to sleep on a couch, floor, or anywhere I could find an empty space. I don't think I ever woke up in the same place twice.

I hated to pack up my tie-dyed t-shirts and my scruffy sandals, comb my own unruly hair, set aside my folk music, and head home to reality. Spending time in the Village gave me the opportunity to escape from the rigors of my frenzied everyday existence, and spend hours with people who simply lived to love life. I had taken an incredible trip into a cultural time warp where material things weren't important. I have always been a closet hippie at heart.

At some point, I hope you have the opportunity to take a break and disappear from normalcy for a while. I highly recommend it! It certainly beats Miami Beach.

Chapter 15

Back we went to the north side of Chicago, to begin a new chapter of our musical saga. We started a run at the Clarite Lounge, a spacious friendly neighborhood bar. My life changed again, this time for keeps.

We were in the middle of our first set, when a raucous group of neighbors came through the door. They were celebrating, showing off a shiny bowling trophy they received for winning their league championship. It took me about 30 seconds to zoom in on a beautiful redhead. I did everything I could to get her attention, but she wanted no part of me. I tried to buy her a drink when we went on a break, but I ended up with the cold shoulder instead of her attention. She seemed to be enamored with Eddie, my close friend who played saxophone. Sax trumps guitar? Oh no!

Eddie had no interest in a serious relationship. He and Brenda shared a couple of casual dates, but birds didn't sing and bells didn't ring. I wanted to take her out. She didn't want to go. Undaunted, I believed in hope eternal!

Eddie headed home for Thanksgiving and I

asked him if he minded if I asked Brenda to spend time with me. He didn't object, so I started planning my stealth campaign. I wore her down and she relented, but only because she thought she could get rid of me. We set up a date for lunch, and she figured she'd antagonize me by making me take her to the laundry, the store, the post office, and every other stupid place she could think of. I knew this insurmountable situation called for drastic measures, so I devised a plan to turn the winds in my favor.

She was chuckling to herself when she loaded up my Cadillac convertible with half of her house, so we could start running all her pesky errands. I drove several blocks, then pulled over to the curb and parked.

She looked at me suspiciously and said, "What are you doing?"

I reached under the dashboard and pulled out a chilled martini shaker. Two martini glasses with olives miraculously appeared, and I poured each of us a drink. She gave me a bewildered look.

"I figured this was the only way I could ever get you to have a drink with me," I sheepishly admitted.

That broke the ice. We ran her errands, and she agreed to go out with me again. Sometimes being sneaky gets things done.

That was the beginning of a beautiful relationship. This year, 2021, we will have been together for over 50 years, all because of two martinis (dry, one olive). There have been plenty of ups and downs, but I still know what I knew the minute I saw her. I'd found the woman I wanted to love forever and grow old with. We developed a wonderful balance of caring and understanding, and we learned to respect each other's space. Yet, we were always just a step away in case one of us fell.

Brenda is a perfect partner in life. Even after all her wonderful qualities, there's one more major perk. She cooks Italian food just like her mother, has a zillion cookbooks, and actually knows what's in them. She is a phenomenal gourmet chef. That 138-pound guy from high school is gone forever. Thank God for Lipitor.

I received a life-changing letter telling me to report to the draft board for my physical. My mother sent me ten sets of x-rays, which showed that my back resembled a pretzel, a leftover souvenir from that old pole-vaulting accident. Down at the draft center, they glanced at the x-rays, threw them in the trash, and classified me 1A.

I was screwed. I started sorting my meager possessions and clearing out my apartment, anticipating the inevitable all-expense paid trip to Fort Dix.

We were working at a nightclub named, "The

Beritz," a semi-classy show lounge. This little fellow came in every night, and asked us to play "Bony Moronie" three or four times. He seemed to be a nice enough guy and the song had become one of our most requested dance-tunes, so we played it over and over. He repeatedly bought us drinks. I couldn't believe I could get buzzed from playing one song. One night he told us he hoped we'd have a long run at the "Beritz." "Bony Moronie" was his favorite song and he'd never heard a band play it so well.

Much to his dismay, I informed him that we might be gone any day, as I'd been classified as 1A and therefore was high on the draft list. He asked me if I had any physical problems, and I explained about my back. He told me to bring him a set of X-rays. I did! After seeing how Rush Street worked, I figured anything was possible. He hemmed and hawed as he scrutinized the x-rays, then he stuck them in his briefcase.

He arrived like clockwork every night, we played his song, and I waited for the letter that would send me camping. I received the letter, but instead of taking away two years of my life, I was reclassified 1Y, a deferred status.

The little guy came in and said, "Did you get your mail?"

"Yeah and I'm reclassified 1Y."

He said, "I know. I'm the head doctor at the draft examining board, and I believe your back injury is legitimate, and you'd never make it through basic training. Now play my song."

We must have played that song ten times that night, and I bought *him* copious rounds of drinks.

When I thought I'd be heading into the army, I had absolutely no reservations about going. I figured I'd end up playing officer's clubs and doing USO tours, if my bad back didn't wash me out in basic training. So, I didn't feel guilty, and this new 1Y classification left me free to pursue my career and my life. Of course, most importantly, I didn't have to leave Brenda.

Road trip! Eddie and I headed to New Jersey in his vintage Corvette convertible. I couldn't pack much, as the trunk in that car might have been two cubic feet. I planned to see my parents, and take a swing through New York to conduct record business.

We stopped to see my folks then traveled into the Big Apple, where I made my rounds to some of the publishers and record labels. We attempted to see Bobby Darin, but found an empty office. Eddie reminded me I stole Bobby's sign that said, "I'm the boss," but I conveniently don't remember doing anything as nefarious as that.

As I foraged around New York, I came upon an elegant nightclub: Toots Shores. A hangout for actors, musicians, and movers and shakers; this place looked like ground zero for entertainment industry figures when they chose to relax.

A friendly old black man, the grey-haired washroom attendant, turned out to be one of the most intelligent and unforgettable characters I met in the city. He made a fortune in tips and wouldn't have given up that job for anything, even though he had a college diploma. He pointed out the stars, the artists and producers. and recited their bios, helping me meet folks and make new contacts. I visited with him for years. He snuck me into the wrap party for *Ocean's Eleven* on a phony press pass, and I got to schmooze with Sinatra, Dean Martin, Sammy Davis Junior, Joey Bishop, Angie Dickinson and all the other stars. I had found my favorite New York watering hole.

We returned to Chicago, and Brenda cooked dinner for Eddie and his parents; a luscious gourmet chicken dish loaded with oregano. The compliments were flowing, as was the wine. The following morning, we woke up complaining that each of us had been plagued with the strangest dreams.

Eddie befriended an actress/singer who was trying to make it in LA, but when she traveled back to Chicago, she crashed at our apartment for a few days. She walked into the kitchen, picked up the oregano bottle (which was empty), shook it and said, "Where's my pot?"

That solved the mystery of the weird dreams.

We inadvertently experienced one of our two brushes with marijuana. We didn't dare admit it to Eddie's parents. They probably would have assumed we were potheads. Funny now! Not so funny then!

My second, and last, drug experience occurred after we purchased tickets for a Kiss concert. We took our kids and ended up sitting way up in the nosebleed seats of the amphitheater. The pot smoke from the audience drifted up and hung in a big cloud by the rafters. Forget about second-hand cigarette smoke. We experienced a major contact high. We left early as the kids were getting loopy, and I knew I had to drive home. Never again!

Brenda and I hated drugs. We saw too many actors, musicians and singers with addictive personalities tragically throw their lives away. The touring/recording rockers and some of their producers, managers, and groupies, seemed to use narcotics more than the professional studio musicians, and producers of radio and TV commercials and films. A tracking date required them to play precise and complicated music, and the musicians needed to hit the difficult film cues the first time they played them.

Chet telephoned us with the news that an old friend of his dropped into town. He asked Brenda if she'd cook her spectacular old-country Italian food for his guest. She graciously agreed and Chet showed up at our apartment with his friend Joe, anticipating a delectable home-cooked feast. For some obscure reason, we had purchased a bottle of Gallo Thunderbird, the wine that made Schlitz Malt Liquor taste like Champagne. Joe picked up the bottle, looked at it, and asked Brenda how she liked it.

Brenda replied, "It tastes like gasoline."

Joe looked at the bottle, studied the label, took off the top, sniffed the wine, pulled a notebook out of his pocket and took extensive notes. I looked at Chet and raised an eyebrow.

Chet said, "Oh, by the way, Brenda, this is Joe *Gallo,*" the son of Ernest and Julio Gallo; owners of the Gallo Wine Company.

In retrospect it was one of those comments that Brenda wished she could take back, but after Joe left we both thought it was funny as hell! Anyway, she made a wonderful meal, and Joe graciously did not mention the wine again.

Chapter 16

Eddie's parents ran into an agent on a trip to LA, and he extended an invitation for us to stay at his house if we ever traveled to California. I thought it might be interesting to fly west, and see what we could stir up. The soon-to-be-known as, Mister Flaky Hollywood Dude, said he looked forward to meeting us.

We walked into a circus. The agent's mansion turned out to be an aging relic, a monument to1940. A couple of threadbare couches sat on ugly grey shag carpeting, and the kitchen and the bathroom were in dire need of an update. I breathed a sigh of relief when I saw a seat on the toilet.

An unemployed actor lay on a blanket in a huge stone fireplace, and a male escort and his girlfriend lived in the squalor of a slovenly back bedroom. The sink overflowed with dirty dishes, and empty pizza boxes, and bags of potato chips were strewn everywhere. I spotted a few pictures of the agent posing with some unknown actresses, hanging on the spackled walls, in cheap plastic frames.

The agent turned out to be openly gay and

immediately started hitting on Eddie, who bolted and ran for the Hollywood Hills. He found an old friend from college to stay with. Traveling on a tight budget, I thought I could get away with sleeping on the couch.

The first night as I dropped off to dreamland, an enormous, ugly, black dog clambered up on the couch and sacked out next to me. I tried to shove his ample butt on the floor, but he growled at me so I couldn't get up until Fido, the dog, decided that I could. The good news: he snarled anytime anyone came near me. Nice doggy! I couldn't really comment on anyone else's lifestyle 'cause I was sleeping with a damned dog.

Our first taste of the alternative side of the west coast show biz, almost ruined my desire to return. Despite the deplorable living conditions, we met some music people to add to my ever-growing list of contacts. The last thing we did before we left LA: we scoped out some motels to stay at the next time we went west. One visit to the zoo was enough.

We headed home, relieved to have evaded the clutches of "Hollyweird." Brenda wanted to send the dog a box of Milk Bones and a thank-you note. I bought him a triple steak burger before I left.

Brenda and I led crazy, complicated lives. She handled many family obligations and worked in a German restaurant at night. Whenever she could break away, she came to visit me on the road, or attempted to drop in and catch a couple of sets when we played locally. We spent most of our days together, and realized that something remarkably special existed between us.

After a whirlwind courtship, and being of sound mind and body, I asked Brenda to marry me. Her traditional Italian mother blessed our upcoming nuptials with a touch of skepticism. ("Marrying a musician? Are you crazy?") She and my father would have agreed on that.

Brenda and I exchanged rings in a lovely little chapel at Northwestern, and moved into a comfortable apartment in the same building I lived in with John Kelley, located near the lake. Three boys appeared as if by magic, and we had a wonderful time in the years we spent between the beach, the recording studio, the clubs, and our cozy flat.

Despite my wondrous dance with blissful domesticity, I couldn't permanently shake the little devil that still sat on my shoulder once in a while. A nasty old man lived across the alley from our back entrance, and he continuously chastised the boys for simply doing what boys do. He cursed at us if we parked in the alley for a few minutes to unload groceries.

Late one lazy fall afternoon, I reclined on the couch as Brenda carried on a marathon telephone conversation with a friend. There I sat, with nothing but time on my hands. I started to think about this mean old man and felt I should rock his ill-natured world with hastily contrived retribution.

It was immediately after Halloween and a sagging jack-o-lantern still sat in our doorway. I pulled out a canvas shopping bag stuffed with fireworks left over from a previous Fourth of July celebration. I crammed the pumpkin full of all the explosives it would hold, and surprisingly found a long piece of Jetex hobby fuse in my bottom desk drawer.

Light sleet filtered to the ground and the skies were overcast and gloomy. I scoped out the alley for kids and pets, but figured they were all inside, staying warm in front of their glowing fireplaces. Perfect!

I put the end of the fuse in a string of 500 firecrackers, and set the pumpkin next to the old grump's house. I took another cursory look around, lit the fuse, and ran back inside. I pretended to sleep, comfortably nestled in my cushy armchair, when "Pumpkingate" went off. Pretty effing loud! Lasted a while too. Brenda got off of the phone in a hurry yelling,

"Dammit, Bobby! What did you do?"

I opened my eyes, shrugged (something I learned from Dave Moore, my pilot), and replied in a phony innocent voice, "Nothin'!"

Then I yawned and casually reached over and picked up a copy of *Guitar World*. I glanced up for a second. She had her hands on her hips, giving me "the look." I expected to be called by all three names. but she shook her head, mumbled something that sounded like "basspole", and withdrew into the kitchen.

We didn't dare walk out of the house for a few hours, but when we finally emerged, the old grump stood in the alley, scratching his head, and frowning at us as he looked at his orange house. He wasn't stupid. He knew who did it, but you can't get a conviction sans evidence. He never yelled at us again, but if dirty looks could kill I'd be a dead man!

I started working at a club in Old Town, appropriately named, "The Outhouse." It was a perfect location. "The Troubadour" (a folk lounge) was to the right of us, the "Plugged Nickel" (a jazz club) to the left, and a gaudy strip club nestled on the corner, where the blinking fluorescent lights sent out a clarion call to those looking for erotic titillation. (Again, no pun intended.)

On band breaks we headed over to the "Troubadour." Bobby, Eddie, and I made the acquaintance of Jose Feliciano, Oscar Brown Junior, and Miriam Makeba. Such beautiful, talented people!

The Plugged Nickel featured small ensembles

of jazz greats, and catered to avant-garde music aficionados. One night we attended a Miles Davis show. Miles, unusually moody, played his trumpet over in a corner of the stage with his back to the audience.

This rather stout obnoxious lady at a front table jumped on his case. "Hey, Miles! Why don't you face the audience? Are you too good for us, Miles," and so on.

Miles finished his set, completely ignoring the woman. He set his trumpet down, lit up a cigarette and casually took a few deep puffs. After he'd smoked about half of it, he sauntered off the stage, and as he walked by the big mouth's table he casually dropped his cigarette in her drink, never bothering to look at her.

As you walked down that block, the signs said: "The Troubadour starring Oscar Brown Junior"; "The Outhouse featuring Bobby Whiteside"; "The Plugged Nickel—performing live tonight—Miles Davis"; and "The Old Town Gentlemen's Club presents Boom-Boom Bazooms and the Ta-Tas."

My dad just shook his head when he came to hear us play at The Outhouse. Mom wanted to know what a ta-ta was. They listened to our music and seemed to enjoy the band. As usual, they told us we should turn the volume down.

We knew we were close to the end of our run at the Outhouse the night the toilets backed up and people continued to dance.

Chapter 17

The legendary company, Chess Records, has been the subject of feature films, documentaries, and books for many years. Brothers Leonard and Phil, Polish immigrants, moved to the South Side of Chicago, and turned it into the heartland of blues music. They quickly learned that the impoverished neighborhoods were starved for their own music. Leonard and Phil signed a handful of black artists, started recording the blues, and peddled the records on the streets in the 'hood out of the trunk of their car. After months of tenacious exhausting work, they established themselves as major players in the fields of soul music and blues records, producing songs that their urban audience could relate to.

Eventually, they acquired a nightclub where they showcased their talented acts, and over time forged close ties with the major R&B radio stations, one of which they were ultimately able to buy. As the label flourished, the Chess brothers collaborated with Sam Phillips (another recording industry pioneer in Memphis), and began to search the entire country for artists to sign to their company. I don't want to bog you down with reams of Chess Records' history, but Google it sometime. It's fascinating reading, and an intriguing success story.

The original Chess studio, located in an unpretentious building at 2120 South Michigan, was well known and world famous. Projects recorded in that sparsely furnished room had an incredibly unique sound. The incessant industry chatter about the "Chess sound," reached the Rolling Stones and they made the trip to Chicago to record an album and capture some of the funk that emanated from the room. The studio, a long narrow space with high ceilings, emerged as an internationally acclaimed acoustic marvel, comfortable enough to put the musicians at ease and let the ideas flow freely. Magic happened every time they recorded an artist.

Leonard knew he needed a mega-studio, large enough to accommodate a full orchestra. He moved his entire operation to a commercial building two blocks further south, where he constructed *TerMar* studios, consisting of the studio of his dreams and a smaller funky facility for the blues and rock groups. He added several simple one-room studios for editing and screening material. He hated leaving 2120. After the agonizing but necessary move, he destroyed the original studio to prevent any of his competitors from buying it and recreating his sound. Today, after a massive renovation, 2120 South Michigan stands as a landmark building, housing the Willie Dixon Blues Foundation commemorating the evolution of blues music in Chicago.

The newly constructed TerMar Studios excelled Leonard's wildest expectations, and the staff continued to produce hit records without missing a beat. As always, one unexpected quirk appeared. The new building had four floors, and the stairwell functioned as an amazing live echo chamber. If someone used a door to the stairwell, you'd get a slam right in the middle of a song, so they had signs on all the doors that said, "Check with the office before opening the door, unless the place is on fire."

Almost all their original hit artists were black: Howling Wolf, Willie Dixon, Lightnin' Hopkins, Muddy Waters, Bo Diddley, The Flamingos, The Dells, Walter Jackson, Fontella Bass, Minnie Riperton, John Lee Hooker, Jimmy Reed, Etta James, Little Walter, and Ramsey Lewis. The label showcased an encyclopedia of R&B stars from 1950 to 1969, when it was sold to *GRT.*

Paul Glass, the owner of my first record label, asked me to come to his office for a meeting with Leonard and Phil Chess. Chess was thinking about opening a white pop division in partnership with Paul, and they offered me a job to produce the acts. My father smiled when he heard I might have a real job.

I gratefully accepted the position, heading off on a 22-month long whirlwind ride that firmly established my deep rhythm and blues roots, and ingrained in me a love for the indelible soul music that would last the rest of my life. I observed hundreds of sessions (they did up to four a day six days a week), and learned from and worked with some of the most celebrated studio musicians in the world. I had the good fortune to land in the midst of brilliant soulful singers, producers, engineers, and writers.

Some days, I'd look around and feel like a paleface at an Indian convention, but I only faced a moderate amount of resistance from one producer. It was all about the music and creating hit records. Race was never much of an issue.

At that time Chicago was experiencing racial and civil unrest in the streets. The sprawling, poorly lit, Chess parking lot happened to be in a late-night low-traffic area. At that time I carried a full-sized .45 caliber 1911 semi-automatic pistol, in a case that looked like a folio. It opened up when I pushed in on both ends. I left the studio at three in the morning and walked to my car, oblivious to the dangers of the night and not paying attention to my surroundings. As I approached my vehicle, two men stepped out from behind it and blocked my path.

One of them said, "Where you think you goin', man?"

There was about eight feet between us, so in a panic, I hastily popped my case and pulled out that formidable pistol. We stared at each other and I finally squeaked out, "Anywhere I want to!" I waved my intimidating pistol around like a crazy person.

For a brief time we had a standoff and the world stood still, then they began to slowly back away. I heard one of them say, "Man goin' anywhere he want to!" The glowing anger in their eyes cut through the shadows as they disappeared into the night. After I climbed into my car, I slowly exhaled. I hadn't realized I'd been holding my breath.

Thank God my survival skills kicked in when I needed them and I pulled through another close call. I peeled out of the parking lot, berating myself for being so careless and clueless. Then, the adrenaline rush crashed and I shook all the way home. Lesson learned!

The house rhythm section included Bryce Roberson, a blue-eyed soul guitar player from Detroit, and Louis Satterfield on bass. Louis went on to play trombone with the Tower of Power horns, after he played virtually hundreds of sessions for Chess and Motown. He helped develop the driving Motown bass sound that you heard on so many hit records. Maurice White, who later started the group Earth Wind and Fire with Louis, performed on drums.

When he left, Morris "Mo" Jennings took over the slot. Morris, a metronome with a smile turned out to be one of my favorite musicians of all time. We worked together for years. Every time he sat at his drums, all I had to do to get a great sound was turn on the microphones.

Leonard signed talented staff writers to his huge publishing company, who cranked out hit after hit for Chess and Motown. Leonard had a discerning ear for finding top-selling artists and an understanding of soul music that led him to sign prolific writers.

The first group I found for my white pop division, had a truly weird name: P-Thoup. They were an incredibly unconventional ensemble that I discovered singing on a sidewalk for tips. They looked like scruffy flower children from San Francisco. I liked the lead singer's distinctive commercial rock voice. I took the group into the studio to evaluate them. What a disaster!

The band behaved like kindergartners, totally undisciplined and obnoxious, and they thought everything was funny. They were stoned out of their gourds. I barely avoided a fistfight with the guitar player, and quickly kicked them to the curb.

They pulled it together a couple of weeks later and begged me for another audition. This one worked out in their favor and I signed them. The actual recording session featured new musical sounds that were groundbreaking and light years ahead of the times.

Marshal Chess, Leonard's son, signed a Leonard Cohen-type singer that he asked me to produce. I'd been sliding down to Nashville to write and record songs, and loved the way those Nashville cats played together. Their tight rhythm sound differed from the Chess sound, but Marshall knew he'd found what he needed to record a commercial album.

I flew in Charlie McCoy, the legendary harmonica/bass player, Mac Gayden on guitar (wrote the timeless hit, "Everlasting Love"), and Nashville's number one drummer at the time, Kenny Buttrey.

Charlie and Mac flew in together and I picked them up at the airport in my tiny Triumph convertible sports car. I must have been brain dead not to have brought a bigger car. We managed to tie their luggage on the back of the little red menace, but three of us were crammed into the two front seats. As we flew down the expressway, Mac held his guitar over the side of the mini-car. I caught a lot of well-deserved flack for that one. Impressed with the Nashville guys,

Marshall whisked them off to Europe, to play on a Howlin' Wolf album.

I selected several other groups to sign to my division. One of the groups featured a pushy, arrogant, writer/musician named Nathan. Bryce Roberson, the Detroit guitarist, had asked Leonard for the chance to do some engineering. Leonard directed him to use one of the small studios and record guitar/vocal tracks of Nathan's songs, so we could evaluate them and pick the best ones to record on their album.

Bryce suffered through a terrible day. (And did I mention he had a temper?) Nathan, an obnoxious handful, stretched Bryce's last nerve to the max by the end of the afternoon. He became belligerent one too many times and that last nerve snapped. Bryce removed the whole roll of tape containing all 18 songs, from the recording machine. He picked up a razor blade, stared at Nathan like a feral animal, and sliced the entire roll into ten-inch pieces.

Nathan turned as white as a sheet. Bryce, razor in hand, continued to lock eyes with his nightmare artist and didn't utter a word as he backed out of the room, muttering ominous threats. The heavy door slammed shut, like the crack of a gunshot. I'm sure Nathan looked up and down the hall before he scuttled to his car. Now that was what I call an attitude adjustment. You didn't mess with those Detroit boys.

I finished up the six albums Leonard requested, but he shelved the project temporarily. He needed time to research what kind of promotion he had to put in place, in order to get airplay on pop stations around the country. In the meantime, I sat in limbo. Every one of the acts I recorded had star potential, but it wouldn't be the last time a project I worked on for months fell by the wayside.

Leonard finally decided to shelve the white pop division altogether. He realized it would be a massive undertaking to set up a new promotion network, so I lost that job. However, Leonard asked me to stay on for a while as an arranger and a floating producer.

Leonard told me to poke my head into sessions and see if I could add anything. It was the opportunity of a lifetime. I stayed in the background and learned more in 20 months than I did in my six years in and out of college. I made small suggestions, and occasionally commented on mixes, but most of the time the producers hit home runs without needing any of my input.

Dick la Palm, CFO of Chess, heard some of the arranging I had been doing. The label signed Woody Herman and his band, The Thundering Herd. Dick asked me if I had time to write a big band chart for the group. I jumped at the chance.

I put countless hours into this project. I wrote my personalized version of "Dreams of the Everyday Housewife" in 6/8 jazz waltz time. I fervently believed this arrangement could be a showstopper. The music featured exciting screaming trumpets, aggressive woodwinds, and a "thundering" rhythm track.

I took the chart to Dick and he showed it to Woody, who put on his granny glasses, studied the score, and turned it down flat. I couldn't believe it! After all that work—zilch!

My keyboard-playing friend from Stan Kenton's Band scanned the chart and said, "Hey, dumbass, Woody's solo is too hard. He's a figurehead, not a virtuoso."

Another lesson learned. Don't write more notes than your artist can play or sing.

Bryce tracked me down one afternoon, and asked me to come into the studio where they were recording Billy Stewart's take on the song, "Summertime." He felt the music needed embellishment and wanted the input of my fresh ears. I listened to what they already recorded, and suggested adding a memorable signature guitar lick in the intro, to set up the song. We worked out an ear-catching solo, they finished the session and the record became a smash hit.

When Motown artists toured in the area, they found Chess Studios a comfortable venue to conduct rehearsals. I found it thrilling to watch The Supremes, The Temptations, The Four Tops, Jerry Butler, Marvin Gay, Smokey Robinson, Stevie Wonder, and so many others as they arranged their songs, practiced their choreography, and polished their shows for their next major road trip.

A Chess recording artist, unhappy with the label, asked me to find him another record company. His current contract expired, and he didn't think he wanted to resign. I flew to New York for a meeting with Columbia Records, and they were so excited about the material I played for them, they offered me $20,000 to record four songs. After that, they agreed to give me another 50K to finish the album (almost unheard of budgets at that time). I flew back, told the artist and he seemed extremely happy. What could possibly go wrong?

I returned home for the weekend, thinking about producing his session. I had never been more confident in my life that one of those songs would be an undeniable hit. Columbia concurred!

Monday morning, Max Cooperstein, the business manager of Chess said, "Come in to my office and shut the door."

He told me that the artist re-signed with Leonard over the weekend. I asked him how that could possibly happen with so much cash available from Columbia.

He replied, "The artist got drunk and needed some money for pot, so he went to Leonard, who gave him a hundred bucks. Then he said casually, "Oh, by the way, sign this contract while you're here." I was dumbfounded! I looked like an idiot when I reported back to Columbia.

The soulful writing and recording flowing from my pen began to formulate the foundation for my own sound. I composed music and enhanced it with unique orchestrations. When my musicians performed the arrangements, they breathed life into them and the tracks soared. The music showcased my new signature, driving groove. I hadn't heard much of this in the pop music world yet, but this style contributed to my success when I changed careers.

I enjoyed a brief stint as an artist on Mercury Records. The song I released; "The Sun is Cold." Unfortunately, it had the same sound as the Sonny and Cher record "I Got You Babe," that they released two weeks after mine. Guess who won that battle!

I independently recorded a mega-talented local band. Lots of turmoil and egos, but they were skilled musicians and featured two strong lead singers. After the band broke up, I signed one of the singers to a personal recording agreement, and secured him an offer to record for Black Sabbath Records in Europe. However, he wanted to be with a band, and an up and coming group was looking for a lead singer.

I let him join the band and we signed a one-inch-thick contract where the band agreed to pay me a percentage of what they accomplished in the first year. The rest is history as their first hit went double platinum. However, the group refused to honor their contract and the only lawyer I could find willing to sue them, wanted a $50,000 retainer, so I reluctantly let it go.

It was my first experience with people whose word was not their bond, and to whom a contract was a worthless piece of paper and, unfortunately, was not the last. It turned out to be a very expensive lesson, as my share of the royalties would have come to a considerable amount, not to mention the fact that I lost thousands of dollars in developmental money I'd spent on the singer's career.

On one of my frequent trips to New York I met Gene Weiss. Gene discovered Janis Joplin and Bob Dylan. I had high hopes that he could ignite my career. Gene loved the existing music tracks on four of my self-penned songs. I climbed aboard a jet plane and headed east to sing the lead vocals.

He booked the recording session at RCA Studio A, large enough to house a 747 and seat the audience from Carnegie Hall at the same time. It resembled an empty shell of an abandoned Costco at midnight. In the middle of this dark chasm of an amphitheater, sat one tiny microphone, one black metal music stand, one solitary wooden stool for me to sit on, and a single spotlight provided a minimal amount of illumination.

Waiting in the shadows, barely visible, I began to eyeball the studio in a fruitless quest to estimate how long it would take me to walk to the bathroom. Gene broke into my distraction when he pushed the talkback button in the control room, and delivered one of the most memorable lines of my career. He said, "Be intimate!"

I blinked, knowing that I was the sole occupant in this vast warehouse. Flustered, I threw my hands up in the air and bellowed, "Are you kidding me? You put me in the middle of a f***ing airplane hangar and you expect me to be intimate?"

That line followed me for years!

Despite the fact that we never quite finished the vocals the way we wanted, Gene's label went ahead and released one of the songs. I ended up with another fizzle. I needed to take a break from recording and focus on songwriting. I hoped that somewhere down the road the ocean would wash ashore more riches than the tide took away.

Chapter 18

I needed to kick it up a notch with the band, or figure out something else to do that made more money. I searched for ways to find bookings in newer venues that provided more exposure. I no longer had the security of the Chess job, and with a family to support I had to build a better mousetrap.

I booked us into a reasonably classy club, and arranged for Herb, the #1 booking agent in Chicago, to come audition us. We'd rehearsed the show to perfection and impatiently waited for Herb. What happened next is referred to as "The Great Rubber Chicken Incident."

Wayne, the bass player, used a rubber chicken as a prop when he performed an occasional magic trick. The funky chicken, usually resided at the back of the bandstand, next to Bobby Delich, when Wayne wasn't pulling it out of unexpected places. The guys became restless, and their boredom increased the longer they waited for Herb. Bobby snatched the chicken and succumbed to a reckless impulse. He whipped it at Wayne, smacking him squarely in the back of the neck. *Thwak!*

At that exact moment, Herb strolled through

the door in time to hear Wayne let loose a tirade of profanity that would have made a stripper blush. Unfortunately, the microphone was on and Wayne's blasphemous blast even made me wince. Herb stopped in his tracks, gave the band a, "you're kidding me" look, shook his head, and trudged back to his silver Mercedes convertible.

That did it! I knew I'd continue playing as long as I could, but it was imperative that I begin to search for a new career. I naively decided to make a foray into the jingle business, writing and producing music for radio and TV commercials. Sometimes not knowing what you are about to attempt is a blessing in disguise.

I cut together a composite tape of the music I'd recorded with my pop acts, and a selection of R&B material produced while I worked at Chess. Eddie and I blindly chased around the advertising agencies and film companies, hoping they would listen to the tape, like what they heard, and throw us an assignment.

My music, a composite of pop and soul music, mirrored the new hit songs on the radio, and sounded more contemporary than the jingles being produced at that time. Many of the current music campaigns were a bit old-fashioned, and square. My music was more *Soul Train* than *Lawrence Welk*.

I plunged blindly into the abyss of the advertising world, but stayed loyal to my rock and roll roots. My hair grew past my shoulders, I wore a Nehru jacket, bell-bottom jeans and sandals, and looked like I just left Frank Zappa's house. I presented a different picture from the usual staid suits and ties the other jingle producers wore. I think one of the most frequent questions at the agencies became, "Who the hell is Bobby Whiteside, and where did he come from?"

I had the good fortune to land an appointment at Leo Burnett, with a brilliant creative director named Hal Kome. Some years later Hal told me, "You looked so stupid when you and Eddie walked into my office that I figured I had to help you."

He gave us our first job! It was a Motorola commercial, with my old friend Peter Cetera singing the lead.

Our second assignment, a Captain Crunch commercial, didn't have a huge budget, but the train began to roll, albeit slowly. In addition, I composed music for the Santa Fe Railroad. We were in a financial hole, but I thought this business had potential. Then, Eddie got drafted and I had to come up with a new marketing plan.

I started to build up my company: The Trendsetters. Tom Hall, a creative director at J. Walter Thompson, hired me to produce a variation on the theme, "I Wish I Were an Oscar Mayer Wiener." We booked a young rock and roll group, Gary and The Hornets, to act and sing on camera. I'd see a lot more of Tom, both as a client and a friend over the years. This moment can be found on YouTube, by searching for "Oscar Meyer Wiener Gary and The Hornets." The exposure from this production started to open doors for me, and I hoped that things would start clicking into place.

I composed a Kentucky Fried Chicken campaign for Hal Kome with the line, "Ain't it fun to lick your fingers." The visuals of people licking their fingers from every conceivable angle were hilarious. Hal thought we created a masterpiece. The client called it advertising porn. Hal loved to walk on the edge. I loved Hal!

Our little apartment became terminally overcrowded when we added a Great Dane, named Snoopy, into the mix. I produced a talented band named, The Family. The man who managed the group informed me he sold houses at a new housing development in Darien, located half an hour from downtown Chicago. He offered to sell me a four-bedroom colonial house on the corner of a cul-de-sac, at a heavily discounted price.

I borrowed $10,000 from my father for a down payment, money he probably thought he'd never see again. *Voila*! We were officially suburbanites. We couldn't pass up the opportunity to own a real home even though finances were tight. I threw myself into my new career. We wanted to pay off my father in a timely manner, and stay even with the mortgage payments.

We watched each stage of the construction from the ground up. As our new home emerged from the original dirt lot, we tried to visualize our future in this placid suburban neighborhood. We had no idea what our neighbors would be like. Some of their houses were being built at the same time as ours, and we looked forward to meeting them when they moved into their new homes.

The construction crew completed the finishing touches and we were ready to move in. We hired a couple of hulking men with two old rickety trucks that looked like they had been purchased from a Mexican Army surplus vehicle pool. With the help of some friends, we loaded up. Chet drove one of the junky trucks, and had a brief brush with the highway patrol when they pulled him over. After he convinced them he wasn't running drugs, he proceeded to the house. The vans pulled in the driveway, and the movers began to unload our meager possessions. All the neighbors came out onto their porches to view the newcomers.

I casually pulled up into the driveway, in my gold Cadillac convertible with the top down. Snoopy, my Great Dane rode shotgun, and VO perched on the center console, scoping out the neighborhood for bushes and fire hydrants. I let the dogs out, grabbed my guitar in one hand, and tucked a stack of hunting rifles under my other arm. As I walked into the house, I noticed that most of the neighbors had gone back inside their houses. Long hair, big dogs, guitars, and guns! Meet the new neighbor! There goes the neighborhood. It wouldn't be the last time I had that effect on people.

After the usual battles about which kid got what room, we settled in. I landed an occasional session and Brenda kept us on a tight budget. Then we made a huge mistake, which taught us a very valuable lesson. We completed a large project that brought in a substantial check. The money covered paying musicians, talent, studio costs, and me. We optimistically thought I'd be working on a regular basis, so we used some of that money to pay a handful of our bills. It didn't work out that way, and we were scrambling to make ends meet.

After three months of ducking musicians and singers who wanted their session fees, we were finally able to pay off all the charges that came with that job. We never spent money that wasn't ours, again.

The dogs loved frolicking on all that property, especially Snoopy, who set out to explore the neighborhood gardens and garbage cans. Snoopy did not endear himself in the cul-de-sac, so we tied him to one of the columns on the front porch. We stopped receiving mail. One of our neighbors reported that when Snoopy spied the mailman, he ran as fast as he could until he hit the end of his chain, then he flew up in the air about five feet and barked and snarled. The mailman wouldn't even venture onto our side of the street.

I built a ten by thirty fenced dog run on a concrete pad in the back yard that severely limited Snoopy's reign of terror. He marked every inch of the fence but he spent hours longing for one real tree. When we put VO in the dog run he sulked. He felt he hadn't done anything wrong, and should have been free to paint all the hedges and the bushes in the area.

Snoopy and Brenda had a love-hate relationship. He loved to aggravate her. She loved to hate him. When she attempted to carry a laundry basket up the stairs, he blocked her and leaned his 120 bulky pounds against her. He'd pounce on the nozzle and bite the hose when she vacuumed the carpets. When I left the house, he climbed to the top of the stairs, came flying down, scattered the carpets in the foyer, tore through the living room, ran through the dining room, and slid through the kitchen like he was on doggy crack.

One day, after he pushed her patience as far as he could, she waited around the corner in the kitchen. When he slid into the room, she wound up and smacked him with a metal broom, and knocked him on his ass. That slowed him down for about a week. At least he looked in the kitchen before he blew through it.

There were lots of Snoopy stories, but one day he busted loose and ran into my neighbors' yard. He started pulling up three-foot long pieces of newly laid sod, and tossing them over his shoulder. This episode sealed his doom. Unfortunately, inbreeding made his brain grow faster than his head. He suffered from headaches, and they made him mean. When he bit a little kid, I had to put him to sleep. I don't think VO missed him. Brenda smiled a lot more than usual.

I contemplated using ten feet of that dog run to put up a shed. I thought I'd install a doggy door, to let VO seek shelter from the rain while he was in his version of jail. I had never built anything substantial before, but being a manly-man, I possessed power tools. This was equivalent to giving your seven-year-old a Harley. Hey, how hard could it be?

I bravely measured and cut, then re-measured and recut two-by-fours, for hours. Surrounded by wasted short pieces of wood, the remnants from my inability to saw boards in a straight line, I finally assembled the framework for four walls. Unfortunately, they were laying flat on the ground. All I had to do was stand them up and fasten them together. Piece of cake! *Not!*

After I'd bent at least 200 nails, and made 17 fruitless attempts to complete the framing, all four walls were finally standing. I rushed into the house, bursting with macho pride, to show Brenda what "Bob the Builder" created.

As she perused my handiwork, all four walls came crashing down. She gave me a sanctimonious pat on the back, mumbled a "harumph" through tightly clenched teeth, and went back to reading Cosmo. I called Jack Flannery, one of my new neighbors, to help me and he did after he stopped laughing. A ramshackle shed became the centerpiece of my backyard domain.

The cul-de-sac started to fill up. Our next-door neighbor sold real estate. The Polish guy that lived next to her, an official in the bakers union, brought us an unlimited supply of donuts. Next to him lived a laconic fellow named Kenny Schlegel, a bricklayer with a beyond droll sense of humor. (Kenny became my fishing partner when I started trolling the waters of Lake Michigan.) Then finally, a grandma and a grumpy Amway salesman moved in.

Jack and Dilly Flannery lived across the street. It took Jack a while to get over his skepticism about our unconventional rock and roll family, but we became fast friends. They were both notable characters. Jack was a gray haired, ruddy cheeked, fun-loving Irishman. Dilly was an ever-smiling, down-to-earth delight to be around, and she ruled her husband with an iron fist.

They arrived in Darien after previously residing in a wild neighborhood in Milwaukee. Jack revealed an unsightly red mark on his stomach at the belt line. I asked him about it.

Dilly chimed in. "Oh yes, Jack and I were at a party and he said he smelled something burning. He looked down and saw his stomach leaning against a hot barbecue grill." She had to borrow the neighbor's wheelbarrow to ferry him home.

After that party, Dilly banned him from guzzling vodka, so he began drinking the cheapest wines he could buy. Note the word "cheap" for later.

Before he migrated from the old neighborhood, Jack and all his male friends assembled every Saturday morning, and each of their wives put a slip of paper with a honey-do chore written on it, in a Mason jar. The men imbibed a Bloody Mary, and performed the assigned task. Then, they drew another job from the jar and went to the next guy's house, had another drink, and did that project. This went on all day.

The following Saturday, they redid all the jobs they messed up the previous Saturday afternoon, in their inebriated state. Then, they started the process all over again. Saturdays were fun in Milwaukee!

Jack and Dilly left on a well-deserved vacation and asked us to watch their house. When they returned home, they found the huge banner we attached to their garage door. It said, "Thanks for making our garage sale a huge success."

Brenda and I went out of town and, to get even, Jack sold our house. He stuck a For Sale sign in the yard and agreed to a price with a passing motorist who expressed interest in buying it. Thank God he didn't forge a contract.

He and Dilly hosted an anniversary party. He showed me his ticket for a flight early the next morning, to go on a business trip. After he shuffled off to bed, his kids and I enveloped his car in leftover streamers, confetti, wrapping paper and Scotch tape, and placed a gaudy cardboard sign on the trunk that said, "Finally Married!" He missed his plane and when I climbed out of bed, I found he had collected all the neighbors' garbage and put it on my front porch.

Brenda and I tirelessly worked for a couple of weeks decorating for Christmas, hanging up string after string of colorful lights. When the house turned into a Christmas cottage, we held a traditional champagne-fueled lighting ceremony.

Jack meandered out into his front yard, hammered a hand-written sign into the ground, and illuminated it with a single spotlight. For those neighbors who could read his writing, the sign read: "See our light display across the street!"

I responded with a billboard out in front of my

Christmas cottage, with a big arrow pointing in his direction. It said:

"Christmas comes but once a year.

For most of us a time of cheer

But not for Scrooge' cause he's too tight

To go and buy some Christmas lights."

We were more fun than those old roadside Burma-Shave signs.

One Christmas, we conspired to create something special for the holiday season. We decided to hang a banner between the houses that said, "Merry Christmas from the Flannerys and the Whitesides."

Jack possessed a sizable piece of shiny canvas, left over from a Chevy trade show. He delegated me to do the artwork, and volunteered to procure the supplies to hang our Christmas greeting. I figured he probably still had all his confirmation money, but I didn't realize he was a total tightwad. He bought the wire to hang it, from a half-price, rusty wire, bargain bin at Ace Hardware. Cheap wine, cheap wire! Cheap Jack! Get the pattern?

Upon inspecting the wire, I questioned his purchase and possibly his sanity, but he assured me it would be okay. After putting S hooks in the soffits of our houses, we strung our banner across the street.

How were we supposed to know you had to cut air vents in a big cloth sign? The first night, it crackled and popped in the wind, driving the neighbors crazy. It sounded like a machine gun combined with Fourth of July fireworks.

I called him in the morning to see if he had any suggestions as to how we were going to fix it. I called him and glanced out the window, just in time to see his cheap-ass rusty wire break. The banner fluttered to the street—directly on top of a police car.

The cop crawled out of his car buried under our Christmas greeting, scratching his head and looking back and forth between both of our houses. As I looked over at Jack's, I could see his shades going down one at a time. Coward!

That was the end of "Bannergate." I never found out the sentence for bannering a police car. I mollified the police officer with a little Christmas cheer in a to-go purple sippy cup filled with eggnog. He reluctantly admitted that it was pretty funny. (Note to self: Buy your own building supplies when working with Flannery.)

One balmy spring day, the smell of flowers wafted through our open windows. I perused Jack's house and I could see right through the screen door on his front porch. He peacefully read the paper as he sat at his breakfast table in the back of his house, drinking Irish coffee.

I purchased a replica of a Civil War cannon that shot sound waves that didn't explode until they hit something solid. I assumed that if I placed the cannon on a bar stool in my window, it would be perfectly aligned with his screen door. I loaded it up with an abundance of percussive carbon and added a little more for good measure. I took careful aim and fired that sucker.

The sound wave passed through his porous screen door, traveled all the way through his house and exploded right behind him on the wall. I caught a fleeting glimpse of a coffee cup, a newspaper, and Jack and his chair flying over backwards. I have a fond memory of Jack standing in his front doorway covered with coffee, shaking one fist at me, and giving me the finger with his other hand.

One night Jack enthusiastically called me to run over to see his new vintage 1958 Chevrolet Convertible with the spare tire that was covered by a shiny continental kit. He purchased it in Ohio and drove it back to Darien. I walked up his driveway and something smelled strange to me. I knocked on the door, Jack answered. I said, "Nice car! Oh, by the way, it's on fire."

He traveled 200 miles to bring the car back. The muffler broke loose, and the heat from the exhaust turned the metal floor white hot and set fire to the carpeting.

He grabbed the garden hose and soaked the smoldering rug. It was a good thing I ran over to see it, or there would have been a 1958 classic, melted turquoise piece of metal in his driveway. There are many other Flannery stories, but it's time to move on.

Jack and Dilly, our two wild Irish Roses, have long since left the garden, but memories of this close friendship comes to mind after a couple of martinis.

Chapter 19

We added daughter Wendy to our brood and let me tell you, it made me really appreciate my sons. Boys raise all sorts of hell till they are about 12, then they discover girls and sports, and if you have succeeded as a parent, you don't see them until they leave for college.

This is true unless they all hang out at your house, which seemed to be the case in Darien. I thought we were going to have to install lockers on one side of the garage for all their friends. A constant stream of neighborhood kids passed through our doors daily. When you have a pool table and a man cave in the basement, at least you know where to find them. We became an adolescent daycare center.

Little girls are sugar and spice until they turn 12, then they turn into she-bats, extraterrestrial creatures that science is unable to explain. They exhibit moods that haven't been diagnosed yet, voice urgent privacy concerns, develop vicious gossip patterns that defy modern communication methods, and they love to wear clothes that you don't approve of. ("But all the girls are wearing them!") A different one of their girlfriends is "really a bitch" every week, and did I mention moods?

It takes considerable patience to learn to live with a little girl, and anyone who claims to have a user's manual for teenage lassies is delusional. Most of the time, our boys gazed at their little sister like she had two heads, though they managed to share boisterous, but pleasant, times when they weren't getting on each other's nerves. They found that on rare occasions, a little sister could be a surprising source of entertainment.

One night the family sat around the table enjoying one of Brenda's gourmet meals. Still a little toddler at the time, Wendy tried to eat her peas with her dull plastic knife. We held our collective breaths and watched in suspense as she balanced one pea on the soft utensil and aimed it toward her mouth. Gravity defied her efforts as the pea fell off onto her plate before it reached the target. She looked at the offending pea for a minute, then in a frustrated tiny voice, my sweet angelic little towhead said, "Oooooh, shit!"

You could have heard a pin drop. We were trying not to smile, but my middle son, Tarrey, giggled. We burst into laughter. She stared at us with this bewildered look on her face like, "What?"

We all agreed that the profanity police had to step it up a notch; little ears, big mouth.

Before my real estate friend Ed suggested we

move to Darien, I had never heard of it. We were part of the foundation of a brand-new town. Darien didn't have a main street. It had a police station and a small city hall, but it didn't emerge as a stereotypical city until much later. The school systems were exceptional, and Little League and other sports programs were very organized and time consuming. A plethora of activities kept our children busy.

We ran our company from a home office. I created music on a piano in the family room, and Brenda set up a small cubicle downstairs to do the bookkeeping. I took charge of the creative side and she handled the bidding and the billing. By doing this, we didn't step on each other's territory, and that's the way we ran the company the entire time we were in business.

When I took a client to lunch, they repeatedly tried to talk me into giving them a price break on a project. I ducked the question. "You'll have to take that up with Brenda." They were all aware of her ferocious negotiating skills. Reluctantly, they called Brenda, and I was off the hook.

Enough business was flowing through the door for us to generate a reasonable cash flow. We were finally ahead on the bills and paid our loan back to Dad. He scrutinized the last check; shook it and held it up to the light to make sure it was real, before he put it in his pocket.

Raising kids took a lot of time. Brenda spent hours in the car taking our three boys to different Little League teams on separate fields, to games scheduled at about the same time. Shuffling them from park to park, and getting them to the right place became confusing at times. I found it difficult to book recording sessions that didn't conflict with baseball and football games, but I attended as many of their sporting events as I could.

My parents moved to Glenview, Illinois, from New Jersey. They purchased a charming two-bedroom cottage a short walk from the beach in Michiana Shores, in scenic Michigan. We enjoyed occasional weekends at the lake, but when my sister, her husband, and her daughter showed up it rapidly became overcrowded. Our family ended up sleeping uncomfortably on the screened-in porch and the aches and pains that resulted from sleeping on a hard surface made me feel older than I looked.

We noticed a Lilliputian cozy cottage on a hill directly across the street from Lake Michigan. The house needed considerable work, but the price was manageable. It was located at the center of an all-Jewish community, so we jumped through some hoops to buy the house. I was the first Presbyterian to break the lakefront block. Damn! There goes another neighborhood.

The house required a total renovation, including a major update of the kitchen and bathrooms, so I took my power tools to Michigan (I'd become a lot more proficient with them) and started to tear the house apart. We decided to create a small lodge. We installed rich wood paneling and brought the kitchen up to speed. I also took my first futile shot at tiling the bathrooms. (Note to self: Find a good tile guy next time.)

The first day we started remodeling, I stood in the front yard, my noisy circular saw slashing strips from a sheet of paneling. My wavy long hair flew in the breeze, and I wore torn jeans and a Rolling Stones' t-shirt embroidered with a disgusting graphic of a large red slurping tongue. The grandmother who lived next door walked over with her granddaughter, a warm smile on her face, and a bottle of red wine tightly clutched to her bosom. "We'd like to meet the new neighbors."

I said, "I *am* the new neighbor."

They held a hasty whispered conference and said, "Nice to meet you," and left with the wine. About an hour later, they sent over a coffee cake.

What was it about me, and neighborhoods?

As the years progressed everyone on the lakefront became wonderful friends. Brenda completely reinvented the house. Twice! It was the beginning of an emerging pattern. If you manage to stay married through one rehab, much less two, you have a really strong relationship.

Overruling my objections (over my dead body), Brenda transformed my hunting lodge into a fairy cottage, with lots of fluffy couches piled with pastel pillows. She also hired a contractor to build five tiers of gardens in the front, then she converted the roof of the three-car garage built into the hill, into a large party patio.

She was on a roll as she directed the carpenters to construct a spacious deck made from weathered grey driftwood, overlooking the lake. In a final burst of creative inspiration, the backyard evolved into a fenced-in space that contained an inviting swimming pool and a spa room that housed a luxurious hot tub. The original residence boasted three bedrooms plus a hide-a-bed on the enclosed front porch, a fireplace and three separate sitting areas on the first floor.

On the second remodel, Brenda installed a spiral staircase and added a second-story open-beamed A-frame loft. I was able to find room for a small recording studio, and I set my writing table in a garden window that offered a sweeping view of the lake.

We constructed two separate bedroom suites on the loft level. Our bedroom showcased a white marble fireplace, brightly colored bedding and pillows, and a plush loveseat. We could walk through the sliding glass doors onto a cantilevered deck that overlooked the pool.

The front suite sat under a cathedral ceiling, containing a king-sized bed, built-in paneled drawers and cabinets, and a brightly colored loveseat sat in front of a sliding glass door. At dusk we could watch the blazingly beautiful sunsets over the lake.

We originally viewed the lake house as our peaceful oasis where we could relax on weekends and recharge our batteries. Hah! As our business expanded, we ended up hosting many clients on Saturdays and Sundays, sometimes entertaining up to 20 folks every weekend. Don't ask me how Brenda cooked for, and entertained, that many people. She was a culinary genius and a consummate hostess, born with the energy of a commercial Coleman generator.

The nearby marina became the hub of my fishing obsession. I bought my first boat, a sleek 21-foot Boston Whaler, one of the safest and hardiest small crafts one could buy. I equipped it with high-tech fish locators to help me in my search for the elusive salmon swimming around in Lake Michigan. Kenny, my terse, but quietly humorous neighbor, drove the boat as I tied lures on the fishing poles and set the lines in the water. Through the years we owned the Michigan house, I worked my way up to a 32-foot Carver cabin cruiser, rigged like a charter boat. It had an abundance of fishing and navigation aids: radar, radio direction finders, and color TV camera/fish locators with transponders that you lowered in the water to pinpoint the fish and what depth they were at. The equipment also fed me the temperature of the water.

My emerging reputation as a skilled fishing guide resulted in Budweiser asking me if they could sponsor the boat in major tournaments. I politely refused. I loved trying out new techniques, and wanted the freedom to select the people who threw up on my boat in rough weather. I tested lures for several companies, designed flashy metal attractors that I sold to sporting goods stores, and especially enjoyed fishing without corporate oversight.

I fished the same way General Patton fought. I strategized and contrived battle plans to launch against those sneaky fish. Fishing became my therapy. All thoughts of business disappeared for a while. I participated in quite a few tournaments. My best finish: one hundred and twenty boats competed, and I ended up in twenty-second place, despite the fact that seventy-five were professional charter boats.

When our friends and clients arrived at the cottage for the weekend, they had many choices. They could fish with me or chase antiques at the homey, bucolic shops and farms peppered throughout the rustic area. They were free to chill out on the deck, or grab some rays at the pool.

I only had two rules. 1.) If I have to entertain

you, don't bother coming, and 2.) talking about business on my boat was forbidden.

Michiana Shores (the small town where the house was located) became a paradise that we enjoyed through all the seasons of many years. In the spring, the summer, and the fall we spent hours out on the lake, and relaxed in our swimming pool. We traversed quiet wooded walking trails, scanned hordes of antiques, visited a various assortment of quaint little shops and cafes, and utilized our boat slip at the bustling marina; usually with friends and clients.

During the winter, Brenda and I were able to spend time alone. We loved being snowbound, gazing at the miles of ice-mountains out on the lake. Sitting by a cozy crackling fireplace, lost in rare solitude, gave us a well-deserved break from the constant march of clients that we hosted and entertained the rest of the year. What else did we need? I couldn't think of anything!

Chapter 20

I began to forge serious inroads into the commercial business. I learned that there were certain unwritten rules I needed to keep in mind.

The problems and complexity of a job were inversely proportional to the budget. With a low budget, the client would probably be difficult to work with, and many seemingly insurmountable problems would emerge. The times I worked with a generous budget, the job normally ran smoothly, as the agency provided enough money to do it right the first time. The clients always managed to find the dollars for the redos, but it would have been cheaper and easier for them if they allocated more money to begin with. It's like painting your house twice because you used cheap paint for the first coat.

Number two related to the clients who stated the one line I never wanted to hear: "I'm not sure what I want, but I'll know it when I hear it."

Shriek!

Next came the client who never accepted what I played them when we started our recording session. I'd run down my recommended music track for one particular copywriter.

She'd say, "No. It needs something else."

I learned to keep generating subtle changes until I traveled full circle back to the track I played her the first time. At that point she would say, "That's it! That's perfect." The band knew the drill and they loved it, as they were on the clock while she made all those unnecessary changes. She'd do it every time.

I worked with another client who waited until the end of our session to surprise me. I looked at her, expecting her to approve the spot and tell me the session was over. She would flutter her eyelashes and say, "Bob! A question?"

And we'd be starting all over again, much to the delight of the musicians.

The band earned a payment for a minimum of one full hour, and more money for each 20-minute segment needed to finish the music track. Some of the veteran musicians tried to take advantage of my "newbie" status, assuming I lacked experience. I'd be on the verge of completing a track within the first mandatory hour, and one disruptive trombone player would raise his hand and ask a stupid, utterly worthless question. By the time I answered, we were paying for another 20-minute segment.

Another "stick it to the producer" trick involved kicking over a cup of coffee in the middle of the last take. By the time the musician cleaned up the mess and the band played it again, the musicians were in overtime, shooting my budget to hell.

I hired one arrogant established musician who constantly wasted time, so I stopped booking him on my recording dates. He confronted me by the coffee machine, in front of all his buddies. He smirked disdainfully, and said, "Hey, Whiteside! How come you never use me anymore?"

Everyone was watching to see how the new kid would handle it. "Because you waste time on my sessions, ask the dumbest questions I've ever heard, and you play out of tune."

I turned and walked away, clothed in the mantle of newly established respect, leaving behind a group of open-mouthed seasoned session players. A few minutes later, when I walked into the studio, all my musicians were quietly sitting at attention. I'd drawn a line in the sand and they knew it was a deep one.

I became beyond busy. I searched for a contractor to book my bands for me, file contracts, and keep my sessions organized. I hired Lennie Druss, a fellow musician and a friend. Lennie played flute, piccolo, English horn, oboe, clarinet, alto, soprano, baritone, and bass saxophones. The musicians respected him, and my recording dates ran smoothly when he was in charge.

In his younger years, he traveled the highways, touring the USA on immense band buses. He told a story about the day they were driving through Kansas and the bus screeched to a sudden stop. All the players jumped off the bus carrying machetes. Lennie feared the band was under attack by a ferocious band of renegade scallions.

The reality? The old-timers were harvesting marijuana plants that they placed in the luggage compartment of the bus to dry. When the group's stash ran low, it called for drastic measures. "What happens on the road stays on the road," remains the unwritten rule everyone follows when they tour.

I could always count on Lennie to arrive on time for sessions, but one morning he staggered in 40 minutes late. I wanted to know what short-circuited Mr. Reliable.

"That's not like you man, what happened?"

"Car trouble!"

I tipped my head to the side and shot him an inquiring look. He shrugged and answered my silent question.

"No driver!"

What could I say?

I'm going to take an educational pause, to teach a mini version of commercials A-101; how I created a commercial. There are several scenarios that I found myself faced with in order to create advertising. I'd like to share some of them with you.

The first is my favorite. This one I call the "I don't have an effing idea, blank page" approach. The client says, "I want you to create a commercial for Widgets." I ask him if he has a slogan or campaign idea in mind. He replies, "No."

At this point in the conversation I tell him I need all the marketing information he has available on demographics, product features, previous radio/TV advertising, target audience, geographical marketing areas, and every other scrap of relevant material he can give me about Widgets.

He thinks about it then informs me they want to target frugal, short people who drive muscle cars on the East Coast.

So, now I have to create an advertising slogan based on his parameters. Hmm! The theme line rolls off my tongue. "Widgets are for midgets who want to save digits and drive a beast in the East!"

The client jumps up and down with joy, so I finish an entire song lyric with the above title, which I will spare you. Then, we decide what style of music we need. In this particular case, I recommend something similar to "Short People." I write the music and we complete our campaign. The next thing to do is to produce it.

If this commercial makes short people buy Widgets we are a success. So, in a perfect world, the advertising campaign will work and Widgets fly off the shelves.

The next scenario is when the client calls you in and *they* have written the campaign line. One client gave me, "Good friends are never far apart" for a telephone company commercial. Now *that* was a strong idea!

Richard Wold (I will introduce him to you in a later chapter) and I wrote a beautiful stirring string orchestra ballad, and Lee Greenwood sang an exceptional rendition of the song. Everyone loved the lyrics:

Feelings never change
It's like time stands still
And everything we share comes from the heart
You know just what to say
It's as though you read my mind
Good friends are never far apart
When I need to hear your voice
You're always there for me
We've shared special moments from the start
Through the good times and the tears
I'll be close to you
Good friends are never far apart

I enjoyed having the opportunity to write something meaningful that sounded more like a song than your standard "buy me" commercial. I think I loved doing those the best.

And then there were times the advertising agency showed large storyboards, drawn on sizable sheets of construction paper sitting on an easel. Storyboards are individual pictures, snapshot or drawn, of each scene created for the film. The lyrics, or dialogue, that goes with each individual storyboard frame is written under the scene. It's the same principle as reading a child a book and turning the pages when the visual needs to change for a new part of the story.

Most of the time, I wrote and produced a rough demonstration music track to this series of pictures, to show how the music, lyrics, and scenes worked together. The agency presented it to the client and as the track played, they pointed to the picture where the film would be, at that point in the music.

Then, a client calls you to the agency, hands you a film and says, "I need a track for this." It wasn't easy to write music that produced smooth transitions between the scenes, but practice makes perfect as they say, and I ended up with hundreds of film scores under my belt to prove it.

Many times we were simply handed an entire lyric and asked to write a song to show the agency our approach to the music. I might have done a demo with a piano, a bass and one singer, to present a sketch of my idea. Agencies customarily requested cheap rough demos. At the point when they approved the rough, they authorized me to produce the final track for broadcast. Then, in a perfect world they came up with an ample budget that enabled me to use a larger band or orchestra, a lead singer, and a chorus.

There were also rearrangements of someone else's music, sound effects, and many other possible combinations, but I think this gives an idea of how flexible I had to be in order to succeed in this business.

Meanwhile, in the jingle world, business continued to grow. My ability to write contemporary music, coupled with my soul and R&B background, gave me the edge over many of my older competitors. For the agency, it became a toss-up whether to go with the tried and the true, or take a chance with the young upstart, the soulful hippie.

One of my biggest problems in booking top session musicians regarded their loyalty to the producers responsible for most of their work. It was mandatory for members of the A-list ensemble to be available to the big guys when they were needed, or the producers wasted no time replacing them. A guitarist would be booked for my session and he'd call me and say, "I can't turn down this date with a certain producer, so you'll have to find another guitar player." I partially solved that by going to my guys at Chess, and finding some new creative musicians who hadn't been discovered yet.

In addition, I came up with a frightening new

concept, the seven a.m. recording session. Sleep in? Nah! Not anymore! If I needed a musician who might bolt, I booked him for seven a.m., as none of my competitors were crazy enough to work at that hour.

They didn't want to admit it, but this worked in favor of the musicians. They'd miss rush hour traffic, and earn a session payment before their gig for the big jingle company at nine a.m. The first morning I scheduled one, the drummer shuffled in at 7:30 a.m. He slithered into the studio and faced a room full of dirty looks, but we all had to laugh when he said, "My six o'clock ran over."

These early sessions were convenient for me. Now that my business had increased in volume, my office/apartment over the recording studio became a lifesaver. If I wrote all night, I could slip on my shoes and traipse downstairs to my recording date.

Those Whiteside wake-up calls provided the opportunity for humorous situations. One early morning, I walked into the studio to find my entire band in their pajamas, their clothes hanging on the microphone booms, and bacon sizzling in an electric frying pan over in the corner.

I ended up in the middle of a self-inflicted, "Oh, crap" moment when I did a funny-at-the-time, but astonishingly stupid thing. I'd been asked to create a six-note tag ending for all the existing Kentucky Fried Chicken commercials. The agency rejected at least 40 I had previously written. Again, I worked all through the night, and exhaustion caused a momentary lapse of common sense.

I unwisely thought it would be entertaining to my musicians if I wrote each individual six-note part on toilet paper. When I went to hand out the music, I ambled around the studio with a roll in my hand, and ripped off two sheets for each musician, one with the music on it, the other to hang over the stand to keep it in place.

Unfortunately for me, the big kahuna, the humorless honcho from the advertising agency, appeared unexpectedly. He found no humor in seeing his expensive music scrawled on scented toilet paper. His crimson cheeks reflected his displeasure.

Despite the egregious consequences, I still think it was funny, and that story floated around for a while, adding to my already questionable mystique.

I helped destroy the archaic recording session dress code. Up until the time I appeared in the business, the producers and musicians mostly wore conservative coats and ties. It didn't take too long to start seeing sandals, golf shirts, and jeans. I loved it. My older competitors hated it. I think it had something to do with dignity, but dignity, a blasphemous word to me, didn't belong in my irreverent approach to the business. My musicians liked having casual Friday every day of the week, and that's all that mattered to me.

I'd become friends with an extremely witty jingle producer named Dick Boyell, a remarkable musician. He stood outside the studio, pounding his forehead against the brick wall in frustration. He told me his client walked into the studio, gave the flute part to the tuba to play, and switched all the other parts around to see what it sounded like. Nightmare! The parts were in different keys for each individual instrument. He looked at me and with a straight face, and uttered another long to be remembered famous line, "Who do I have to f*** to get *off* this job?"

Chapter 21

I found it imperative that I build my bands around a rock-solid keyboard player. One of my terrific finds: Fred Kaz, the genius piano player/music director from "Second City." Second City, the legendary impromptu comedy theater in Chicago, became the castle of improvisation where John Belushi, Chevy Chase, Dan Aykroyd, Gilda Radner, and a host of others served their apprenticeships and honed their craft.

Fred extemporized music for the comedy review every night, without one ounce of pre-written sheet music. He reminded me of an old-time piano player, who brilliantly reacted musically to whatever was happening on stage or on the early silent movie screens.

I hardly noticed that Fred lacked parts of two fingers. He cut them off working on a punch press, trying to pay his way through music school to be a classical piano player. I asked Fred how he kept going after that.

"I just made up my mind that I could play the hell out of anything using eight and a half fingers."

And could he ever! In fact, he performed chords that no one could duplicate, as he created new unique combinations using his stubby fingers to play notes no one else could reach.

Fred was an old soul, undoubtedly a full-blown hippie in a past life. A gentle, laid-back man with sad dark eyes that had witnessed volumes of life, he created melodious magic in his own unique way. He had long jet-black hair, and a speaking voice that sounded like Leonard Cohen on pot.

Every once in a while, Fred would come out with one of his famous *Freddyisms.* This soft-spoken beautiful man once said, "If I was to ever get in a war, I would hope that everyone on the other side would be a vegetarian."

Fred possessed an astonishing musical second sense. We finished a music track for a film and felt it lacked something, but we couldn't put a finger on what. We asked Fred to check it out. He watched it, nodded his head, and said, "I got it! Let's record it!"

We ran the film. Two thirds of the way through, Fred reached over and played one note. We looked at each other. We listened to a playback, and damned if that wasn't exactly what it needed. I felt honored to work with this talented piano wizard, who so graciously added his immeasurable talent to my music. The Chess players loved him, and we recorded hundreds of sessions together.

Bobby Christian and Frankie Rullo, two

notable characters in my musical world, played innumerable percussion instruments, and performed on drums with many of the vintage big bands.

Bobby played with a combo at the landmark Edgewater Beach Hotel in Chicago. The band consisted of piano, bass, drums, and a passel of horns. In this particular group, it took a complete rhythm section (the piano, bass and drums) to play as a unit to hold the band together. Every time the bandleader permitted the bass player to come up to the microphone to sing, he stopped playing and set his bass down on the floor.

This infuriated Bobby. He had to try to fill out the sound by playing his drums loudly, without the help of the bass. So every time the self-proclaimed crooner got up to sing, Bobby poured a cup of sand through the holes in the front of his upright bass; sand he retrieved from the beach on band breaks

A month later, Bobby got his revenge. The bass player looked at him one night and complained. "I have to go to the doctor. I don't know what's wrong with me. I can hardly lift my bass."

Bobby and Frankie played an assortment of instruments on some of my wild percussive tracks: kettledrums, marimbas, slide whistles, xylophones, and chimes. A cartage company that delivered a storehouse of equipment to the studio for their sessions, sometimes made more money than they did. They left their stamp on tracks that ranged from Spike Jones' crazy music to cartoons, and songs that required soft lush vibes and bells. They also powered out classical percussion on my big orchestral symphonic tracks.

Frankie, a consummate schooled musician, was precise to a fault. He lost his temper if someone in the band screwed up the tempo. One day, in a moment of mischief, we conceived a way to play a trick on Frank. Usually, the band recorded to a click track, a metronome that was fed to each musician through individual earphones, which kept everyone playing at the same tempo. We decided to feed 24 of the musicians in the studio one tempo, and we fed Frankie one at a completely different speed.

We ran the track down and 24 guys played the track together, as Frankie confidently played at the wrong speed, nowhere near the click we fed the other band members. At the end of the take, Frank exploded into a tumultuous rant, threw his headphones on the floor, sneered at the other 24 guys and barked, "You a******s are all wrong."

When he found out what we had done, he was...um...really mad. You used Frank on the serious stuff if you had any common sense.

At that time, I recorded almost all my tracks at

Universal Recording Studios in Chicago. Murray Allen, the owner of the facility, developed a formidable, well-equipped studio; a wonderful place to work. He tried to stay up on and ahead of the emerging technology, to make sure we had the finest up-to-date versions of studio equipment.

So many fantastically talented musicians and engineers passed through Universal Studios. Bruce Swedien, one of my first recording engineers, moved to LA and engineered all of Michael Jackson's records. His talent helped him to become Quincy Jones' favorite mixer.

Pat Leonard, one of our keyboard players, went west to become Madonna's music director and co-writer.

CJ Vanston, another brilliant keyboard player, is currently one of the hottest, sought after producer/engineer/arranger/players in LA. Early in his career he accepted an offer to become Dolly Parton's music director. CJ performed as one of the members of Spinal Tap, and added his distinctive sound to albums by Toto, Celine Dion, Prince, Barbra Streisand, Tina Turner, Joe Cocker, and a host of other acts. He scored at least seven movies.

Bobby Brooks, one of the young assistant engineers, became another one of the hottest mixers on the West Coast. He recorded Rick James, Supertramp, Tina Marie, Prince, Stevie

Wonder, Stephanie Mills, Diana Ross, The Temptations, and too many others to name. He wrote me a note last year thanking me for my help in his early career. It read in part:

If I haven't said it before, I learned so much from working all those sessions with you, and that knowledge became the brick and mortar of my decision making in the studio. You worked for the level of quality I would come to strive for in my records. You showed me what really mattered... the little things...getting the parts to feel right...the stuff most people couldn't learn, but you intuitively knew...searching for that element that makes a human being reach in their pocket and pull out an Andrew Jackson for a recording. It was truly other worldly, and spiritual in nature, and time so well spent. Again thank u for that gift...homie for life.

I met Bobby at the inception of his career, and I could see he possessed a formidable amount of ambition and a serious work ethic. It all paid off, and his tremendous success was well deserved.

The fact that I could help guide the careers of some of the younger emerging talents became one of the biggest rewards of working in the music business. Sometimes, I stopped them from heading in a wrong direction, or making a mistake that could cost them work, or their careers. I continually searched for promising young talent to help keep my music fresh.

Having the apartment upstairs probably saved my life, as there were so many nights I had to work until three and four in the morning. Driving home cost me a couple of hours of potential sleep. If I slept at the office, I could get three to five hours a night. I learned to hypnotize myself by reciting the mantra, "You will wake up and feel like you had eight hours of sleep." It worked more times than not, and I woke up after a short nap feeling completely refreshed.

One night, I arrived home at 9:30 p.m., with eight commercials to write for an eight a.m. session, the biggest challenge I'd faced yet. I sat at my piano, my head in my hands, wondering how I could get these spots done. A little voice bannered across my brain. "Start with the first one, stupid." I wrote all night, hired a limo, and finished the music in the back of a "stretch" limo stuck in rush hour traffic on the way to the studio. And after that, I always started with the first one!

It was important that I accept any work that was offered to me, because bad times always seemed to follow good times. I tried to build up a nest egg when we were working, so I could tap it when we were slow.

A music score is the big stack of papers the conductor places in front of him on the podium when he conducts the orchestra. This shows him what every instrument is playing. After I wrote a score for a session, each part had to be copied off that composite sheet to a separate piece of music paper for each player.

Some nights, a copyist worked right behind me. When I finished a score page he grabbed it and started copying off the individual parts. A good copyist saved my butt quite a few times.

I did some copying when I had time, but professional copyists made the musicians' parts look like printed sheet music. The ones that I copied were not. The musicians became used to my sloppy notes, and fixed the mistakes before I had to suffer through hearing them played incorrectly.

Every bar of music was numbered, so if I had to change a note during a session, I could just say, "Trumpet! Bar six! That third note should be a B flat."

Some of the copyists were also orchestrators. The few times that I fell behind schedule while writing a big symphonic score, I could call in one of those multi-talented magicians. I'd write lead lines and chord placements on my score sheet and they would finish the arrangement.

For example, I could write out a trumpet lead line and the copyist could fill in the other two harmonizing trumpet parts, or I could write a lead violin line and he could write in all the other viola and cello parts to go with it. I didn't have to face this situation very often, thank God, but my orchestrating copyists bailed me out of several sticky situations.

I did all my own arranging. I refused to add another writer to the company the way many of my competitors did. I had no desire to expand. I wanted to keep the music under my control, and give every project my personal touch and my undivided attention.

There were only a few times that I made exceptions to this rule. I assigned a couple of horn arrangements to Jerry Hey, an A-list arranger from LA, who arranged the Michael Jackson *Triumph* and *Tribute* albums.

My brilliant friend Robert Bowker, wrote gorgeous and complex vocal arrangements that far exceeded the scope of my musical knowledge, he added his personal touch to some of my favorite tracks. Robert is an incredibly accomplished singer, composer, arranger and conductor; who will be mentioned later.

I continued to take occasional trips to New York, where I focused on assembling a nucleus of top local musicians and singers, and scheduled appointments with record companies and publishers to keep my contacts current.

This also gave me an excuse to visit my parents. On one particularly memorable evening, I arranged for my mom and dad to meet me in

New York at the end of the day. I escorted them to my favorite classy bar, Toots Shor's. My mother, in a rare burst of courage and adventure, decided to order her very first martini *ever*! My father asked for his monthly highball.

Toots made his martinis in a rather bulbous glass. I doubt my mother had ever received a drink served in a fishbowl. She certainly never consumed one. We shared a wonderful visit, ate lots of cashews and pretzels, and my mother sipped away at her gigantic beverage.

My plan, to treat them to dinner at the Playboy Club, materialized sooner than I expected. I began to realize my mother was becoming *slightly tipsy* as she put it, so I decided it was time to amble over and have dinner. The wind had started to blow and the temperature dropped through the teens, so we collected our coats and headed up the sidewalk.

I noticed my mother holding her fur coat strangely. I understood why, when she pulled her hand out from under a beaver and took a swig from her purloined martini. Mom and I had the giggles. Dad wouldn't walk with us. He gave us "the glare," and that set us off again. Steaming, he walked five steps behind us, red-faced with embarrassment, fearing a visit from the imaginary martini police.

His worst fears were realized. Not only was I *just* a musician, I succeeded in corrupting my mother. We arrived at the Playboy Club where a very understanding bunny gave Mom a small to-go bag for her hot souvenir beaker, along with a coaster and a matchbook cover embossed with the world-famous Playboy bunny-head. We enjoyed every bite of the gourmet dinner. The music, elegant and soft, created the perfect mood, and Mom and I shared a special evening. I think Dad started talking to us again... maybe a month later. Mom said, "Let's do it again, but next time we won't take Scrooge."

I was very close to my mother, my biggest cheerleader. I talked to her almost every day on the phone. She always found sunshine where my father perceived doom. Mom proclaimed that I would complete my own album, and she couldn't wait to see the day. My mom and dad were exceptional parents. My father started to come around and see that I might actually have a real career, and he was off the hook... almost.

Chapter 22

When I turned 27, Les Bridges, a feature writer for *the Chicago Tribune*, wrote a piece on me for the Sunday supplement magazine. His article articulates where my career had landed at that particular moment in time, so here are some excerpts and thoughts from his perceptions of my life:

"Whiteside typifies a Chicago phenomenon. He illustrates how someone young, aggressive, and talented can shoot to the top very quickly, especially in music. I was intrigued by how well this young guy worked with older musicians, even though he's not super organized. Whiteside's music is a little raw and unpolished, and he does a lot of improvising, with both the musicians and the engineers. He'll spend time overdubbing, adding reverb, echo, and other electronic effects that are so important to the success of rock music. Anyway, it works.

Bobby is doing okay. At 27, this musician, singer, songwriter, arranger, record producer, jingle maker, and artist manager sits atop 5 companies. His little empire of two song-publishing companies, an artist management wing, a jingle-making house, and a record production company nestles under a parent company called Trendsetters Inc.

Bobby said when he first started out in the business, he starved until the advertisers got onto the "youth thing." Young guys were the future of the business. The young guys were creating the new music; the music of the future. At this point, Bobby is probably ten years younger than the "old pros" that dominate the jingle airwaves. Youth seems to be the magic ingredient. One advertising guy said, "There are guys who are technically a lot more knowledgeable about music, but Bobby has a verve, an unexpectedness. He may not deliver the slickest arrangements, but his stuff has guts." You'll find him sitting in on all these gleaming conference-table, coffee-cluttered meetings, discussing strategy, market share, and demographics. He takes the input and runs with it to create their music.

In the studio, a lot of the musicians are much older than you'd expect, lots of beer guts and bald heads. There are also the Chess guys, the famous black session players who have played on hundreds of hits. It's a great combination. They listen carefully when Bobby gives directions. He hired them. He tells them he wants a Motown feel. Bang! You feel like you are in Detroit. He finishes the track. The advertising agency producer and the client look at Whiteside. He says, "I think we have it." They nod, and Bobby moves on to his next session.

I questioned Bobby on the integrity of doing commercials when his heart was really in records. He tells me that the commercial business is instant gratification. You cut a track, someone else pays for it, and you get to hear it without having to wait. It also gives you a budget to experiment with, and to look for new players, singers, and sounds that will make your next record better. He takes off his sunglasses. His eyes look tired and decades older than he is.

We talk about managing acts and working with groups and I get the feeling he also loves this part of the business, the opportunity to be in on the ground floor of developing talent. But he has no delusions about the cost of developing an artist, and the disloyalty factor of artists as soon as they get a better deal. He also has to take into account the amount of work it takes to launch an act. But somehow he finds the time to promote and hustle the songs of stars that haven't been discovered yet, and he makes a concerted effort to continue to build a nationwide network of record producers, publishers and booking agents from coast to coast.

I ask him what makes a hit record and he answers with words that seem to say volumes about what he knows of the realities of the music business. He says, "Clever arrangements will never replace dumb luck!" We thought about that for a minute, *and laughed. I ask him about drugs. He laughs and says, "Some musicians stay high for a couple of days. I don't even have a couple of minutes to waste." Then it's time to go. Tomorrow, Nashville! The next day, the world! Run, Bobby! Run!"*

Les' article articulated the high points of life in the jingle business. We spent uncountable hours together and he witnessed the unshackled chaos, first hand. Thanks, Les!!!

I received a tap on the shoulder from Don Novello, a hilarious, creative writer from Leo Burnett. Don needed a series of spots for Schlitz Malt Liquor, in the style of "50's" doo-wop music.

One of the commercials talked about taking your girlfriend bowling. I remember the first line of the commercial. "A gu, gu, gu, gu, gu, gu, gutterball...kind of love...dooby doo wah." Another parody titled, "You're a Schlitz Malt Liquor Kind Of Girl" turned out to be a vintage gem.

We hired eight original doo-wop vocal groups to sing the arrangements. We completed all the band tracks and started on the vocals. Problems! Only half of the groups could say Schlitz. The rest of them couldn't get past "Slitz." We tried and tried, and finally gave up and let a couple of the spots be Slitz Malt Liquor commercials. We *did* succeed in prodding several of them to sing

"Schlitz." We dropped the four groups with the worst Slitz mindsets. Minnie Riperton, with her five-octave range, soloed on one of my favorites and, as usual, she nailed it.

Don told me about a character he created, to use in a comedy routine. At the time I wasn't sure if it was funny, or even a good idea to have a priest do jokes. However, I knew his instincts were right when I tuned into *Saturday Night Live* and saw Don do his Father Guido Sarducci bit. Whodathunkit? People never believed me when I told them he was an advertising client of mine. You have to admit that a priest doing stand-up was kind of bent.

Then I participated in "The Raid Mexican Misadventure." I jumped at the chance to create a Raid commercial for the Hispanic population of Harlem, written by Foote Cone and Belding. The agency generated the script and went to Berlitz for the language translation. I knew the people of Spanish Harlem spoke in many dialects, so I questioned the script. They assured me they had done their research.

So where do we find Spanish musicians? A Mexican restaurant! After three pitchers of margaritas and numerous red plastic baskets of crispy nachos, we hired the band. The commercial consisted of numerous Spanish lyrics, which led up to the campaign slogan: "Raid kills cockroaches dead!"

The recording session turned into a royal mess. Most of the band showed up high, or drunk on tequila. In addition, none of those boys had ever been inside a recording studio. What a fiasco. It took awhile, but we finally finished the commercial. The clients returned to the agency, and rolled out the finished product for national radio play.

Several months later, a Raid sales rep visited a store in Spanish Harlem. When the commercial blared over the radio, the customers started to laugh. One lady grabbed a can of Raid off the shelves and sprayed her husband's groin.

"What the hell?" the rep said in dismay.

The storeowner delivered a startling piece of information. "Oh, man, you don't know about that commercial? Says...Raid kills cock dead." Then he laughed and slapped his thigh as he enjoyed the rep's obvious discomfort.

So much for agency research! I did my own after that. It set a record for the shortest amount of time it took for an agency to pull a commercial off the air, in the history of the advertising business.

Chapter 23

I loved the convenience of renting an apartment above the recording studio, but my proximity to Louie's Cantonese Restaurant two floors below me, made it two for two. Where do I start with talking about Louie's? I guess... with Louie.

Louie, known as the Cantonese version of Don Rickles, gave everyone a hard time. You could tell how much Louie liked you by the number of times he insulted you. Louie's became a favorite lunch hangout for legions of advertising people. The ad guys accepted me by assimilation due to the numerous times I frequented the place.

The creative folks from J. Walter Thompson rapidly became my favorite new friends. Louie, who was tuned into the whole ad thing, always stuck his nose into creative conversations. When the agency won the Schlitz Beer account, he bought a dozen cases in their honor, only to find out that the JWT dudes hated the taste. So he unloaded his stock of Schlitz Beer on unsuspecting outsiders who simply wandered in for the food.

As most restaurants do at one time or another,

Louie's developed a *small pet* problem. One afternoon, Brenda pointed out a cockroach. Louie said, "That is Elmer. You leave him alone."

When the pest control company treated the restaurant, the bugs ran upstairs to my office. When I exterminated, they ran back down to Louie's. We finally saw the collective light, and fumigated the entire building on the same day.

I suggested that Louie install a dumbwaiter so he could winch up food to my office. Louie said, "Got dumb waiter here who carry food upstairs."

I once opened a Chinese fortune cookie to find a hand-written note that said, "Pay your bill!"

The size of a drink at Louie's was comparable to the huge martinis at Toots Shor's. He concocted pink umbrella drinks using bottom shelf liquor for the tourists, but he always kept the good stuff stashed away for the regulars. One day, I brought a prospective client in for an introductory business lunch. I think you will enjoy the following conversation.

Louie: "Whadayouwant?"

Client: "I'll have a very dry gin martini, two drops of vermouth, with one olive and a slice of lemon peel, stirred and not shaken."

Louie: "You want all that s***, you get it yourself."

Then he turned around and harrumphed all the way back to the kitchen.

The client sat back in his chair. "Did he really

say that?"

I said, "The bar's over there."

Surprisingly enough, he ended up hiring me to write some music, and walked away with a great story to tell his friends.

It didn't matter what I ordered, Louie brought me whatever *he* wanted to serve. In resignation, I reached the point where I didn't bother to pick something out, because what he brought me was always better than my original choice would have been.

I have never found another Chinese restaurant with food as tasty as Louie's. His Hong Kong steak, a juicy T-bone on the crispiest vegetables possible, delivered a colorful, delectable, gourmet experience. His sauces, specialties, and curry: award winning. He threw together a big bowl of soup for me, packed with ham, chicken, shrimp, pork, whole mushrooms and an assortment of pea pods and bean sprouts. He named it "Bobby's Soup." It seemed funny to have a dish named after me on a menu!

I boated a trophy-sized 14-pound Lake Michigan Coho salmon, and asked Louie if he would prepare it for Brenda, a group of our best friends and clients, and myself. He committed to a Thursday night, so we invited a dozen of our favorite people, tantalizing them with the promise of a spectacular Chef Louie oriental aquatic feast.

Everyone showed up licking their chops, waiting for that delectable masterpiece that they knew only Louie could create. We waited impatiently as we sat around an extended table, acting like a bunch of hungry Vikings.

Louie served some flavorful appetizers, but then he emerged from the kitchen and said, "The fish is spoiled."

A dark cloud swirled across the room. He held up his hand and told everyone not to worry, that he would cook some other "good stuff."

I thought, "The best laid plans..." when Louie walked out of the kitchen proudly carrying a huge steaming platter spotlighting the fish, surrounded by a culinary display of colorful Chinese vegetables that should have been featured on a cooking magazine cover. For a minute I was ready to kill him, but only for a minute. That went down as one of the best meals I've ever consumed, and more importantly, the clients loved it. Brenda and I were both able to give a sigh of relief by the end of the night.

I would drop into the restaurant late at night and Louie and I would just talk for hours. Louie shared stories about his fascinating life. When he first opened the restaurant, he lived in the apartment that was now my office. Not believing in banks, he stashed his money under the mattress and got robbed. He opened his first savings account, and decided to add some stability to his life by getting married. So, he sent home for a bride. He really did!

His relatives shipped him one, and he dragged all his employees down to meet her when she arrived. Louie took one look at her and frowned. The people he brought gave her an indisputable thumbs-down, and he sent her back. Yup! He sent her back! Only Louie!

He accepted the next one and stayed happily married for years. His wife was lovely and his kids were smart, polite, and nice to be around. I think they took after their mother.

Chapter 24

Joel Slosar, one of my JWT (J. Walter Thompson) buddies, told me about a package of 7-Up commercials he wanted to enhance with my creative touch. The commercials revolved around a box; a square black box sitting on a table covered by a white tablecloth. Surrounding it were two cans of Coke and one can of 7-Up. The top of the box popped open, a white-gloved hand emerged and fished around for a soft drink. When the hand touched a Coke, it pushed it aside. When it found the 7-Up, the hand picked it up, and lifted it back into the box and the top slammed shut. I admired Joel's flair for the unusual.

We finished the project and the commercials went on the air internationally. As sometimes happens with worldwide advertising, a problem emerged. A black box in Italy meant death, so we had to redo all the spots with a green box.

Joel came up with another brilliant idea for Kraft Salad Dressings. His line was; "If you don't have Kraft dressing, you might as well toss the salad." It looked like a winner to me. The client hated it! They said salad was sacred and that line reeked of blasphemy.

Sacred? Are you kidding me? These people had the imagination of a kumquat. We lost so many terrific ideas to untalented, non-creative, narrow-minded, stubborn corporate executives, who ignored agency recommendations and showed absolutely no vision, or advertising acumen.

A client called me to tap into my knowledge of soul music. He asked me to create commercials for a company who made hair products for the black market. This was right up my alley. I booked my mind-blowingly talented Chess musicians. Minnie Riperton, Marvin Junior from the Dells, and singers from top R&B hit groups agreed to sing on the project. The commercials turned out to be in sync with the soulful songs that people were listening to! The music ran on every R&B radio station in the country. They sounded like mini hit records, and the phones lit up with callers expressing their delight with our music.

The client acknowledged the success of the spots and the agency signed me to do a second package. I suggested we head for New York and utilize the talent of the original cast of the cult play *Hair*, in its first run on Broadway. Talk about a marvelous experience! We attended a matinee, then headed backstage to meet the cast. There were very few actors who couldn't use supplemental royalty money, and they were grateful for the opportunity to broaden their resumes.

We rented Media Sound Studios on 57th street, a converted church with a regal sound. I worked with an engineer named Joe Jorgensen who became my go-to-guy in New York whenever I flew in to produce music. The session rocked the room! Our singers were total pros, and the spots were one of a kind. When they went on the air, it looked like I created another series of winners. The phones lit up at the stations as listeners requested to hear the commercials, almost unheard of in the jingle business.

I never had a reason to meet the client. I heard the president of the company listened to each commercial, leaned back in his chair, and nodded his head up and down to signify he approved it.

The agency took an inexperienced young copywriter to his first client presentation at the corporate office. Trying to make a relevant contribution to his initial meeting, this doofus piped up and remarked, "Can you imagine that those spots were done by a white guy?"

The president sat up straight in his chair and shook his head from side to side signifying, "No!" Oof! I lost the account. In the music business we never considered that aspect of life. The guy lost his job, and I lost a very lucrative account, but I had those commercials on my demo reel for years.

A matchless "name" singer flew in to do a commercial. He arrived at the studio with a young maiden he met at the airport, who looked like a younger version of his wife. She left her luggage in the reception area and came into the studio to hear him sing. She did not realize that Universal's foyer doors were open to the outside.

When our singer finished weaving his tapestry of advertising ideas, they walked out of the studio to find her luggage missing. It probably ended up on Maxwell Street on the South Side, where unscrupulous vendors hawked hot items at the Sunday flea market. So not only did he have to entertain her, he had to buy her a new wardrobe. Karma is a bitch!

Paul Wimmer, part owner and manager of Mr. Kelley's and the London House, two historic jazz clubs in Chicago, asked me to check out an artist he was interested in signing. I attended her show and she blew me away. Paul asked me what I recommended. She performed a song called, "Do You Wanna Dance," in her act. I thought it could be a hit record if we produced it with a full orchestra. He asked me how much that would cost. I told him five or six thousand dollars. He wanted to know what I could do for a couple of grand and I told him, "Nothing right!"

So, he passed on the project!

One evening as I drove home, I heard Bette

Midler's number one song, "Do You Wanna Dance," on my car radio. I never let Wimmer forget that. Unfortunately, sometimes it happened that way: clients try to save a buck and end up completely missing the brass ring.

Chapter 25

I met the incredibly talented Curtis Mayfield during my stint at Chess, and we developed a comfortable congenial relationship. When people looked at Curtis, they saw a diminutive African American man, emotional and quick to smile, with eyes that sometimes reflected the pain he felt for people who lacked opportunity and the necessities of life. His friends, as well as his business associates, called him the "gentle genius." This beautiful soul became a never-ending source of many compassionate, powerful, memorable songs that often conveyed his dedication to righting perceived injustices he witnessed in his life.

Born on the often volatile, poverty-stricken South Side of Chicago, he beat the odds and grew up to be a highly successful legendary R&B writer, performer, guitar player, and producer. Curtis sang with a gospel choir as a youth. In the years that followed, he and Jerry Butler linked up to form the well-known musical group, The Impressions.

Curtis became one of the first artists to merge social consciousness with memorable songs. He wrote "People Get Ready," number 24 on the Rolling Stones' list of greatest songs ever. He added "Gypsy Woman," "Amen," "Keep on Pushing," "Move on Up," "He will Break Your Heart," "Freddy's Dead," "Superfly," and so many more R&B anthems, to his burgeoning catalogue of hit records.

Curtis listened to my music, and asked me to come and see him. He formed *Curtom*, a Chicago-based soul, R&B record label. He signed me as his only white artist and gave me carte blanche to write, sing, and produce an album.

I decided to do six of my own songs and chose five by other writers. Curtis singled out one in particular named "Pity the Poor Ghetto Child," penned by Bill Dean, a singer friend of mine from New York. This song pointed to children who never had the opportunity to experience life outside the small 'hood they were stuck in.

(Got to) Pity the poor Ghetto Child
Flappin' his wings and got nowhere to fly
Pity the poor ghetto child
Mama what's a buttercup, Daddy when's the sun come up
Is a country hill the same color as a dollar bill?

The Impressions added background vocals and Curtis loved the finished product.

I listened to a copy of a song named, "Easy

with You," written by my friends Richard Mainegra and Rick Yancy; two wonderful accomplished singer/songwriters from Nashville. They reached the top of the music charts with several memorable hits in a group called The Remingtons.

Rich devised a complex guitar solo on the demo, and I couldn't find a guitar player who could duplicate it. I flew him and Rick into Chicago. They shared the guitar work and sang harmonious backgrounds. It turned out to be my favorite song on the album.

Then, I recorded "Wendy Wakefield," a beautiful ballad about a blind girl who could only see the world through *my* eyes. I composed an eerie all-vocal intro, a combination choir-Gregorian classical piece of music that lasted for about 35 seconds. It must have been unique, as I heard it being used as a chant on a tasteless rap record last year. They sampled my intro, stole it, and used it as a background melody for profane lyrics (which I didn't appreciate) 44 years after we completed the album.

Theft of creative property is becoming a way of life these days. Damn this modern computer technology that lets anyone steal your music.

Minnie Riperton, Kitty Heywood, and Bonnie Herman performed background vocals on another of the songs. While we were recording, Minnie celebrated the success of her number one hit, "Loving You." Kitty, an up-and-coming incredibly soulful singer, performed with a voice that guaranteed she would have a long, successful career. Bonnie Herman, the reigning sweetheart of the commercial business, deserves a book all by herself.

Bonnie appeared on the music scene through the efforts of a prominent musician and an advertising executive, who decided that Chicago needed some new singer choices. They auditioned vocalists all over the country and discovered Bonnie. They brought her to Chicago, trained her, and she became the number one lady jingle singer in the Windy City. Bonnie's best commercial? A 30-year run of singing, "State Farm is there!"

Bonnie, one of the sweetest people in the business, could sing in any style and do it to perfection. I have to give her credit for one of the pivotal moments of my career.

I arrived at the studio after a frustrating non-productive business lunch, to find myself working with an extremely difficult client. I felt myself snapping at everybody. When the singers and musicians are in the studio, they can't hear what you are saying in the glassed-in control room until you press an intercom talkback button. So, all they were hearing were my terse commands when I *did* use the button. They had no idea of the stress, and the annoyance, happening behind the scenes.

We took a break and I walked out into the hall.

Bonnie came up to me, put her hand on my shoulder, looked at me with those soft beautiful eyes and said, "Honey, have you listened to yourself today?"

She stopped me in my tracks. From then on I tried to let my talent be aware of the happenings in the control room. I continually focused on the thought foremost in my mind. I wanted them to feel like friends and part of my musical family, rather than employees.

I didn't mean to get off the topic of the album, but I have so many things to share that sometimes it's hard to not get sidetracked.

I found working in Curtis' studio to be a liberating experience. The engineer let me do anything I wanted. In fact, when it came to mixing the album, I ended up engineering most of it myself.

I recorded another up-tempo song by Rich and Rick called, "Valerie." The harmonic background vocals they created turned out to be unquestionably some of the finest I ever recorded. Those Nashville boys were something else!

Some of the other titles on the album were "Pen of a Poet," "Play It, Piano Man," "Up on Living," "Footprints," and "Why Don't You Grow Up." The final record contained compositions that held touching themes and heartfelt lyrics. Today, you can find copies of my collection of poignant

Bittersweet Stories on eBay for $15, iTunes for $9.99, Amazon for $9.49, or in your local bargain bin for 99 cents.

Curtis authorized me to use any musicians of my choice. I hired my favorite horn players, Chicago Symphony strings and, of course, my sensational rhythm section.

One day as I began to record with 23 string players, Curtis came charging into the studio. He frantically said, "I need your strings, man. I need your strings."

Noting his desperation, I simply said, "Have at it!"

Hired to score the cult detective movie *Superfly*, he faced a two-day deadline to send the theme song to the film company in California. Curtis, a brilliant performer on stage, had no idea how to write music down on paper. So I watched in amazement as he sang the signature string parts off the top of his head, to 23 Chicago Symphony musicians. What a tough day for them! I bet they had never seen that before.

The parts were genius and the record turned out to be a smash, but I'll never forget the process. Neither will the string players who were schooled to read music, and known for preferring structure. With Curtis, they were a bit out of their element. They were most comfortable having the notated parts sitting in front of them.

Curtis released "Easy with You" as my first

single. Unfortunately, he faced the same problems as Leonard Chess. His promotion network, geared to R&B stations, found it difficult to get pop stations to open up the airwaves to a new artist. The album did as well as could be expected under those circumstances, but most of the reported sales were probably purchases by my friends and relatives. We did score some airplay, but not enough to be significant and make the record a hit. Even after 44 years, I still love that song, "Easy With You!"

On a sad note, a light tower fell on Curtis in a concert in 1990, and he ended up paralyzed. He continued to perform, but it wasn't the same. He will always be one of my favorite people. I'm grateful that I had the opportunity to work side by side with a legendary artist like Curtis, and become his friend.

On a much sadder note, my sister called me and told me my mother suffered a heart attack. I rushed to the hospital. I picked up the first copy of my album that morning, so I brought it with me. Mom told me she felt like an elephant was sitting on her chest.

I put my album in her hands, and she smiled and whispered, "I knew you would do it, honey."

It meant a lot to me to be able to share it with her. Mom always had faith in me, and she always believed that I'd get to complete my album. I wish she'd had time to hear it. I still miss her beautiful heart. That day in my life was the ultimate *Bittersweet Story*.

Chapter 26

On the next spin of the wheel, the arrow pointed back to Darien. Our sons were fully entrenched in sports, and the incessant flow of neighborhood gals and pals wore a path up my driveway. Gym shoes piled up in the garage, and the yard looked like a used bicycle shop. Even today, I keep running into my children's old school friends, whom I don't remember. They tell me what fun it was to grow up at my house. Go figure. I must have lost some memory cells, or there were too many of them to count.

As usual, Brenda somehow managed to juggle the house, the business, our client entertainment, the lake retreat, and our burgeoning social life. In addition, she became the ultimate supermom. To this day she is the perpetual Energizer Bunny without the bass drum. I was the dummy with the pencil and the music paper. Strangely enough, life seemed surprisingly smooth.

Wendy, our five-year-old munchkin, had been asked to sing a commercial for Cindy Dolls. She possessed a delightfully cute voice, and one of my clients thought the fledgling Shirley Temple would be a perfect fit for her commercial.

Picture a tiny curly-haired cherub standing in the studio, wearing unlaced pink gym shoes, jeans from the Gap Kids, and a once-perky wine colored hair ribbon with white polka-dots squished under a giant set of headphones. She sang, "Cindy is my friend," into a microphone that sat three feet off the floor. It was a picture worthy of a *Life Magazine* cover.

She finished her first take, put her hands on her hips and said, "Gimme a playback." We shook our heads in astonishment and laughed out loud. Where did she learn that? Little Miss Diva!

The commercials were perfect! She collected her first royalty check and held my hand as a dignified silver-haired banker filled out the papers for her to open up her first bank account.

Buoyed by Wendy's success, Tarrey, my middle son, asked if we thought that he could do commercials. We hooked him up with a friend of ours named Bob Ebel, the best youth photographer/producer in town. He placed Tarrey on two singing spots and finally landed him an elusive on-camera film role. The day before the shoot, he fell out of a tree and cut his face. Panic mode! Makeup fixed it, but filming ran over, he missed his school dance, and he wasn't a happy boy. His disposition significantly improved when he saw his first residual check. There it was—his introduction to the downside, and the upside, of show business. He started saving his royalties to buy a car, and it all worked out when he drove his shiny white Triumph sports car to school.

Wendy experienced one of her first exciting show biz moments when she sang a duet with the talented Richard Marx when she was seven. Her first older man! Richard's father was the top jingle producer in Chicago and he started Richard singing at an early age. Richard's developmental training paid off for him when he moved to LA and recorded the first of many hit songs. Richard's dad had been a long-time established producer, and his mother sang on sessions. Even though we were competitors, I hired her to work with my young talent, as she knew how to make them feel comfortable in the studio. My other two boys dabbled a bit, but they were more into baseball and football, and doing commercials became old really fast.

We were having a profitable year. I wanted to give something back. I launched a Christmas charity that I named, "The Children's Festival of Giving" to provide toys for underprivileged, troubled, and handicapped kids at various facilities around the area. I cajoled my musicians to shake loose some bucks, put the arm on anyone else I could hustle, and hit the stores for overstocks, broken boxes, and Christmas toys I could coerce them into donating.

It started as a charitable thought, then turned into the perennial "fish that ate Pittsburgh." I ended up leaving our family celebration every Christmas Day, to deliver the toys I had been unable to distribute the week before the holiday.

I called the Chicago Cubs organization. They graciously hooked me up with some of the ballplayers, to make appearances when we passed out the toys. Ron Santo, Billy Williams, Don Kessinger, Steve Stone, and even Ernie Banks, graciously appeared at different functions. For the kids, an autograph constituted another Christmas gift. It made the occasion a memorable experience for them, and the players were as friendly as they could be.

I received a call from Rick Monday, the Cubs' center fielder, offering his services. I scheduled a delivery of toys to a mission on the South Side of the Windy City, and he agreed to meet me there.

When I arrived at my destination I freaked out. As usual I hadn't done my research. I found the mission to be in the middle of the worst neighborhood in Chicago. I pulled up in front of the address they gave me, to find a depressing storefront, masquerading as a church. I thought, "Holy smokes, Batman. I think I did it again."

The decrepit spiritual retreat loomed before me. I double-parked and waited for Rick. After he arrived and found a space for his car, we threw anxious glances from left to right, then entered the dismal "chapel."

We found the shabby sanctuary to be rank, dusty, and smelling like urine and stale booze. The "bouncers," two huge black ladies wearing flowing white angel costumes and giant wings, were primed and ready to maintain order at all costs. A smattering of people sat slumped in ancient folding chairs. A notably intoxicated bum snored in the front row, and in a far darkened corner, an old wino sat, nodding off from time to time.

The miniature minister, clad in a worn thrift-shop suit, danced and waved his arms as he preached in a surprisingly loud, high-pitched voice. His meandering message soared to the stained yellow ceiling as sweat poured off of his egg-shaped balding head. As I approached the warped plywood pedestal to tell the pint-sized pontificator I was there with the toys, the drunk came to life, staggered over and started to urinate on the radiator.

Wham! Those two "angels" sacked him like Green-Bay Packer linemen, with ferocity and vigor. They lifted the poor, dazed soul off the ground and threw him through the doors that were closed at the time.

Rick looked like a deer in the headlights as he took in the situation. I felt a dire sense of insecurity myself. We asked the winged enforcers to help us bring in the toys and decided to leave the baseball bats on top of the pile, to grab as a last defensive measure. This had to be the one damned time I wasn't carrying my gun!

We weren't eager to stay there, but the flailing pastor spewed an uninterruptible flowing pattern of words and remained completely immersed in his sermon. We sat down in the squeaky chairs, hoping he'd need to catch his breath at some point. Here was a bit of the interaction he had with a member of his flock.

Preacher: "So let's be thankful for Lord God almighty!"

Drunk jerks his head up and shouts: "Amen!"

Preacher: "And let's be thankful that the spirit of Jesus will be with us on Christmas Day."

Drunk wakes up again and shouts: "Amen!"

Preacher: (the air whistling through the space in his teeth). "And so we celebrate the birth of Jesus... and yo' shut yo' mouth!"

The front row mumbled a raggedy "Amen!"

We became aware of gang members poking their heads in the door, giving us the evil eye. The word spread through the 'hood that there were two lambs on the alligator farm.

Finally, Rick and I broke into the preacher's marathon mumblings, wished him a Merry Christmas, left the toys behind, and bailed out the door.

Rick went to retrieve his car, after he told me I'd better be there to lead him out when he got back, or he'd hunt me down and kill me. It was an inauspicious start to a long friendship. We'll return to Rick in a minute, but I need to finish the charity episode.

By Christmas the following year, the festival had exploded and my garage bulged with toys, ready to deliver to hundreds of kids. I had only managed to make a few early deliveries. I thought I'd take a whole slew of toys to the police department by Cabrini Green, a high-crime housing project. The police hosted a Christmas party every year to try to bolster community relations.

My kids and I loaded up boxes of toys, and I drove to the precinct where the police liaison tapped some folks to carry in the cartons. The toys were displayed all over the big room where they were going to try to show the neighborhood children that men in blue were the good guys.

Then it was time for a shift change, and the cops filed into the room and plundered the toys, taking armfuls for their own kids. I hit the ceiling. I created such a stink, that they forcibly removed me from the building before I ended up in jail. I hadn't done all that work collecting all those gifts for a bunch of greedy crooked officers of the *law* to pillage the designated peace offerings and take them home.

I found it ironic that this was the same precinct where we were arrested when we worked on Rush Street. It was obvious that not too much had changed. Anger didn't come close to how I felt.

To cap it off, some gifts remained that were too large to give to a group home: a chemistry set, a telescope, etc. I fielded a last minute Christmas Eve call from one of my old DJ friends, who received an on-air plea for toys, for a needy family. I felt gratified that I could help make their holiday special, so on Christmas Day I loaded up the rest of the merchandise and drove to the designated address.

The family lived in a second-floor apartment in a decent neighborhood. I walked up and knocked on the heavily fortified door. Much to my horror, a chubby welfare queen dressed in a red-velvet bathrobe answered the door. I gazed at a Christmas tree larger than mine, an apartment filled with fancy furniture, three obnoxious snot-nosed kids, and a room *full* of freebie gifts. Son of a bitch! That did it! I unceremoniously dumped the gifts on her lush white shag carpet, and begrudgingly gave her a card that said "Merry Christmas from the Children's Festival of Giving." In a cloud of disgust, I returned to my car.

All of a sudden one of her whiny kids knocked on my side window. He was shaking the open card in my face like he'd had a lot of practice. He said. "My mother wants to know why there isn't any money in the card."

I lost it! I told the kid, "Tell your mother to go f*** herself." Not one of my prouder moments.

My charitable spirit fled into the wind, and the Children's Festival was over! Done! Finished! I realized how much I'd missed not spending time with my family on Christmas Day, so on subsequent holidays you could find me sitting at home by the fireplace with Brenda, some close relatives, and my beloved bambinos, trying to make up for some of those lost moments.

Chapter 27

Brenda and I treated Rick and his wife, Teri, to dinner to thank him for his help and offer an apology for getting him involved in a life-threatening, stressful appearance at the toxic mission. The more time we spent together, the more we realized we had a lot in common. He had two cute kids, a boy and a girl, and we started spending more time together. My boys were in Little League heaven. None of the other teams enjoyed visits from a real live professional baseball player. Rick attended an occasional game, and very generously took the time to hang out with the players and sign autographs.

The crowd increased at our house, if that was at all possible. Rick offered free passes to our boys for all the Cubs' home games, and we were inundated with baseball, baseball, and more baseball! When the team left for a road trip, Teri and the kids spent a lot of time at the house, adding two more munchkins to the mob.

And then Brenda said the "C" word…"Cat!"

Teri owned a beautiful, longhaired silver Persian, and Brenda decided she wanted one. The only thing that tore up my allergies more than scouting equipment, had to be longhaired cats. I bravely stocked up on Kleenex and Actifed, and Tiffany, possibly the snottiest cat west of Lake Michigan, became an unwelcome member of the family. Even the dog hated her, after a couple of inquisitive sniffs and the resulting clawed nose.

Tiffany wasn't stupid. She either curled up in someone's arms, or climbed on top of something. Miss Pris, The Cat, noticed VO's viperous looks, and his bared teeth every time he spotted her, and knew if he ever cornered her the fur would fly, along with jumbo chunks of cat!

I wheezed and sneezed and hoped Brenda would take pity on me. Ignoring my snorts for help, she bred the cat and then we owned seven longhaired silver Persians. I have to admit I kind of liked the runt of the litter. I called him Spud, a very un-cat like name. The kittens were amusing to watch—from across the room.

Thanksgiving rolled around, and after we finished our epicurean Thanksgiving feast of fowl, Brenda stripped all the remaining meat from the turkey. She thought it would be cute to put all the kittens in the bathtub with the turkey carcass. She did, and those little scavengers attacked the remnants of that bird like roaches in a bakery going after the crumbs on the floor. I watched them attack the empty shell for a few minutes, and went in to check out the football game. I felt a compelling need to do something manly at that point.

All of a sudden, Brenda and the kids were in a panic. My favorite little buddy disappeared from the tub. So we embarked on an exhausting, futile quest to locate the truant kitten. We finally put our search on hold, and Brenda went to lift the turkey carcass out of the tub. All of a sudden Spud's little grease-coated head popped out of the turkey's body cavity. Our perceived runaway had crawled inside the turkey and become immersed in his own flavorful private Thanksgiving feast.

We eventually sold all the kittens. Although I don't remember how we got rid of Tiffany, I remember that I was deliriously happy when she was gone and I could stop going to Walmart for bulk Kleenex. The loving look returned to VO's eyes.

A quick aside: we threw a costume party. Rick came with Steve Stone (the Cubs' pitcher), dressed as pregnant cheerleaders complete with flashy pom poms, platinum bouffant wigs, and false eyelashes. They wore splotches of bright red lipstick smeared in the approximate area of their lips. They encountered a minor problem when they were stopped by the police on their way to the house, and a bigger one trying to explain it to a burly macho motorcycle cop. Rick did like the blow-up inflatable doll we got him, although she was hard to dance with.

Rick was responsible for what the press called

"the play of the year." On April 25, 1976 at Dodger Stadium in Los Angeles, two protesters ran onto the field and tried to set fire to an American flag.

As the two radicals started to burn the flag, Rick dashed over and grabbed it away from them. He ran through the infield to thunderous cheers, the Stars and Stripes billowing behind him.

The ballpark police swooped in, arrested the two illegals, and escorted them from the field. When Rick came to bat, he received a standing ovation from the crowd, and the big message board behind the left-field bleachers flashed the message, "RICK MONDAY... YOU MADE A GREAT PLAY!" I still see the film clip of his flag rescue in the news highlights on Memorial Day.

I added my own touch to the many awards being sent to Rick, from groups of patriotic Americans. I made up a plaque with the picture of him running away from the two pyros, carrying the flag. I captioned it "Crazy man steals American Flag from two bewildered Boy Scouts." My personalized award became one of his favorites.

Rick's wife still travels around the country proudly displaying that flag, reminding Americans that patriots and unsung heroes still exist, and Rick Monday really made a great play.

Being an avid fisherman and an occasional hunter, Rick spent a substantial amount of time with me on the water. When I motored out of the marina and turned left, I cruised out onto Lake Michigan, where we fished for salmon and lake trout. If I turned right, I meandered up a tranquil river stocked with bass, catfish, and other small pan fish. Occasionally, we limbered up our shotguns and missed a duck or two.

One cloudy morning, Rick and I fished at a fork in the river. I purchased a new pole for my kids, loaded with light six-pound test fishing line, and I wanted to try it out. For some reason, we were casting into an unusual number of snags, and losing lures when we couldn't pull them out of the bushes. I threw out a little Mepps spinner, and started to reel back toward the boat. It snagged! I looked at Rick, muttered a curse under my breath, and prepared to break another line.

Rick said, "Don't look now but your snag just moved," and I experienced the best fishing adventure of my life.

That fish ran up one channel and down the other. I could tell I'd hooked a big one, but with that feeble pole I couldn't do anything but try to keep him from breaking the line. I had a fleeting hope he would tire himself out, and Rick could gently net him. The battle went back and forth for about 30 minutes. The fish finally came closer to the boat. We saw a silver flash in the water and caught a brief glimpse of a monster.

I finally eased him close to the boat and Rick went for the landing net. He knew he'd only have one shot at getting him on board, so he stealthily dunked the net in the water and waited. I gave one last pull, the line snapped and Rick netted the fish before it could swim away.

We were admiring a 29-pound king salmon (actually a 28-pound 10-ounce salmon, but we fisherman love to exaggerate). The fish had been swimming up the river to spawn. I mounted the marine monster, and it hung on my wall for a long time. No one believed I caught it on such a light fishing line. I wouldn't have believed it either!

Some years later, Rick retired from playing baseball and became a sportscaster. On one of my trips to LA, I took a detour to San Diego to see Rick and his wife, and enjoy a couple of Padres games. I sat in the booth with him as he announced the games. In the middle of the night, my bed started to shake and pound on the wall. I started to cuss Rick out for playing a prank on me. His wife rushed in. "Get into a doorway! It's an earthquake!" If you want to feel powerless, get caught in an earthquake. It is the most frightening experience you will ever have.

We remained friends for a long time after he moved, and I ran into him on some of my LA and New York trips. We'd catch dinner, reminisce about the fun times we had with the kids, and laugh about our near death experience in the ghetto.

Back in Darien, I'm not sure what possessed us to poke a hole through the mantle of parental responsibility and buy our boys dirt bikes, but we did. We were surrounded by acres of woods and fields, so the boys had plenty of space to ride with no traffic worries. Late one afternoon, my daredevil son Torrey, and his brother, arrived home from riding the trails. Soaking wet, he pushed his bike into the garage. I asked him what happened. He said he ran into some water.

Torrey laughed. "Yeah, Dad. He drove it into a stream, but he was standing on the seat at the time."

A large tract of vacant land that sat near our house was being cleared for a new housing development. This property looked like a perfect place for me to test out my shiny new toy. Despite the overcast skies, we headed in that direction. Tarrey carried my new pride and joy, a Fox double-barreled shotgun, that he expressed the desire to shoot. With a burst of youthful enthusiasm, he clambered up to the top of a formidable mountain of wet topsoil, where he stood like a mini-king of the hill, perusing the land for storybook invaders he could repel.

The muddy mountain sat adjacent to a deep

drainage ditch partly filled with sludge. The only trace of civilization in the area was a lone, elderly watchman in a crude, ramshackle shed on the other side of the property, so we were free to fire away.

Tarrey aimed at an imaginary bad guy and prepared to take a shot. I forgot to tell him to only pull one trigger at a time and he pulled both of them, discharging the two barrels simultaneously. Being a miniature soldier, the recoil from the shotgun forced his slight body to do a backflip and land with a splash at the bottom of the ditch. If I'd been a judge at the Olympics, I would have awarded him a nine.

The shotgun went barrel first into the slime. I skidded down the side of the pit into the water next to him. I wiped the mud out of my eyes and carefully pulled the shotgun from the muck. We slithered our way out of the ditch and headed for home. We looked like two drowned rats that got caught in a sewer-pipe after a monsoon. Not so funny then, but funny now!

Brenda and I ushered our sons, and my friend Jim Ross' kids, to one of the world's oldest cons, a trout farm. "This will be fun!" we said.

The sullen shady-looking man who ran the farm informed us that if we decided to keep the fish, he'd clean and scale those plump aquatic critters and prepare them for the frying pan. Our extended brood landed a fair number of fish, and they wanted to keep them. I wondered why the old geezer seemed so disgustingly happy. He gleefully scaled and gutted them, I pulled out my wallet and we were ready to leave.

Always read the small print! If you kept your fish, they charged five bucks a pound (weighed before cleaning). It ended up costing me $200. Fortunately, Jim was a good sport about it and split the cost with me. So at the end of the day, we tossed down a couple of beers and enjoyed a terribly expensive "gourmet" fish fry.

Chapter 28

I loved living the life of a wandering gypsy. My West Coast trips became more frequent, and I zeroed in on some of the best studio musicians in LA. Hal Blaine and Earl Palmer, members of the famous "Wrecking Crew," were two of my drummers. The Porcaro brothers, and some of the original Toto players, were available and I auditioned some marvelous guitar players.

James Newton Howard played keyboard. He scored over 100 movies, including *Pretty Woman, Prince of Tides,* and *The Hunger Games.* He was also fortunate enough to tour with Elton John, Toto, Crosby, as well as Stills and Nash.

Michael Boddicker and Craig Hundley added some brilliant synthesizer parts and created sound effects that placed a unique signature on many of my music tracks. Craig appeared on the *Johnny Carson Show* playing piano at the age of six. Boddicker exhibited Einstein's imagination when it came to programming, and performing on electronic instruments. These two incredible musicians were the backbone of my LA bands for a while.

Every time I traveled to Hollywood, I booked a room at the Sunset Marquis, a boutique hotel half a block from Sunset Boulevard. I usually ended up in a first-floor poolside room. Paul Schaeffer, from the David Letterman Show, occupied the room to the left of me, While Jim Belushi and Brian Doyle Murray (Bill Murray's little brother), were to the right. We ran into each other all the time, shared cocktails on the veranda and became friends. Paul Schaeffer offered to contract my bands for me when I started recording more sessions in New York, something I looked forward to doing.

Every time I walked out of my room, I encountered a swarm of music and movie stars, sitting on the palm-lined patio immersed in their Hollywood meetings. Actors rehearsed lines at the pool. The Sunset, a melting pot of industry activity, became a very "in" place to network.

I enjoyed a fascinating discussion with Ron Kovic, the pre-eminent, paralyzed ex-sergeant, anti-war, activist from the Vietnam War. We talked extensively about constantly changing world affairs, and I listened to his personal views until the sun came up. *That* was a conversation. Ron ended up the subject of the movie, *Born on the Fourth of July*.

Before Jim Belushi's acting career went into high gear, I found him some music to help him put together a commercial demo tape. He presented it to the advertising agencies and landed enough voice over work to tide him over.

I became a regular at the Sunset and they stored my electric piano and some custom music writing supplies in their storage room. The hotel staff delivered them to my room and set up the keyboard before I arrived. Brenda and the kids joined me anytime they could break away. The Sunset became our LA getaway destination. On one of our trips, Wendy tagged along with Bruce Springsteen every morning when he went down to get the newspaper, one of every kid's dream experiences.

On the rare times I couldn't get into the Sunset, I checked into the Chateau Marmont, the hotel where John Belushi overdosed. On one of my visits, as I attempted to write, the guys in the next room were tearing up the place with music. I found it incredibly hard to concentrate, so I knocked on the door and asked them to tone it down.

The fellow who answered the door gave me a disdainful look. "Stevie (Wonder) is almost done writing his new song."

I slunk back to my room.

I worked for a client, a gourmet chef, who always stayed at the Chateau. They stored a full sized stand-up steamer trunk full of his cooking supplies, and set up a gourmet kitchen for him every time he dropped his anchor there.

The chef was one of my J. Walter Thompson guys and he tapped me to do a 7-Up (The Uncola) Bubbles Commercial. Robert Abel, the film director, excelled as a technically superior, brilliantly innovative, man way ahead of his time with the computer animation techniques he developed. He found a way to create fluid character animation at a time when such lofty goals were someone else's dream.

In addition to working on commercials, he produced award winning work on the films *Tron* and *The Andromeda Strain.* He also contributed graphics for that outstanding Michael Jackson video, "Can You Feel It."

This 7-Up commercial can be viewed on YouTube. Google: "7-Up Uncola 1975." (There are several of them, so look for a picture of a lady dressed as a butterfly.)

Robert Abel's early sample reel can be found on the net. Google: Robert Abel and Associates, computer animation.

I mentioned this 7-Up commercial earlier, the music track containing six tempo changes in 30 seconds. I had never made as many adjustments at a recording session. Every time we looked at the film with the music, we saw another little nuance we wanted to embellish.

The commercial won seven Clio Awards (the advertising Oscar, better known as an "attaboy" for ads).Best of all, I scored one of the seven, for excellence in music. It was a highly successful collective effort by everyone involved, and the advertising agency's creative concepts were outstanding.

I had the opportunity to write a rollicking Harley Davidson radio spot with the line, "If you haven't been on a Harley Davidson, you haven't been on a motorcycle."

When I appeared at the Clio's, not only did I pick one up for 7-Up but, much to my surprise, I received another one for the Harley commercial. I also garnered several honorable mentions for other spots. I must have been doing something right, or the mythical Jingle Fairy was waving her magic wand in my direction. Through the years, I won three Clios and received 23 nominations.

I found a business partner/sales rep in LA, named Steve Siegel, who agreed to present my music to West Coast advertising agencies. I worked from his comfortable office a few blocks from the hotel writing, making phone calls, and hosting creative meetings.

On one corner of Steve's block sat Giuseppe's, a comfortable Italian restaurant adorned with decorative terrazzo tiles, pastel décor, exotic plants, and white villa-plastered walls. A wood-burning oven sat in front of an open kitchen. The ambience was relaxed, but classy. I found the food to be *fantastico*, a combination of flavorful old family recipes and modern European cuisine.

Giuseppe's family immigrated to the States from Italy. Giuseppe, a small, suave gentleman, exuded magnetic charm, and embellished his sparkling personality with a touch of sophistication. He greeted us with open arms, and served a meal that tasted like it had been cooked by the ultimate Italian chef, Brenda's mother.

In the fickle LA restaurant scene, he struggled to keep the doors open. I simply thought he hadn't been discovered yet. I recommended Giuseppe's to anyone looking for an exceptional restaurant. I relentlessly introduced every one of my friends and clients to this previously hidden gem. My partner Steve did the same thing, and gradually Giuseppe's became one of the hottest restaurants in Hollywood. He bought a white grand piano so he could sing duets with Julio Iglesias. From time to time, celebrity cabaret artists performed a song or two.

Giuseppe, the newly anointed consummate maître d' to the stars, greeted customers at the door, wearing his white tuxedo and a warm friendly smile. He made his patrons feel like they were coming to a family dinner. He sat Steve and me down one afternoon and thanked us for helping him get through his rough times.

I said, "Hell, now we'll never be able to get in here."

"Any time for you, my friend!"

One Friday night, Brenda and I finished a taxing recording session. I called Giuseppe to see if by some miracle he could squeeze us in. He told us to come right over. The valet opened the car door and whisked us past a line of waiting celebrities, straight into the restaurant, to a lovely quiet table on the upper level.

Coming from a session I wore jeans, a casual faded shirt, and an old denim cap. The tuxedoed waiter came over with his nose in the air, sniffed and said, "Oh, yes! Bobby Whiteside! Living proof that Giuseppe doesn't have a dress code."

Subtle? *Not!* We ate there for years. Giuseppe was to Italian food what Louie was to Chinese— simply the best.

I had to laugh at one indelible experience that occurred with an LA client who never seemed to be happy about anything. The recording session ran smoothly and we finished in record time. The client seemed miffed.

"You just did that commercial in an hour. What am I paying you four thousand dollars for?"

I looked her squarely in the eye and answered, "My ability to *do* that commercial in an hour."

By now I was hanging out and working with Skunk Baxter from the Doobie Brothers, along with some other accomplished and well-known musicians. Nathan East and Ray Brown played bass. Harvey Mason, Earl Palmer, and Hal Blaine sat in the drum chair. They were the beginning of a long line of superb LA musicians. I spent many evenings visiting the famous Chyna Club, listening to some great West Coast bands and vocalists. Almost any night, we could find musicians from all the hit bands: The Doobie Brothers, Toto, Jack Mack and the Heart Attack, and some top studio players jamming in a variety of obscure nightclubs. I relaxed and listened to some of the most incomparably spirited music I'd ever been exposed to.

After an extensive search, I found a cadre of impressive studio singers beginning with Edie Lehmann (one of the vocal directors of *The Voice.*) I reconnected with Patti Austin, whom I had been working with in New York, and became friends with Rosemary Butler, one of the finest singers in the country (sang with Linda Ronstadt and James Taylor). They were the heart and soul of my outstanding talent pool. Edie booked my vocal groups. The musicians and singers in LA were extraordinary, and my commercials kept sounding better and better.

One afternoon, I met Don Piestrup, one of my California competitors, when we were conducting sessions back to back in the same studio. He turned out to be one of the funniest characters I met in the business. Don, reputed to be a remarkable musical talent, made a fortune from a lucrative client base consisting of major corporate names like Ford, Chevy, Dodge, and so forth.

Don accumulated a legendary wine cellar, and he brought cases of fine vino to his recording sessions. This worked out for me when we were using the same singers on the same day. When Don finished his recording date, he sent Edie and the vocal group over to my session, carrying bottles of leftover wine... and I mean fine wine.

The funniest Don story came about because he "stacked" his clients. I always worked with one client at a time. Don would do all the band tracks for three or four clients in the morning, and then do all the vocals for the same clients in the afternoon, one right after the other.

This turned into a nightmare for him, when he created advertising for four different car companies on the same day. All the clients sat in the waiting lounge at the same time. After the wine flowed, they began to go into the studio and critique each other's commercial campaigns. Two of the clients almost engaged in a fistfight when the Ford client didn't like the Chevy spots. I can picture him getting a bang out of the whole thing. He was a rare soul.

One evening Don invited me to dinner with a few of his friends and clients. He insisted on picking up the tab and started ordering bottles with embossed labels. His guests drank ten bottles of wine. Cost? A thousand dollars! To say that Don had developed a successful business was certainly an understatement.

Some years down the road, I heard a rumor that invisible people chased him through a glass door, so he liquidated (no pun intended) his wine cellar.

Skunk Baxter, one of my mainstay guitar players, must have been a chameleon in a past life. A superb musician, blessed with a high intelligence, his life experiences molded him into an incredibly diverse and interesting person. He attended a prestigious prep school then studied Communications at Boston College.

In the 60's Skunk played bass in a band with Jimmy Hendrix. Then he worked at Manny's Music, where he repaired amplifiers, and became a guitar tech at Jack's Drum Shop, two iconic music locations in New York. In 1968, he scored his first hit as a member of a psychedelic rock band tagged with the bizarre name: Ultimate Spinach.

Following that, he shifted coasts to LA, and became a founding member of Steely Dan, one of the great musical ensembles of all time. He earned a fabulous reputation for his solid guitar grooves, and his exciting and distinctive sound.

Upon the dissolution of Steely Dan, he joined

The Doobie Brothers. After a basket full of hits, he left The Doobies. As a studio musician, he played on recording sessions for almost every big-name talent in the country, so his writing and producing credits are lengthy and wildly impressive.

He had a natural affinity for, and a curious interest in, electronics and the newly emerging digital world filled with algorithms and 0's and 1's. He also absorbed every bit of information he could find about military, missile, and defense systems.

He wrote a paper about converting the Aegis missile into a rudimentary missile defense system, which brought him to the attention of certain government officials, and his career as a defense consultant began. He now holds top security clearances, sits on many important committees, and is known for his out-of-the-box thinking that is so badly needed to protect our country.

He is still a master guitar player, working on a new album as I write this book, and continuously performing timeless music for the ages. Over the years, he's retained the signature Baxter Look: a green beret and long bushy sideburns that merge into a generous mustache. His appearance reminded me of some old sepia photographs of the gunfighter Wyatt Earp. I'm sure he is the recipient of some surprised looks at Congressional hearings.

One of Skunk's favorite stories relates to a Saturday afternoon recording session for Hyatt Hotels. Skunk was staying in my apartment over the studio. I ran into the session with a last-minute rhythm chart and the band killed it! The musicians magically filed in the blanks in a burst of creativity. It was on that session that he met, and was impressed by, CJ Vanston, the sensational producer keyboard player I mentioned earlier. They became best friends, and currently collaborate on numerous projects. That chance meeting resulted in some brilliant compilations by those two. (You're welcome, Skunk.)

Skunk and I produced several tracks for my daughter. Her voice mirrored Belinda Carlisle's commercial sound(lead singer of the girl group The Go Go's). We loved the way they turned out, but when we balanced out the toll a recording career on the road would take on a 16-year-old, versus not doing it, we figured it prudent to shelve the project. It would have been way too much for us to handle, as Brenda and I were short on time already, and constantly under the gun running the business. The responsibility of overseeing the formative years of an active teenager's recording career would have been overpowering.

We recorded Wendy on a version of Chad and Jeremy's "Summer Song" with that famous Skunk Baxter grooving guitar. I added some intricate background vocals. CJ created a soaring synthesizer sound, and it's still one of my favorite music tracks I ever produced, both for personal, and professional reasons.

There's so much more to his story, but I think I've given you the encapsulated version. Skunk's Wikipedia page is fascinating.

Chapter 29

I had the good fortune to be in a life that constantly produced interesting people. Although he started out in Chicago, Mike Lesner already looked like a well-tanned blue-eyed LA guy. Mike weighed about 150 and proudly sported a bushy Afro hairdo. I found it to be an interesting combination. Mike was as cool as his hair.

The first time I worked with Mike, we traveled to Nashville to record an International Harvester project with an authentic country sound. We landed at the airport, took a cab to our destination, and when we arrived we found musicians picketing outside the studio. They were protesting the use of one of the first synthesizers, a Mellotron, which electronically reproduced certain instruments, depriving live musicians of work.

So began another auspicious beginning of a lucrative business relationship, and a lasting friendship. Nobody remembered me, but they never forgot Mike's hair.

The rhythm section for the session was composed of some of the best of the best pickers in Nashville. David Briggs played piano, Norbert

Putnam strummed bass, Mac Gayden added tasty guitar parts, Kenny Buttrey played drums, Ron Oates (one of the gifted Nashville players who sight read music and composed orchestral scores) played keyboard number two, and last but not least, Charlie McCoy added some melodic flourishes on harmonica. Some of them were part of the legendary Muscle Shoals rhythm section, and collectively they recorded or played with Elvis, Waylon Jennings, George Harrison, Joan Baez, Dolly Parton, Kris Kristofferson, Linda Ronstadt, Bobby Goldsboro, Henry Mancini, Jimmy Buffett, Roy Orbison, Bob Dylan, The Allman Brothers, Simon and Garfunkel, Willie Nelson, Dolly Parton, Keith Whitley, and a host of other entertainers.

Mike and I were fascinated by musicians' use of the Nashville "numbers" system. Instead of notes or chords on a music part, the musicians used a surprisingly simple technique. Trained musicians sometimes picked up a part and stated, "What the hell is this?"

Let me see if I can explain it to you. A music scale has eight notes. A music scale in the key of C would be C, D, E, F, G, A, B, C. The chords in music correspond to one of these notes and are represented by a number. In the key of C: C=1, D=2, E=3, F=4, G=5, A=6, B =7

Jingle Bells in the key of C would be written and played like so:

Jingle Bells, Jingle Bells, Jingle all the way
EEE EEE EGCDE(melody notes)
333 333 35123(numbers)
The accompanying chords are
Jingle Bells, Jingle Bells, Jingle all the way
C C C FG C(chords)
1 1 1 45 1(numbers)

Let's say one key is too low for the singers so you need to play it in a higher register. The beauty of this system is if someone needs to change the pitch of a song, they don't have to rewrite a new chart, as the same numbers relate to every key.

I was used to writing orchestral scores and real music notes, but this system intrigued me and I wanted to learn to use it to notate music. Some of the musicians in Nashville who played on hundreds of hit records, are among the most accomplished players in the world, yet don't read a note of sheet music.

I was amazed when I watched my first group of Nashville singers work from one of these parts. When the singers read the page stacked with numbers instead of music notes, it looked like they were reading shorthand, or interpreting a math problem.

Anyway, back to Mike Lesner!

Michael, having dumped the Afro years ago, is currently a producer for the longest continuously airing health show, airing on television, *The*

American Health Journal. Earlier in his career, Mike served as an Executive Producer for Animax Entertainment, as well as the President of Animax Health.

An ad agency veteran of Leo Burnett, Y & R, J. Walter Thompson and McCann-Erickson, Lesner also created Michael Lesner Productions, a freestanding promotion unit for *CBS Network Television.*

The music we created in Nashville for International Harvester, received many compliments from the discerning executives at the advertising agency and an extremely happy client. A few months later, we traveled to New York to Media Sound, Joe Jorgensen engineering, to create driving EXPerience commercials for California Ford Dealers.

While Paul Schaeffer contracted my New York bands, he hooked me up with an A-list rhythm section named Stuff, and we generated some remarkable music through the years. They were one of the finest groups of musicians in the country. I'll tell you more about Stuff in a subsequent chapter.

We returned to New York to produce Levi's commercials for the Moscow Olympics. The commercials won the coveted, prestigious Best in the West award.

Mike is homeless. I mean he doesn't have a

290

house. He lives on a boat. A ship! A 93-foot yacht named the Kinsai that he keeps docked in a marina located at Long Beach, California.

The Kinsai is a classic in the world of boating. The solid teak hull is fastened together with bronze fittings. This is not a multistoried fiberglass boat like the mega-yachts you see in Monte Carlo; it is a single level of elegance that sits low in the water. Kinsai is the kind of storied yacht you would see in an old time movie, where a head of state attends an elegant party on the water. Mike found her when he visited Hong Kong to set up a company, and bought that wooden beauty on the spot.

The only boat Mike had ever set foot on, my 32-foot cabin cruiser, opened the door to his desire to own his own floating getaway. When he spotted the *Kinsai*, he pulled the trigger and bought it immediately. Then Mike did the unthinkable. He hired a crew and sailed it from Hong Kong to California. (And you thought I had a death wish.) I bet *that* was a learning experience.

He spent $600,000 refurbishing it, and masterfully engineered almost all the woodwork by himself. The lavish interior is enhanced by solid polished teak floors and walls, lush leather burgundy furniture, and has a hot tub on the bow. The yacht is the unmistakable jewel in the Long Beach marina.

So, today, Mike stays in shape, looks like Paul

Newman's brother, drives a Jaguar, lives on a yacht, runs a bunch of companies, and dates supermodels. Okay! We're still close friends, but officially I hate him!

While recording in LA, an agency contracted me to produce a commercial with Davy Jones from the 60's boy band, The Monkees. I found him to be serious, but friendly, a classic commercial rocker with a British accent who was extremely focused and surprisingly easy to work with. He invited Brenda and me to his house in the Hollywood Hills after the recording session. We shared a friendly drink, and engaged in a lengthy discussion about the music business.

The Monkees had been under contract at a set salary, so they missed a lot of the benefits, royalties, and financial perks of having all those hit records. His "focking" business manager disappeared with a lot of the money he thought he saved, so he basically had to start over.

Sad story! It happens way too many times when fast-talking managers are driven by greed, and short on honesty and morals. And we have to give honorable mention to the record companies, who simply screw the artists.

These situations happened more often than you can imagine. My friend, Butch Baker, now a successful, well respected music publisher in Nashville, exhibited star potential as a singer.

Sony Records signed him and kept promising him they would release his album. This went on for years, and left Butch in limbo, unable to sign with another company as Sony kept him under contract. This practice became known as the "Sony artist protection program." Sorry to say, they never did release his album, a tremendous loss for the music business, and fans like me!

I signed several artists to production/management contracts, but tried not to hang them up if they wanted to go someplace else. It was interesting to watch how many of their careers fizzled when they thought they had all the answers, and the grass was greener someplace else. Keeping them under contract became more trouble than it was worth. I didn't have the time, or the inclination to be a babysitter and they probably would have stuck it to me in the end.

Chapter 30

A friend introduced me to a lovely model/singer from Milwaukee, named Lane Brody. This beautiful girl exhibited an exceptional voice, and seemed like a viable talent I could work with. I felt she had the potential to become a terrific writer. We began cranking out songs and doing artist demos.

I helped her finish a partly written song, a lush, emotional ballad that the talented Paul Anka wanted to record. I floated visions of the record, produced with dreamy strings and an ethereal vocal chorus. Just shows you how wrong you can be!

I flew to LA for the session. I arrived to find the veteran engineer Al Schmittt and Anka's arranger working with a big band better suited for a nightclub performance: ten funky horns, no strings...and no vocal chorus. Melanie's hit song from the "60's" floated through my brain. "Look What They've Done to My Song, Ma." My high expectations were flushed down the commode of things that were out of my control. At least we scored a major artist "cut" for the resume.

Lane progressed quickly, reaching new

artistic and creative goals every week. She embarked on an international tour with a monster singer/guitar player named Thom Bresh. Thom's father, Merle Travis, the father of finger-pickin', led Bresh to develop his own amazing techniques. Thom so impressed the legend, Chet Atkins, that Chet immediately mentored him. His voice had the same texture as Kenny Rogers. He played both parts of "Dueling Banjos" at the same time, did impressions, and I couldn't believe the effortless way his fingers moved when he performed his unique thumb-picking guitar solos.

If you want to hear this virtuoso, he's all over YouTube, or Google: Thom Bresh guitar.

Already a one-man super-show, Bresh rocked stages all over the world sharing vocal duties with Lane. I'd fly them back into town for commercial work, and continue to help develop Lane's songwriting skills at the same time.

She began to round out her catalogue with quality compositions. While searching other sources for songs for her to record, I found several potential hits through my New York publishing contacts. She recorded a catchy tune named, "You're Gonna Make Love to Me." The A&R guys at GRT, a medium-sized record label, were excited about the song and eager to run it to the radio stations. We shook hands on a deal.

Within hours, Sony begged me to give them the record. They were a much larger label, with sweeping promotion and formidable clout. If I had done my job as a manager, I would have pulled it from GRT. For better or for worse, I had this funny thing about a handshake. I couldn't go back on my word, but my artist probably had a better shot at a hit record with Sony. Lane and I shared some groundbreaking musical adventures, but her career needed more time and energy than I could give it.

I steered her toward a contract with Steve Wax at Cleveland International Records, and they recorded a notable album. Lane had a definitive vision for her own music and ended up collaborating with several top-notch producers over the years. She sang a hit duet with Johnny Lee named, "The Yellow Rose."

She continues to release CD's filled with lovely songs and is deeply embedded with a group that rescues wildlife. Always a true patriot, she often entertains military personnel with her exceptional emotional music.

Lane brought my attention to Richard Wold, a multi-talented singer/songwriter, also from Milwaukee. He performed in many local clubs and slowly built up a sizable fan base. When she played me his tape, his warm contemporary voice impressed me, and his potential songwriting ability seemed unlimited.

I asked him to drive down to Chicago to meet

me and we headed to Louie's for lunch. Big mistake! Richard was a bit nervous so he didn't eat much. I should have warned him about Louie's drinks. I finished my tasty Cantonese luncheon and we climbed the stairs to my office where he proceeded to initiate my wastebasket.

Despite our unusual first meeting, I realized Richard had the potential to be a creative success, both as a writer and an artist. He intrigued me and we began to work together. He didn't disappoint, and we succeeded in creating some commercial, but eloquent, music. Whenever possible, he commuted down to Chicago and we wrote all night. In the morning he would head back north to the Badger State.

Richard and his wife Chrissy, performed all over the country with a popular song and dance troupe named, The Brothers and Sisters. Between his touring experience, and his well-received appearances at various nightclubs in Milwaukee, I had no reservations about booking him into top clubs in our area.

He finally moved to Chicago with his two boys and Chrissy, also a talented songwriter. Brenda searched the area, found them a house, and they settled comfortably into the 'burbs. That made it convenient for us to get together and write, and we became best friends. He started performing in clubs on Rush Street to packed houses, giving me an excuse to return to my old stomping grounds.

He knew an innumerable number of songs: Kenny Loggins, Don McLean, Bread, and The Beatles...he skillfully covered them all. People enthusiastically applauded Richard's voice, and his skilled guitar and piano playing, and his fan base continued to grow.

Ad folks began to notice he had a versatile singing and speaking voice, appropriate for music commercials and voice overs, so he picked up some vocal work that helped pay his bills. We demoed our freshly minted songs in the studio, as time permitted. Our hard work paid off. Richard and I achieved tremendous success from 1979-81 that I will cover in another chapter.

An agency hired me to write a Kellogg's corporate commercial. The theme line was, "Kellogg's in the morning, is a very smart, very smart... start." I composed a lilting old-fashioned music track, and my versatile singer-arranger friend, Robert Bowker, came up with a perfect imitation of Rudy Vallee, the 1940's heartthrob. He turned it into a Prohibition Era love song. The spot ended up being one of the best commercials I'd ever done. The agency missed the message, *and* the boat, and killed it.

Have you ever felt like you just couldn't let something go? Normally, I'd shake it off and move on to something else. For some inexplicable reason, this particular rejection seemed offensive and demeaning to creativity in general, so I submitted it to the Clio Awards; neglecting to consider the possible fallout. In order to be eligible for a Clio, a commercial needed to run on the air somewhere. It obviously hadn't, but I really didn't care. And wouldn't you know it, the commercial won another one.

All the agency creative boys and girls at the Clio Awards wore puzzled looks. No one remembered the commercial. When they figured out what happened, I got called on the carpet. Several angry agency executives demanded that I appear before a review board to explain what I had done. They ordered me to give the Clio back.

I'm afraid I wasn't at all remorseful. I looked at the VIPs and said, "So you're going to tell the advertising world that you didn't recognize that you had a Clio Award winning commercial after you created it?"

The pot boiled over, but after the furor fizzled, they decided to simply sweep it under the carpet and never mention it again. However, if it ever came up, they'd blame me. It cost me some agency work for a short time, but they got over it.

Fortunately for me, the story hadn't wound its way around the entire agency, and I kept the clients who loved my work. The copywriter who wrote the commercial took me out to dinner, and we shared a bottle of Champagne, and a few giggles.

One afternoon, while recording with one of my favorite clients, she began to complain about her back. She'd recently had surgery, and sitting for a long time could be painful for her. She asked me if she could go up to my office and lie on the carpeted floor and do some back exercises. I finished the session and walked up to my office/apartment. Upon opening the door, I observed my client lying on the floor, facing the door with her legs spread, holding them up 18 inches off the ground. (Don't panic, she was wearing a granny skirt.) She looked at me. I looked at her and said, "A simple thank you would have been enough." I'll just leave that one there!

Leo Burnett asked me to do the music for a huge Kentucky Fried Chicken campaign, and my love affair with New York blossomed. I had already found a cadre of first-class New York musicians, but the "salt and pepper" guys that Paul Schaeffer pulled together for my sessions had already become legends, or about to become legends.

The salt, the blue-eyed soul members of the group, were Steve Gadd and Chris Parker, who both played drums and percussion. The pepper, the "soul brothers," consisted of Gordon Edwards on bass, Cornell Dupree, and Eric Gale on guitars. Add in Richard Tee on keyboards (Paul Simon,

The Bee Gees, Streisand, Aretha Franklin, Billy Joel, Eric Clapton, Peter Gabriel, et al.) and they were at the inception of musical magic. This group formed the core of the legendary band about to be called, "Stuff."

Paul Schaeffer slid another well-known guitar player into the mix when Eric Gale was on the road. His name: Elliott Randall (early member of Steely Dan and the guy who played the famous opening guitar riff on Steely Dan's hit song, "Reelin' in the Years.") We became fast friends.

Elliott also played the solo on Irene Cara's recording of *Fame*. He started on piano at five, switched to guitar when he was 9 and started gigging with Richie Havens when he turned 16. He played with Jay and the Americans and Sha Na Na. He held staff positions with two major organizations and cut his first band album in 1970. Robert Stigwood owned the rights to *Jesus Christ Superstar* and hired Elliott's band to back up the show. He turned down offers to be music director for The Blues Brothers, and join the band Toto. He became a music consultant for *Saturday Night Live* and performed with artists such as Carly Simon, Sly Stone, The Doobie Brothers, Peter Frampton, two symphony orchestras, and many other acts.

He recorded with John Lennon, Art Garfunkel, Gene Simmons, Peter Criss, Laura Nyro, and hundreds more. He composed jingles and played on movie scores. He has released more than six of his own CDs. Today he lives in London producing albums and working with many superstars. He wears his incredible success well. He remains modest, friendly and unpretentious, but his genius guitar playing makes him a formidable force in the music industry.

Chapter 31

Gordon Edwards started Stuff's train rolling, when he booked a gig backing up a singer at Mikells, a well-known jazz nightspot in Harlem. Gordon, Cornel Dupree, and Chris Parker were the original members. Richard Tee, Steve Gadd, and Eric Gale sat in one night and liked it so well that they immediately became members of the band. They churned out a toe-tapping funk rhythm and blues sound that had not been heard before.

Their individual careers exploded as they joined the elite group of the most in-demand studio players in New York. They performed with Aretha, Paul Simon, John Lennon, Joe Cocker and many others. Stuff wanted to do an album, but it seemed an unrealistic goal, as they were all so busy on different projects.

An engineer/producer, named Herb Lovell, found his recording studio in dire need of business. He thought he could get Stuff's album recorded by whisking them out of town to his studio at Long View Farm in North Brookfield, Massachusetts. He took the train into New York City to see Stuff's manager and offer him a deal he couldn't refuse. They decided to go for it, and the group left for Herb's farm to start recording.

For reasons no one could later figure out, someone decided to record at a low tape speed with no noise-reduction gear, leaving the possibility of tape hiss and other extraneous distracting sounds on the tape. When the band played loud it was fine, but when it was soft you heard an annoying sizzle.

The engineer who started the project bailed out, leaving Herb to inherit recording at that slow speed of 15 inches per second with no noise reduction. On top of that, the band continually partied into the late hours and major hangovers slowed the project to a crawl.

Most of the songs Stuff recorded ended with a long instrumental section, and that's where the band really hit its groove. So, they cut some of that music out from the end and edited it into the body of each song to make it feel like it cooked from the beginning. The music seemed to be taking forever. They were also burning up a lot of tape that cost a small fortune.

Tommy LiPuma, from Warner Brothers, arrived to monitor the session's progress.

He was increasingly irritated at the lack of progress, and rumor has it that he was overheard muttering a lot of words like: "Undisciplined," "Rowdy," "Unmixable," "The whole bottle (?)," "14 minutes a song," and "Are you kidding me?"

All Herb could do was shrug. Tommy left in

disgust after a particularly unproductive night; another rowdy recording session. His alleged last words were, "This project has about as much chance as a fart in a windstorm."

Herb finally had a come-to-Jesus meeting with the guys, and they went to work and nailed it! Al Schmitt, the engineer from our Anka session, showed up and signed on. They settled down and finished a fantastic album by the middle of the following week.

They sent the immense pile of tapes off to Warner Brothers Studio in LA. The record company responded a few weeks later with a letter stating the tapes were technologically inferior, and unmixable due to the hiss on the tape. To further complicate things, they refused to pay Herb's bill. He knew there had to be an answer.

He heard about an innovative piece of equipment called a gate. If you applied it to a single music track, it cut off the loud hiss and let the softer notes slip through. When the gate opened up, the louder notes covered up the hiss by themselves. Herb rented ten of them, convinced the band, and the record label that gates were the solution to the problem, and he successfully mixed the record.

Finally! Stuff became a giant success in the United States and a smash in Europe. The band followed up with several more records. Scan the album *Stuff* in iTunes and be ready to start tapping your foot. You'll quickly understand why Stuff became so popular.

Steve Gadd remains one of the best drummers in the country. When he wasn't available, Paul Schaeffer booked Billy Cobham, who recorded at least ten solo drum albums.

Some of my other notable New York session musicians were the Brecker Brothers, Marvin Stamm, and jazz great Urbie Green. Neil Steubenhouse and Will Lee played bass. Jeff Beck, David Spinozza, and John Tropae on guitar which took me on a whirlwind tour of exciting musical milestones. These guys played on hundreds of hit albums. Just for fun, Google any one of them! It will make for some fascinating reading.

Out of all my New York guys, Elliott Randall (on guitar) was my favorite. I worked with him on both coasts and flew him into Chicago from time to time. If I booked a low budget commercial in New York, I slept on the couch in his spacious apartment over by Riverside Drive. I used Elliott on sessions with Skunk Baxter every chance I could. Skunk set the groove, and Elliott did the fill work. That electrifying combination was the envy of my competitors.

I flew Elliott into Chicago to play in a commercial. A very difficult agency producer wanted something similar to the solo on the Steely

Dan song, "Reelin' in the Years." The client showed up with a room full of corporate executives and agency people, and set out on a mission to show everyone how important he was. Every time Elliott played a part, the guy would say, "No, I want it like the solo on, 'Reelin' in the Years.'"

The conversation became increasingly, and tiresomely, redundant.

At one point, Elliott climbed up on his chair. The client asked him what he was doing, and Elliott answered, "I always play better, when I'm high."

The coup de grace came when the guy pounded his fist on the console and emphatically stated, "No! No! Play it like the solo on the Steely Dan song."

Silence filled the control room. The ad folks held their breath and wondered what was coming next. Elliott wore a look of frustration on his face and they all heard him quietly say, "I played the solo on 'Reelin' in the Years'."

Bam! Instant karma!

New York offered a veritable fountain of talent. The singers performed with a distinctively edgy sound, and the bulging talent pool offered many options. The jingle singers you never heard about that graced your radio and TV waves every day, were some of the most financially successful people in the music business.

Linda November, the unofficial Mother Superior of the New York jingle singers, broke the mold. The self-titled "Jewish American Empress" hit a high C just for the hell of it, then let fly an occasional F bomb. Linda called her marriage a merger, sang the "Meow Meow" song, could sing any style, wore jewelry (lots of jewelry), and mink coats; her little gifts to herself for making megabucks. I loved her wonderfully rowdy sense of humor.

Leslie Miller, Maeretha Stuart, Toni Wine, Patti Austin, and Stephanie Fuller filled out my soulful, female vocal contingent. Valerie Simpson, who sang on "Ain't No Mountain High Enough" with Nick Ashford, put in an occasional appearance. They rocked the house with an attitude that was unmistakably New York, and their powerful voices grabbed attention, a trait very important to the impact of a commercial.

Kenny Karan (exceptional singer and brilliant songwriter), Bill Dean (penned two songs on my first album), and Ronnie Dante (lead singer of the pop band The Archies), filled out my group of male singers. Even Michael Bolton did commercials.

The New York Times called these guys the "secret singers," as almost all their work happened behind the scenes. The good news; if you were at the top of that game, you were a millionaire. There was no bad news!

It must have been my year for strange projects.

An agency assigned me to do two commercials, the first one with Lloyd Price, the hit singer of the fun song "Stagger Lee." For the second commercial we booked a Richie Havens sound-alike, Billy Eaton.

In the studio, my client pushed buttons, poked into drawers, talked loud on the phone, and did everything else listed under the topic of disruptive studio etiquette. He drove Joe Jorgensen and me, nuts. Billy Eaton added a little levity to the session when he asked us if we wanted him to sound like Richie Havens with or without his teeth. "With" worked fine. We finally got to Lloyd.

Lloyd was doing a fabulous job, but the client didn't like anything. He nitpicked, and finally blew the lid off the session when he told Lloyd, "Sing it like you live, you know, in the gutter."

Joe did his best to calm Lloyd down so we could finish the track. After he left, we let the client back into the studio. He was like a fly on a cow's butt. Flick him off and he'd bite you somewhere else. Joe sent out for Jack Daniels. That didn't help either! We were close to having all the volume faders on the recording console where we needed them, and one or two small adjustments away from a final mix.

The client waved his arms. "Shut it down."

Joe looked at him in exasperation, and with both arms he swiped down, (turning off) every volume fader on the console. We both looked at the client waiting for the inevitable question. He said, "What does that little red light do?"

Joe jumped to his feet. "That's it," Joe said, along with a few additional words.

Joe, a big guy, seemed ready to pick him up and set him outside on the sidewalk. Fortunately for him, he left on his own. Joe locked the door and said, "If I see him again tonight, I'll kill him."

When we last caught a glimpse of our client, he was flagging down a cab.

We went back into the studio and started from scratch. Fortunately, Joe had a terrific memory, and he rebuilt the mix in a short time: easy to do without the interruptions. We put the project to bed, Joe and I shared a high five, and I took a taxi back to the Waldorf. The agency loved the spots.

The recording console we worked from offered 32 tracks. Think about owning a stereo with 32 tracks, each containing a separate instrument. Every track has its own volume, echo, bass, and treble knobs; that would have to be adjusted before the record is sonically sound. This is what an engineer does. He combines those 32 tracks down to two, so consumers can play it on an uncomplicated home stereo. The quality of the finished product depends on the competency of the engineer. Looking at a recording console is like viewing the cockpit of an airplane. You are surrounded by a daunting array of complex buttons, sliders and switches, and it takes years to learn what they all do.

Media Sound, with Joe Jorgensen behind the console, became my home base in New York. Every time I traveled to the Big Apple, memories of my early days of listening to jazz flashed across my mind. The clubs had changed, and so had the music, but we were never lacking for entertainment. Some of the best little restaurants on the Upper West Side became familiar hideaways.

At the end of a recording session Joe said, "C'mon, we're gonna go eat some raw fish."

I thought he was kidding, until I arrived at my first sushi bar. I looked at that stuff. "No effing way!"

After a couple of hot sakes, and watching my musicians put away at least $150 worth of sushi without getting sick or showing symptoms of salmonella, they cajoled me into trying a piece.

It didn't taste like fish.

I thought, "What the hell?"

Joe said, "Oh, if it tastes like fish don't eat it. It's probably bad."

The bottom line: I ended up "hooked." Many years, and thousands of dollars later, I knew I'd always be a sushi junkie, and converted a "boatload" of Chicago doubters to join me.

We finished up a night session with Sid Simms, my bass player friend from Chicago. Joe and Sid and I left the studio at about three a.m., and tried to get a cab. As usual, we wore jeans and less than casual clothes. Sid and Joe had hair down to the middle of their backs, and mine grew past my shoulders.

We couldn't get a cab to stop for us, even when I flashed a $50 bill. Finally, with a squeal of brakes a yellow rattletrap came to a smoking halt ten yards past us. We pried open the back door and climbed in.

The driver, a wild-eyed Rastafarian wearing a torn tie dye t-shirt, looked like a serial killer. We thought he might be a demented reggae singer. The only thing missing: war paint, a bone in his nose, and a shrunken head air sanitizer hanging from the mirror. We thanked the driver for picking us up.

He said, "Oh hell, mon! I always stop for freaks."

I guess he didn't have a dress code either.

Joe shared occasional memorable anecdotes about his recording sessions. He engineered a

Frank Sinatra date with Charlie Callelo arranging. The full orchestra played flawlessly, and Frank seemed to be in a reasonable mood, which could sometimes change in a split second.

Joe thought he heard a couple of bad notes, but he didn't feel he could say anything to Sinatra, so he mentioned it to Charlie. Charlie pushed the talkback button and said, "Hey, Frank, the engineer thinks you're singing flat."

They finished the session after they talked Joe into crawling out from under the console.

I continued to work on a huge package of Kentucky Fried Chicken commercials and my client loved the New York sound. The client needed everything done on impossible deadlines, so I sometimes found myself flying to New York two or three times a week.

Media Sound, an absolutely gorgeous facility, had originally been a lofty old church. When they converted it to a recording studio, they kept the exquisite stained glass windows, all the beautiful architecture, and even the choir loft. That high ceiling gave orchestras a magnificent cathedral sound that no other studio could match.

The chapel had been converted to Studio B, a smaller version of the main studio. One night, I worked with my favorite band in that room for the first time.

To say the boys were behaving badly was

putting it mildly. A bathroom adjoined the studio, and it became a very busy place between recording takes. I don't want to say marijuana, but something certainly smelled sweet. In fact, the intoxicating blue cloud that flowed from the washroom fogged up the control room window.

We kept the door closed to avoid wearing hazmat suits. One of the drummers did not participate in the recreation. He sat peacefully behind his drums, holding his nose, watching the night slip away into the bathroom. On one of my brief forays into the studio to check a loose microphone cable, he uttered one of the subtlest lines that I remember. He looked at me, nodded at the bathroom door and said, "I know! Never again!"

He was right. I never recorded that band in that studio again. Hey, I may be a slow learner, but...

I composed some screaming trumpet parts for an exciting, but complex track, and I noticed one of my big name trumpet players subtly giving me disdaining looks. I asked him if he had a problem.

"All you guys from out of town come to New York, and write impossibly hard parts just to challenge us."

Huh? I scratched my chin and thought about it for a minute, then I looked at him and said, "I could play that trumpet part when I was 17. If you don't want to play my music, I'll find some younger musicians who are up to the challenge. I bet there are plenty of guys that would love to be sitting in your chair."

I witnessed the quickest retreat in music history as he quickly tried to undo the damage. "No! No! I love your writing, man."

After we crossed that hurdle, we made some incredible music together. Jorgensen laughed, and said it was about time someone put him in his place.

It wasn't unusual for a producer to go into a new city and be met with skepticism, as I found out the first time I recorded in London. We'll get to that in a minute.

The few times I couldn't get into Media Sound, I went over and recorded at A&R Studios, owned by Phil Ramone. Phil a world renowned music man, produced and engineered for The Band, Chicago, Bono, Billy Joel, Bob Dylan, Barbra Streisand, Luciano Pavarotti, Elton John, Gloria Estefan, Aretha Franklin, Simon and Garfunkel, Frank Sinatra, Madonna, Ray Charles, Cindy Lauper, Celine Dion, Barry Manilow, Peter, Paul and Mary, Paul McCartney, Tony Bennett, and just about every other major artist in the country.

A&R was to Media Sound what a haunted house would be to Peyton Manning's estate. It was the funkiest studio I'd ever been in. Although, with Phil at the controls, the place took on its own

317

magic as we recorded in the ghostly presence of some of the greatest artists in musical history.

After we were done for the day, I enjoyed fascinating evenings in Phil's wood-paneled office. He sat pensively behind his well-worn desk in a massive red leather swivel chair, while I nestled in a beyond-comfortable silky suede recliner, enveloped in the shadows of all the superstars who sat there before me. I loved listening to the stories of his incredible career, and looking at his walls overflowing with gold records. Plus, there was always the smooth taste of his private stock of aged single malt scotch that he pulled from his bottom desk drawer, and graciously shared with me. Surreal!

New York, New York...a wonderful city!

Chapter 32

As I screened demo tapes at my desk, I fielded a call from a radio station in Cleveland. The proposed project entailed composing music for 15 separate tracks. The client needed a three-minute theme song in supplementary jazz, easy listening, and classical versions, in varying lengths. They intended to use the music, to enhance the station's image, play at sales events and create the station's on-air promotional commercials.

It sounded like an exceptional job, until they quoted the budget. The station requested a large symphonic orchestra, but they only offered the bucks for a smaller not-so-symphonic orchestra. As much as I wanted the work I didn't see any way to do it, until I spoke to Dick Reynolds, one of my competitors. He said, "Go to London. The musicians are fabulous, and you should be able to stay within your budget."

My wheels were spinning as I researched recording music in London. It seemed that Americans were not allowed to set up sessions personally, but you could hire a "fixer" to book the studio and hire the players. You were not permitted to take money out of the country, but they were more than happy to welcome you to London if you wanted to spend it.

I jumped on an international telephone line, and called an English man named Derek Wadsworth. Derek came highly recommended by several of my colleagues, who had used him as the liaison to set up their sessions in England. He turned out to be a charming, affable man, and we shared a productive conversation. A talented and well-respected musician, he contracted sessions all over Europe, so it appeared I'd hit the jackpot with my first phone call.

When we talked about finances, it became obvious that the budget would work. Their hourly rates for sessions were substantially lower than ours in the States.

I decided to go for it. I asked him to book ten solo violins, eight first violins, eight second violins, six violas, four cellos, two double bass players, two orchestral percussion players, a heavenly harp, three trumpets, two trombones, two French horns, a bass trombone, baritone sax, tenor sax, oboe, clarinet, and two flute players who were all members of the London Symphony. (Sorry! Big orchestra = long sentence!) He finished up by hiring a solid rhythm section composed of two guitars, electric bass, drums, and two keyboard players. I was so ready to do this, and couldn't wait to land in London!

I climbed on an airplane later that week and rapidly learned two facts about transatlantic flights:

1. Those coach seats are a bitch-to-sleep in.

2. As soon as the doors close, run over anyone who gets in your way, little old ladies and children included, to stake out three seats in a row to give you room to stretch out. Those outgoing planes were rarely full, unlike the return flights.

I considered myself a veteran traveler, so it surprised me that I could be so cranky and tired when I climbed off the plane in London. The clock read 11a.m, when I went to pass through Customs, I found it surprising that there were no check-in points, or long lines. I wandered into a spacious room, where a collection of agents dressed in dark suits stood against the wall.

As I made my way through the room, one of them stopped me and asked to see my passport. We chatted for a short while and he queried me about my reasons for being in England. Would I be taking any money out of the country? Did I happen to be bringing money in? Although his demeanor was rather formal and distinctively British, I found the exchange to be surprisingly pleasant. Convinced that I didn't pose a threat to London, he let me pass through to the terminal. When I reached the sidewalk, I caught one of those ugly hump-backed black cabs and headed for the city, on the wrong side of the road.

I checked into a hotel situated in the towering BBC building. A uniformed assistant manager presented me with my room key. When I opened the door, and caught the first glimpse of my accommodations, I flashed back to memories of the austere decor of my college dorm room. I reminded myself that as a fledgling tourist, it might take me some time to find a place comparable to a Hyatt. Derek met me at the hotel, treated me to a late lunch, and we worked out the details of our session that started at ten a.m. the following morning.

After he left, I went exploring. I took the obligatory trip through Harrods, the city within a department store. I walked past Buckingham Palace, Big Ben, and Buckingham Fountain. I found myself gazing at breathtaking classical paintings at the British Museum. I knew I could spend days in this timeless vault and not scratch the surface of looking at the numerous magnificent masterpieces exhibited on the walls. I wanted to spend time inhaling the beauty, and absorbing the glorious essence of each marvelous painting.

I hated to leave the museum, but I knew I should grab a bite to eat before I returned to my depressing room. I tasted my first kidney pie, and managed to down a pint of warm ale in a local pub. Re-energized, I wandered over to Carnaby Street, where I added several unconventional shirts and jackets to my already eclectic wardrobe.

My sleep cycle was off kilter due to the time change, so I had no reservations about meeting Derek again. He whisked me over to Ronnie Scotts, a landmark London jazz club that had been in existence for years. Where every major jazz musician who toured the United Kingdom ended up sitting in, and performing, when they dropped into this historic venue. Derek played an early set with a big band, and it was wonderful hearing some of the brassy music that I'd loved for years.

I experienced my first dose of British culture shock when I ordered a scotch on the rocks. My glass contained one tiny ice cube and a thimble full of single-malt. I found out that hard liquor was measured in gills, a fraction of an American ounce. I didn't have to be a brain surgeon to figure out that if I ordered a normal size drink, it would probably cost $40, and if, God forbid, I wanted one in my mother's souvenir Toots Shor's glass, I'd be applying for a loan.

So, I settled for another traditional lukewarm ale from the cooling shelf. On my way back to the hotel, Derek ran by a discount liquor store where I picked up a bottle of vodka for $14. As you can imagine, sleep did not come easily. Running on full adrenaline, I couldn't wait for dawn to break over foggy London.

At eight a.m. Derek picked me up in his Mini-Cooper, and we threaded our way through

London rush hour traffic. We crossed the Hammersmith Bridge over the Thames River, and entered a posh suburb known as Barnes.

Derek parked in front of the huge commercial building that housed Olympic Studios. Faded white paint flecked off the walls of the immense main room, and the ceilings were breathtakingly high. Other than that, the studio resembled many other studios I'd worked in, but my gut told me the sound would resonate in ways I could never have imagined.

Derek recited an impressive list of composers who had previously recorded in that room. Our engineer, a jovial burly Brit named Keith, welcomed me with a loud "Hello, mate," a firm handshake, and a slap on the back.

All around the studio, musicians were tuning their instruments, drinking coffee, and lost in conversation. Trying to ignore the raucous atmosphere, I set my music score on the podium and Derek handed out the parts for each instrument. Now we get to that respect and skepticism thing.

In the United States, when a composer steps up on the podium, the musicians find their seats and respectfully wait for him to start the session. Either this group missed that class, or they were viewing me as the unproven "ugly American." When I stepped up on the podium, they didn't even look my way. I stood there, feeling like a substitute teacher in a class of troubled children, wondering what to do next.

A posture-perfect gentleman with steel blue eyes sat quietly in the first violin chair. He rose from his seat, walked over to me, stuck out his hand and introduced himself. "Pat Halig!"

I introduced myself. We perused the room.

"Are we having a bit of a problem here, Bobby?

"I guess so, Pat!"

"Would you like me to help you with that," he inquired in a sympathetic voice.

I told him any help would be appreciated.

He turned around, faced the studio, and in a voice that cracked like a whip, he authoritatively vociferated one word. "*Boys!*" The room immediately quieted.

"This is Bobby Whiteside from America. You will show him some respect!"

Wow! Pat had the golden touch. You could have heard a feather flutter. I immediately knew he would serve as concertmaster for all my future sessions in London. I later found out that Pat commanded a destroyer in the Royal Navy, which explained his leadership ability. Nobody argued with Pat. I found out in subsequent sessions that he was a good guy to have on my side.

I conducted the orchestra through the first version of the theme song. It sounded wonderful, but I had no idea *how* wonderful. Keith pushed the record button, and the musicians played flawlessly. The track came to the end and he clicked on the talkback button in the control room. "Playback!"

I waited in anticipation.

The music flowed into the room on a breathtaking wave of majesty. The strings soared, the trumpets played like they were welcoming royalty, and the entire orchestra sounded like they were transported to my studio from another place, somewhere very beautiful.

I never witnessed anything that magnificent in my entire life. A chill started in my toes and flowed up my body. The hair stood straight up on my arms, and I felt a surprising swell of emotion. I caught my breath at the end of the playback and took a minute to compose myself. I looked up at the orchestra, the skepticism had disappeared, and I had been accepted into the ensorcelled, glorious world of London music. I floated back to earth and we continued recording.

On a lighter note, I discovered the recording sessions in London ran under a different set of rules than I was used to. The musicians played for 50 minutes, but when the big hand of the clock said ten till the hour, they stopped whatever they were doing, even if they were in the middle of a take. They quickly put down their instruments and headed for a pub to down a pint of ale on their break.

Every studio either had a pub in the building, or one next door. I personally had a hard time swallowing warm ale, but my new British friends drank it down in buckets. I now understood why so many Englishmen had ruddy red faces. At lunchtime, one of the neighborhood ladies brought in a savory one-pot stew, soup, or shepherd's pie for the producer and engineers to eat. We consumed our comfort food while the musicians drank. Derek remarked about the importance of London's extensive public transportation system, as most of the musicians and singers had been cited with at least one DUI. The Bobbies were tough on Brits who drove while tippling.

We resumed recording after the players quenched their thirst, and finished an extraordinary day with no perceptible problems. Enchanted with the talent and the sound, I knew I'd be coming back as soon as I could. I made many new friends, and found another favorite city.

Tapes in hand, I boarded my flight home, eager to share the music with Brenda and my clients. The following year I returned to record in London nine times.

I was still riding the crest from my first London session, when a client who heard the tracks asked me to go back overseas. This posed a new problem. I needed to use a full orchestra to

327

score his corporate film, but the musicians had to be paid in cash at the end of the session. I had no idea what a nightmare this was going to turn into.

No way could I carry $11,000 in cash, to London, so I made other arrangements. My Chicago bank partnered with a sister bank in England, and they issued me a cashier's check to take with me. In a perfect world, the bank in England would cash it, and convert it to pounds. I'd take the money to the session and pay the players. Derek told me to be extremely careful. If there were any problems that affected the payments, it could cause an international incident.

I told the client I needed my business manager to travel with me, so with a check in one hand, Brenda's hand in the other, I arrived in London. Laden down with music paper and a keyboard, I intended to finish composing my score when we reached our lodging.

Derek drove us to a beautiful private flat in downtown London that a cello player rented out to traveling producers. We arrived at the picturesque brownstone building, outlined in gingerbread trim and covered with sculptured carvings of angels and demons. Crimson roses that freckled creeping vines of ivy, climbed the walls, and the fragrance of the flowers in the gardens added to the aura of this stately mansion. When we entered the flat, we saw that the furnishings consisted of precious antiques. Rich oriental carpets adorned the floor, and the art and the tapestries on the wall were beautiful. We felt like we'd been transported to another time.

Our thoughtful landlord stocked the icebox with fruit, milk, eggs, bread and several other staples, and of course tea—lots of tea. The patio doors in the sitting room opened to a small balcony that looked out over downtown. It surely topped that industrial-strength hotel room I'd been housed in on my first trip.

Brenda did a bit of sightseeing while I worked on my charts. We met Derek for dinner, and I learned that one of the favorite cuisines in London was Indian food. We feasted on tandoori chicken then retired to the flat, so I could get an early start on my writing when we got up in the morning. My session started at six o'clock in the evening.

Mid-morning, I cautiously navigated my way through the London underground tubes, way across town to the financial district, where I expected to cash the check. The tubes were a far cry from the elevated transit system that honeycombed Chicago. Three flights of long rickety wooden escalators descended to the tracks below ground. An eerie vision crossed my mind. Trapped in a bad movie I traveled into the abyss, a forbidden dark hole, never to return to civilization.

Two hours later, I reached the financial

district after riding on three wrong trains. I searched for the bank. I found it and entered into the hallowed halls of British finance. Formal? You bet! Of course I hadn't planned my wardrobe around a trip to a dignified establishment. I wore a pair of embroidered bell bottom jeans, leather Jesus sandals, a crinkled cream-colored shirt, and a blue denim Irish fisherman's cap cocked at a jaunty angle. The security guard gave me the stink-eye as I walked in, and I could tell he had the urge to escort me right back out to the sidewalk.

The bank bustled with conservative clients dressed in Savile Row suits and polished pointy shoes. I ignored their disparaging glances. Heaven knows it had happened before! I asked the greeter if I could see the contact that my bank supplied me with, and after a cursory search of her Rolodex, she told me that he wasn't in.

I proceeded to a teller's window to be greeted by a skinny, snippy, dishwater blonde. She looked me up and down, sniffed audibly, and asked how she could help me, as if there was no way. I expressed my desire to cash a cashier's check. When I handed it to her she glanced at it, did a double take, and seemed surprised by the amount. She looked me up and down again, pretended to shuffle a small stack of papers, and told me she wouldn't cash it. We went round and round. I explained about the sister bank thing till I was blue in the face, but she wasn't buying it.

Finally, I asked to see her supervisor. Enter snippet number two, an even bigger bitch. We did the financial mambo, and she turned out to be ruder than the first girl.

She finally called for a bank officer, Percival Snodgrass, who turned out to be the unchallenged new inductee into the asshole hall of fame. He reluctantly searched the registry that listed the signatures of all the officers authorized to cash my check, to no avail. I felt a panic attack coming on.

In the end, facing an impenetrable wall of derision, I created such a stink that I almost started an international incident on my own. The glowering security guard gave me a toothy grin, and grabbed my arm with fingers that felt like they were made of steel, as he not so gently threw me out of the bank.

Despondently, I took a cab back to the flat. It would be several hours before I could reach my bank in Chicago, due to the five-hour time change. Knowing the seriousness of failing to pay the band in cash, I called Derek to apprise him of the situation. According to international law, I could not cancel the session either.

"My, my! That is a sticky wicket!"

I'm not kidding... he really said that. We agreed to wait until I talked to my bank before we freaked out. I wrote furiously, trying to finish my music scores, but due to the wasted time at the bank I still had a long way to go.

Finally, the clock told me my bank in Chicago opened up, and I placed a frantic trans-Atlantic call. They immediately put me through to the president, and I briefed him on my dire situation.

He said, "I'll call you back."

That wasn't very reassuring, but at least we were communicating. I waited for what felt like days. The afternoon passed slowly. I had now reached full-blown anxiety mode. I finally received a call—from the president of the English Bank. He apologized profusely, and asked me if I could return to the bank to pick up my money. Crap! It was almost rush hour; the financial district was on the other side of town, and the studio on yet *another* side of town. However, I had no other options, so I had no choice

Brenda helped me gather up my remaining music, and we climbed into another one of those dreadful black hump-backed cabs to fight our way over to the financial district. To top it off, our driver was the British version of a nervous old Barney Fife, who drove like a little old woman wearing bifocals with the wrong prescription. Brenda restrained me from smacking him over the head with my music and hijacking the cab. I wrote frantically as we experienced a tooth-jarring, seemingly endless, ride with our languid driver. He meandered down narrow streets and barely went with the flow of thousands of bumper-to-bumper subcompacts.

We finally reached the financial district and double-parked in front of the bank, much to the consternation of the autos behind us. I jumped out and vigorously pounded on the enormous translucent glass doors. Dressed in his flawlessly tailored grey Oxford suit, the president of the bank unlocked the entrance and let me in. He stood next to that bastard, the thuggish, unsmiling security guard. Eleven thousand dollars in cash converted into pounds sat in neat stacks on the reception desk.

In a very stately manner, he apologized profusely, and asked me how I planned to transport the currency. Hell, I never even thought about bringing a briefcase. After a fruitless search for an appropriate repository, we couldn't find anything that would accommodate the sizable stash of British money.

In a flash of random luck, I found an emergency solution in a wastebasket. The president grudgingly stuffed my cash into a brown, wrinkled, grease-stained paper lunch bag. He looked at me skeptically and said, " We had to convene an emergency meeting of the board of directors to reopen the vault for *you*."

I knew he was thinking, "Who the hell is Bobby Whiteside?"

He bowed slightly, and asked me if there was any other way he could "serve" me. I told him it would make me exceedingly happy if three of his employees found themselves looking for work the following day. Angered at being called in off the golf course, he seemed profoundly happy to say, "Done!"

I flipped the humorless security guard the bird, and ran for the cab. As we continued on our nail-biting, stop-and-go journey to the Hammersmith Bridge, I finished copying the charts by the light of his flickering dome light. We finally arrived at the studio 25 minutes late, where a 65-piece orchestra sat restlessly twiddling their thumbs.

After I settled down, we had a smooth session—until 10:40 p.m. The pubs closed at 11p.m., so Union rules stated that the orchestra could take a double (20 minute) break. We were booked until midnight.

I don't know how much ale an Englishman is supposed to be able to pour down in 20 minutes, but I'd say there were a few record breakers in the studio that night.

Fortunately, I held back a simple piece of music for last. Those drunks never could have navigated through a difficult one. It was amazing to see so many inebriated people in one room at the same time. If anyone lit a match, the place would have exploded from the pungent cloud of alcohol vapors floating in the air.

The music ended up way beyond my expectations, and the session finally finished.

Derek sat at a small table and doled out $11,000 in pounds from our greasy paper vault. There were a few raised eyebrows at the sack, but no one questioned the validity of the cash. The musicians pocketed their wages and all of them mumbled some version of, "Thanks, mate and g'nite."

I think I downed the British equivalent of a $60 drink after we got back to the flat.

The following day, I called my bank in Chicago to thank them for their efficient problem solving, and find out how they were able to get my check cashed under such duress. It seems that my bank threatened to withdraw three million dollars from the London Bank upon their opening if they did not find a way to get me my payroll.

The president of the British bank had to call an emergency session to convene the board of directors in order to re-open the vault. This meant pulling them away from any personal and family activities they were in the middle of. They had to put their spiffy suits back on, come back to the bank, and do their convening thing. It gave me a warm fuzzy feeling when I thought about the fate of those three pretentious employees...and that the Bank of England no longer had a dress code.

Chapter 33

Brenda and I relaxed after the session and took some time to continue exploring London. We toured the Tower of London and watched the Changing of the Guard at Buckingham Palace. We munched on fish and chips in a sidewalk café in Piccadilly Circus while we were entertained by sidewalk performers and artists. Derek invited us to dinner at 6:30 p.m. so we returned to the flat to freshen up.

We found it difficult to catch a cab during rush hour, so we arrived at Derek's house at 6:35 p.m. His wife didn't speak to us all evening. We found out later that it really angers the British if you are not *exactly* on time. From that day on, if we booked an engagement, we arrived early and waited out front until the precise moment we were expected to show up.

We collected more information on Pat Halig who was a 70 year old nudist windsurfer with a beach house in Wales. He and his wife, Annie, lived on the Thames River, about 45 minutes out of London. They invited us to travel to their humble abode, spend the day, and join them for a home-cooked supper. We set out for his house, and relaxed during the cab ride through the scenic countryside. Pat owned a cozy ranch-style cottage. A boardwalk ran outside his flower-covered, freshly painted, picket fence, adjacent to the river.

We shared a bottle of wine, and accepted their gracious hospitality as we kicked back in cushy reclining chairs in his tranquil screened-in summer room. We noticed 15 small sailboats facing up the river hardly moving at all. After watching the mini-flotilla for a while, I asked Pat what the boats were doing.

"They are having a sailboat race."

He told us he belonged to that tiny yacht club and participated in a lot of those "races" himself. He explained that a real sailor could sail up a river into the wind, not very fast, just a few feet at a time. It sounded like a wasted Saturday to me. I asked Annie what happened when the wind died down and all the boats ended up down the river.

With a straight face she replied, "That's why Pat bought a Boston Whaler with a big motor on it." I assumed it was to tow a chain of stranded sailboats back up the river.

Pat told us we were in for a surprise, and as he spoke, a behemoth of a black cast-iron watercraft slid up to dock at his boardwalk. The helmsman Keith, our engineer from Olympic Studios, threw Pat a rope so he could tie up to the dock.

I had never seen anything like this aquatic

apparition. It was a captured German combat troop carrier left over from the war, that he purchased from a British army surplus depot. The boat was silent, as it ran entirely on electric batteries.

Commander Pat ordered us on board for our first river cruise. It seemed weird, traveling in a boat without hearing the muffled roar of gas engines, but cruising in the unbroken serenity of the ride enhanced the sightings of the famous landmarks and some gargantuan sprawling castles.

We returned to the house, and Annie served supper. They purchased steak: a big deal at that time. Annie baked tantalizingly fresh bread and made a rich dessert pudding from a special old family recipe. We hated to return to the city, but as the old adage goes, "All good things must come to an end."

The following day, I pretended to have a level of confidence I didn't feel, as we rented a car and drove over to Brighton Beach, quite a distance from London.

I don't know how in the world those people drive on the wrong side of the road. It took a lot of getting used to, and I had several close calls with Englishmen who had no patience with newbie drivers. Those Brits can really swear, and I guess the middle finger is an international symbol.

Despite my lack of backward driving skills, we

reached Brighton after a picturesque ride. We realized why so many painters captured the countryside in brilliantly colored oils, and became mesmerized viewing the manors, fountains, and the castles. I stuck my toe in the English Channel; then we turned around and carefully headed back to London. After Brenda unstuck my hands from the steering wheel, I made a solemn vow that if and when we returned to London, I'd never drive one of those left-handed hire-cars again... and I didn't.

My next trip to London turned out to be almost as eventful as the previous one. A client commissioned me to produce some edgy rock and roll tracks, so I rented the studio owned by George Michael and Wham!. Derek put together a talented group of English rockers, and we began to record. We were at Angel Studios, one of the first places to incorporate a computer into their recording process.

Halfway through the session, Tony Burrows, the lead singer from the band Edison Lighthouse, began to sing the lead vocal. The computer crashed and the session ground to a halt. The staff tried to reboot it, but nada! I started to sweat my budget.

Finally, one of the engineers said, "Call Charlie."

Charlie, the stoop shouldered techie-looking

electronic boy wonder that built the computer, shuffled into the studio. He zeroed in on his invention. He started twirling knobs and I swore he talked to the damned thing. When it started back up, he patted it and said, "There!"

Charlie shuffled back to his dark space. The next half hour ran smoothly then, *crash!* Call Charlie! Charlie stomped back into the studio. He cussed at the computer, pounded on it, twirled knobs, spun dials, and almost turned that stubborn metal mess inside out. I expected to see it disintegrate under his violent ministrations. Finally, it booted up again. Charlie gave it a couple of smacks for good measure and hobbled out. Well, you know it had to happen again.

This time Charlie simply stepped inside the door, leaned against the wall with his arms folded and glared at the computer. I swear to you, that computer gave a sigh and came to life again. Charlie stood there until the end of the session and we left, never to return.

Before our exit, I asked one of the sound engineers about Charlie's relationship with the computer. He said, "It's eerie, but it happens all the time. The computer is like his kid."

I ran late getting to the airport as I carried heavy tapes, my guitar, and a duffle bag. Heathrow is an airport built with miles and miles of walkways. Wouldn't you know it, my flight sat at the last gate, Z-56. I dragged my load up to the check-in counter to discover I didn't have my ticket. Panicked, I looked everywhere. A very British voice came over the intercom. "Will Mr. Whiteside please report back to the customer service desk in the main terminal. We have his lost ticket."

The lady at the flight counter told me they couldn't hold the plane, but there had been a slight delay and she would leave the door open till they had to pull out. I tore back to the main lobby and grabbed my ticket. I almost had a heart attack as I gasped my way back to the gate, juggling my cumbersome crap. I swung around the corner just as they were closing the door, and skidded into the jetway in a jumble of paraphernalia. I think I caught my breath somewhere in the middle of the ocean. From that day on, my ticket and passport were sheathed in a case on a chain wrapped around my neck.

When I deplaned in Chicago, I felt that I needed a two-day nap. A distinctly American voice came over the intercom.

"Will Mr. Whiteside please dial the operator. We have an important message for him."

Oh Lord! What now? I called the desk and retrieved a message that asked me to call an advertising agency immediately. I did, and they asked me to come straight to their downtown office for an emergency meeting. I loaded my bulky cartage into a cab and motored to their headquarters. They tried to catch me before I left England, but not in time. They needed me to return to London that night.

It seemed that Delta Airlines needed a version of "When You Wish Upon a Star," recorded with a full orchestra and a gorgeous celestial lead vocal. They were under an almost impossible deadline. During negotiations with Disney to use the track from the movie, the film company jacked the price up to a preposterous amount, which killed the deal, but not the date the commercial had to air.

I took another cab home, downloaded a copy of the original song onto a cassette, and quickly repacked. I grabbed a pocket-sized cassette player, a ream of music paper, and a tiny keyboard with a set of headphones. I kissed Brenda, hugged the kids, and shuffled back to the airport.

I called Derek, and he started putting an orchestra together. He contacted Tessa Niles, one of my favorite lady singers, who had the perfect voice for this project. I needed to know the key she wanted to sing in, so I could write the score during my flight.

Fortunately, I grabbed a row of seats upon boarding. I spread my music scores all around me, and composed from Chicago to London.

Derek picked me up, with a copyist in the car, waiting to transcribe all the original parts from my music score. Exhausted, I handed him the completed chart and headed for my hotel to grab a couple of hours of sleep. "Jet lag" didn't come close to covering how tired I had become.

To this day, I don't know how we pulled it off, but the session was stunning. The beauty of Tessa's lilting soprano voice made her sound like an angel, and the orchestra performed as well as the one in the movie. The choir sang like heavenly beings, and I ended up thrilled again!

An agency courier waited at the studio, hand carried the tracks on a charter flight back to Chicago, and they made their deadline. Needless to say, I slept for a full day. With my ticket firmly encased in the travel wallet hung around my neck, I made sure I arrived at the airport two hours early for my flight back to Chicago.

I flew across the pond to London as often as possible. It had become a music mecca for me, and a treasured travel destination. Brenda and Wendy accompanied me when I scheduled a session at CTI, the recording studio at the famous Wembley Stadium. I didn't realize that we were booked on the same day as the Live Aid concert that featured every music superstar imaginable.

I took Brenda and Wendy across the parking lot to the stadium and did the Chicago thing. I bribed a security guard to let them in. They were excited to be at this star-studded event, but quickly returned to the studio. I asked them why they came back so soon. They said the rowdy crowd frightened them and they were pawed at and pushed against the wall. The crowded stadium, packed with drunks, stoners, and violent gangs, seemed a risky place to stay; and they worried about ending up as victims of a savage attack. I guess concerts in England are like European soccer matches; a riot a minute.

We worked well into the night, and the pub in the studio had long since closed. We were ready to leave and we looked out the window. The Live Aid concert had come to an end. The uncontrollable highly impaired fans were all leaving. I was taken-aback by the sight of the most unbelievable traffic jam I had ever been a witness to. No cars were moving due to gridlock. I released most of the musicians earlier, but I still had a horn section. Two charts resided in my briefcase that I had hoped to get to, so it seemed as good a time as any to take a shot at them. The horn players said they would stay if we brought back the bartender. We woke him up. He returned, reopened the pub, and we continued on.

It was markedly late in the evening, or early in the morning, depending on how you looked at it. My two screaming horn charts were so difficult they had to be recorded in short segments. We finally finished the arrangements. They were exciting and a conquest for the trumpet players. Derek Watkins, one of the best horn players in England, rubbed his bruised lips and summed it up. "Love your writing, mate, but I wouldn't want to go on the focking road with ye. I'd be dead from blowin' so hard."

Traffic finally eased up, and we crawled into Derek's tiny car and made our way back to the city, another happy ending to an epic musical episode. And as always, I looked forward to the inevitable next time.

You are probably wondering who took care of the kids while we traveled. The answer is Idabell, a robust, white-haired, soul-sister grandmother from the south side of Chicago. She raised four boys, so she knew most of the tricks. Our kids couldn't treat her like a substitute teacher. Our brood loved her! She cooked comfort food Southern style, so we knew they would always be well fed.

In all the years Idabell worked for us, we only had one sticky incident. Tarrey had a bushy afro hairdo, and thought it would be cute to drop a couple of his pet white mice in his fluffy hair and let them play around. Mice on top, he headed downstairs. Idabell headed upstairs carrying an overloaded laundry basket. She saw the mice, screamed bloody murder, and did a backflip; scattering clothes everywhere! Then, she ran outside the house and wouldn't come back in. The kids finally coerced her into returning by promising to keep the mice in a sealed container in Tarrey's locked closet while she was there. Crisis averted! Whew!

We took many more trips to London, but looked forward to the challenges that appeared, as new projects came over the horizon back in the States.

Chapter 34

There were times that a family incident interrupted my sometimes way-too-serious focus on the music business in a humorous manner. We inadvertently ended up with a couple of new additions to the family.

Wendy started to lock her bedroom door, and act strangely. Brenda's curiosity, and her motherly BS antenna, kicked in and we decided all was not as it should be. We felt it necessary to investigate the obvious mystery in Wendy's room. As we stood in the doorway of her powder-puff environment, everything seemed relatively normal, other than the fact that a larger than usual amount of the clothes from her closet were piled on the floor, or strewn across the bed. It was unusual to see her louvered closet doors pulled tightly shut.

Suddenly we heard a muffled squeak coming from her half-empty clothes repository. Brenda slid one door open, and there on the white carpet sat a small cardboard box lined with Wendy's pink baby blanket. Two adorable, tiny, black and white kittens blinked their eyes at the sudden invasion of light. They were obviously brothers.

Brenda removed the flimsy makeshift shelter, carried it downstairs, and placed it in a prominent place on the kitchen counter.

At three o'clock Wendy came flying through the front door, dumped her schoolbooks on the hall floor and dashed up the stairs to see her open bedroom door. Then: a moment of silence. She slowly descended the stairs and peeked her head around the kitchen doorway. She knew she'd been busted!

"Do you want to explain this?" asked Brenda in a stern voice.

Wendy gave us a plausible explanation, even though we were unhappy she didn't level with us to begin with. It seemed our little animal rescue princess discovered both the kitties abandoned in a trashcan, so she brought the little rascals home. Wendy correctly assumed I had become a lifetime cat hater, since I had openly, and loudly, spewed my displeasure with Tiffany, the snotty silver Persian.

What could I say? It looked like I'd be taking massive doses of Actifed again. Those little guys had me at that first pitiful meow. We named them RC and Sox, sometimes known as "pile of cats," since they always slept on top of one another. I surrendered my heart, stocked up on Kleenex, and reversed my "no stinkin' cats" resolution; for the time being. I had to reluctantly admit that they provided a bubble of entertainment. In short, they were fun to watch.

I won't regale you with cat tales, but one anecdote emerges from my memory. Sox and R.C., no longer kittens, were inseparable. They played together, ate together, slept together, and hunted together. We never knew when we'd run across a dead mouse, or another lifeless critter in the house; their idea of a loving gift to Brenda. Yuck!

Standing by the sliding glass doors in my den, gazing fondly at our two little black and white stooges, I couldn't help but think that things were too quiet. At that moment their world seemed to be a peaceful place as they lay in sleepy-eyed repose, enjoying the summer warmth.

A meandering duck flew into the backyard, flexed his wings, and arrogantly quacked like he owned the bar.

Sox and R.C. perked up, took one quick look at the intruder, and transformed into attack cats. Sox scampered down from the top of a fencepost, hunkered down, and froze close to the ground. R.C. jumped off his nesting place on a chaise lounge, and imitated his brother.

They moved as if they were telepathic; they simultaneously dashed ten feet closer to the "quacker," who was waddling in a circle with the smug arrogance of the AFLAC duck.

The cats attacked. Clumps of fur flew as the menacing mallard trounced the perky pampered pets, and kicked some serious feline booty. I witnessed the most inglorious retreat I have ever seen as my two vanquished critters tried to escape from Chuck Norris the duck.

Sox shakily climbed back up on his fencepost, and R.C. slithered back onto the chaise. They licked their wounds and tried to pretend that nothing happened; that they were still kitty cat cool.

The gloating duck flexed his feathers, flew into the wind, and honked with glee as he tried to get the cat fur out of his beak.

Several weeks later, another duck landed in the yard. Sox looked at R.C., and R.C. looked at Sox. I could almost read their minds. "Nah!", and back to sleep they went. At least someone in the family learned a lesson once in a while.

Changing gears, I came home after an exhausting recording session and opened the refrigerator to get a cold drink. I spotted a bottle of wine at the rear of the top shelf. I glanced at the label, then did a double take. Much to my astonishment and vexation, the half-empty, distinctive bottle was one of two $500 Chiantis that a trombone player friend had given me as a gift. I went ballistic!

Brenda told me that our son cooked something and needed a cup of wine to complete the recipe. She told him to grab any bottle from the wine rack, forgetting about my two prized glass containers of vino.

After my inevitable diatribe, she calmed me down and assured me that it had been an oversight. Yeah...a $500 oversight!

Still seething about my loss, I returned home one afternoon to find Brenda knocking back a couple of glasses of wine with the girl who did her nails. Scratch my other expensive bottle. From that point on, if I had a primo bottle of liquor in the house it nested in a toolbox, hidden in my workbench.

The following spring, I came home from a trip to London to find a Harley Davidson parked in the lobby of Universal Studios, and the elevator completely trashed. I walked in to see John Belushi and Dan Akroyd recording the *Blues Brothers* album. Reluctant to leave his Harley on the street, John drove it up to the studio in the elevator. It went downhill from there.

Akroyd focused on business. Belushi wanted to party. Continuously "under the weather," John needed a convenient place to lie down. They set up a cot for him under the stairs, right outside the control room of Studio A. When they needed him, they'd wake him up, frog march him into the studio, prop him up in front of the microphone, and record every sound he uttered or sang. Then, he'd go back to the little cot, and Akroyd and the engineer would splice together a full vocal that made sense, taking pieces from all the vocals that John sang when he stood upright.

It took a while, but when they finished the project the movie grossed a fortune, and the album became a smash. No one had any idea what went into making that record.

When they finished the project, John climbed on his motorcycle to go home, and broke the elevator again.

About six months later, as I walked down the hall, I spied an exquisite young lady standing by the coffee machine. She looked familiar. This stunning woman had gorgeous violet eyes, and I found it hard not to stare.

The door to studio B opened and Prince walked out. The lady: Apollonia, his exotic girlfriend. He booked the studio on a "lockout" for two days. No one entered, but him and the lovely brunette. He handled his own engineering, played all the instruments, and sang all the parts. It gave me an eerie feeling. I felt like a ghost haunted the studio for two days. He finished whatever he was recording, walked out of the studio with his girlfriend on one arm, and the tapes under his other one, disappeared into the office, paid his bill with hundred dollar bills, and no one ever heard from him again. Weird!

I received an interesting call from a client,

absolutely insistent on using a singer from a successful 70's group. Sensing a myriad of problems, I tried to talk her out of it, but she remained adamant. The aging warbler, a flower child rocker, had virtually no commercial studio experience, and I knew I'd have to go back to my roots to find a way to produce this guy.

I submitted the budget and put in a huge amount for the use of the studio for two days. She hit the ceiling. I told her I felt it was necessary, anticipating working with a rock and roll artist, not a professional jingle singer.

She reluctantly approved it with a lot of misgivings and skepticism, and asked me to try to bring the job in under budget.

It took no time at all to record music tracks for a 60 and a 30-second commercial. Then, we waited for our troubadour. Wearing a gaudy paisley outfit, he arrived an hour late, and it was obvious he wasn't ready to sing. He did some crazy vocal exercises, gargled with warm water, then sat in a yoga position on the carpet in the studio to meditate.

My client said, "Is he kidding or what?"

"It's gonna get worse."

Sure enough, he came out of his trance and asked us to brew him some of his special herbal tea. The client went quietly ballistic.

I bit my tongue. I tried to tell her! Two hours after he arrived I started to teach him the song. He was one of those guys who would keep singing it wrong and I would keep correcting him, but wrong becomes right and gets stuck in his head. Then, you have to un-teach wrong and start over. I began to worry that two days wouldn't be enough.

Between yoga breaks, herbal tea, meditation, and trying to relearn what he had learned wrong, the first day was coming to an end and we didn't have squat. I gave him a cassette to take back to the hotel, with the correct version of the melody on it, and told him to listen to it a hundred times.

We went through the same routine the following morning. This guy's Zen was a mess. We started recording one line at a time. Get one, go on to the next. At three o'clock, we actually had a vocal done on the 60-second spot. The client was fist pumping.

I looked at her and said, "Um, he still has to do the thirty."

She said, "How hard can that be?"

At 11 p.m. we finally pulled an acceptable performance from our moonchild, a workable vocal for the 30. I had to pull out every single trick I learned when I was producing those inexperienced garage bands in the 60's. It was a fight to the finish with this one. Déjà vu! We mixed it down, and wrapped at three o'clock in the morning.

The client looked at me and said, "How did you

know?"

I simply laughed, "How much time do you have for me to explain the failures I had in my early career, working with guys like him, before I figured it out. All it took was time and money!"

She never questioned one of my budgets again.

It rankled me to see guys professing to produce records and raking in big bucks who took neither the time, or had the inclination, to hone their craft and actually learn what they were doing. It was sinful to watch them stand in the studio, either making stupid comments or no comments at all, and end up taking credit for the artist's creativity.

I was passing by Studio A one afternoon, where a "producer" friend of mine was having seemingly insurmountable difficulties, trying to produce a drum album featuring a big name percussionist. I smiled when I saw the clueless dude had 24 microphones surrounding the drum set. It sounded awful. He looked at me helplessly and said, "Any ideas?"

I whipped a tape out of my case and played it for him. An awesome drum sound burst from the speakers.

He said, "How did you do that?"

"With Morris Jennings, my Chess drummer, and five cheap microphones," I replied.

He asked me if I could help him out of this jam, so the engineer and I tore down that birds-nest of unnecessary recording devices. We set up six or seven of our personal cheapo favorites. In addition, we hung a large beach umbrella off the end of a heavy-duty microphone boom, about eight feet in the air directly over the drum set. It consolidated the sound, and made it tight and powerful. The drummer finally sat down on his stool, played his butt off, and sounded fantastic.

The producer finished recording the album and took it back to the label. Everyone gushed over his drum sound. Wanna' bet I never got any credit for it? You'd be right!

Chapter 35

Lennie Druss, my contractor, booked the orchestra at Mill Run, an immense in-the-round theater. Lennie convinced me to play guitar at a Bobby Vinton concert. Bobby Vinton: "Roses are Red"! "Blue Velvet!" How hard could that be?

I entered the enormous theatre, wandered over to the orchestra pit, set up my guitar, and waited with the rest of the musicians. Finally, the conductor passed out the charts for the show.

Uh-oh! Most of the songs were new to me, and the show only contained three of the banal rock songs that Vinton habitually recorded. All the other parts were written out note by note! I thought I'd just be dealing with simple rhythm charts. I was totally *screwed*!

There wasn't an empty seat in the house. My blood pressure soared. Here I sat, a clueless guitar player, with less than stellar sight-reading skills, and no place to hide. Apprehension washed over me as I geared up to face the daunting opening overture. The second I played my first chord it all hit the fan. It was piercingly loud, carelessly confident, and absolutely *wrong*!

I didn't dare look up. I was convinced I'd find

a sea of disapproving, mirthless faces, sullenly staring at me in condemnation. I was dead and buried; wishing the cemetery dudes would hurry up and fill the hole.

I flashed back to a day in high school when a fellow student, a quiet studious guy, but a loner with inept social skills, tried for a silent slider to no avail. His colossal fart shattered the cloud of silence in the acoustically perfect high school auditorium, startling all 163 drowsy students in fourth period study hall. They all turned around and stared at him with accusatory looks. Boy, could I relate!

Pat Ferrari, one of my best studio guitar players, sat next to me and that's the only thing that kept me from being lynched. He laughed uproariously. Then, he patiently threw me a lifeline by looking over my shoulder and playing all the written solos from my chart. Thoroughly embarrassed, I chunked away on whatever chords I could figure out, just to look busy. I presumed I'd owe him a car by the end of the night.

I spotted the conductor talking to Lennie on a break. I lip-read the words, "Where the f*** did you get this guy?"

After the show, I crawled out from under my folding chair and tried to get lost in the crowd as I bolted from the theatre. I made Lenny carry my guitar so no one would recognize me as *that* guitar player. I sat very low behind the steering wheel of my car, and didn't show my face until I was at least one town away from Mill Run.

I saw Lennie the day after the show and he couldn't stop laughing! My humiliation seemed to wane a bit after two or three months had passed. I tried to forget the incident, but musicians have long memories and warped senses of humor. From time to time I was forced to revisit my mantle of shame.

One of my keyboard players bought an Arp Odyssey, one of the first synthesizers that emulated other instruments. It produced a nice piano sound and mimicked some orchestral instruments. Lennie Druss performed an oboe line at the beginning of a commercial. We listened to it after he left, and it became painfully obvious that Lennie played the part out of tune.

I looked at my keyboard player and asked him if he had an oboe sound on the Arp. He did, and we replaced Lennie's part with the artificial part. Surprisingly, it sounded like a real oboe. As we were mixing, Lennie returned to the studio, listened to the track, cocked his head, and said, "My, I played that well."

The engineer and I glanced at each other and tried not to smile. I felt a brief moment of retribution for the Vinton thing.

Dave Moore, my airplane pilot and Sigma Chi buddy, reached out to me. At the time he worked for Oral Roberts, the televangelist, running his audio-visual department. I didn't know too much about Oral's ministry, and I didn't think that much of televangelists in general, especially after Oral locked himself in a tree house. He refused to come down until he collected a certain amount of money from people like my father. Dad was a sucker for all those guys.

Dave told me Oral constructed a new hospital and expanded his university. He needed a three-minute inspirational theme song, and some supplementary music to use in commercials and informational films. The only catch: he wanted to use the university's 60-piece orchestra and 50-voice choir, in his own studio in Tulsa, Oklahoma.

While flying in to meet Dave, I enjoyed a refreshing Bloody Mary with my minuscule airline breakfast.

Dave picked me up, took one sniff and said, "Oh no! You didn't have a drink on the plane, did you?"

"*One* Bloody Mary!" I replied.

He said, "I can't have you anywhere near Oral, or his family for three or four hours."

I told him I'd chew gum, inhale a can of Velamints, and drink a bottle of Listerine, but he was adamant. This job was becoming a pain in the butt already.

To kill time, he led me on a tour of the enormous and amazingly beautiful campus. I found the new hospital to be astounding, the architecture and the statue of folded hands at the entrance, tasteful and timeless. Everywhere I went I saw nothing but clean-cut kids and happy faces. I had a nagging urge to slap one of them, as it seemed unnatural to me that there were so many dazzling smiles in one place.

David introduced me to a very pretty TV spiritual leader named Vickie Jamison, who plays a part in my saga later on. Oral's son, Richard, finally granted me an audience, and we came up with a game plan to produce the music.

They agreed to let me record the rhythm tracks in Chicago, which enabled me to format the music, then return to Tulsa to add his orchestra and choir in his studio. The project proceeded smoothly. I never managed to meet Oral, but it was effortless to work with his son. His orchestra and choir were competent and professional, so we easily completed the assignment with soaring orchestral and choir music tracks.

My distrust of televangelists took another upward nudge, due to a phone call. After we finished the last mix session, we attended a Kool-Aid and cookies wrap party for the singers and musicians in the big studio. Oral and his wife were away on a trip to Arizona. Richard called his parents and put them on speakerphone. The conversation went like this.

Richard: "Hi, Mom!'

Mom: "Hi, sweetheart."

Richard: "How are you and dad doing?

Mom: "Well I'm just relaxing in the sun, curled up in this luxurious lounge chair by this inviting swimming pool, inhaling this beautiful view, and Daddy—"

Richard interrupts: "Um, Mom, I'm here in the studio with all of our musicians and singers, who are listening to your every word.

Silence! Then, a speedy defensive recovery!

Mom: "Da...Daddy's out in the middle of the desert on a retreat."

I almost choked to death trying not to laugh. I didn't dare look at Dave. I packed up my music and climbed on a plane back to Chicago; enjoying two Bloody Marys on the flight home.

Later that year, I suffered from a terrible attack of vertigo. I couldn't stand up and walk without holding on to someone, or leaning on a wall to stop the room from spinning. Fortunately, it didn't prevent me from working. When I sat down, my head didn't spin. I stayed in my upstairs apartment, and there were walls to lean on all the way down the stairs to the studio. Louie sent me up food so I wouldn't starve. This persisted for a couple of months.

Desperation set in. We had to do something! Brenda guided me onto an airplane, and we flew out to California, after booking an appointment at one of the foremost inner ear clinics in the country. They performed a rigorous examination, and concluded that they had no solution.

Dave Moore, now living in LA, worked with Vickie Jamison, the televangelist I'd met when he was employed by Oral. Dave and Vickie invited us to a banquet for 40 spiritual leaders. The music I created for Oral had been the talk of the holy-rolling industry. They seized the opportunity to welcome me to California to thank me and acknowledge the work.

Somehow or other, we made it. I staggered in on Brenda's arm and sat down at a lengthy oblong table ringed by evangelists.

Vickie Jamison gracefully rose from her chair, pointed to me, and said, "Brothers and Sisters, Brother Bob has an affliction. We must pray for him."

I thought, "WTF?"

We all joined hands around that table and they began to pray. I swear to you, the feeling of power that filled that room was not to be believed. (I didn't *want* to believe it.) I experienced an eye-opening vibration as a zinger shot from one held hand through my body to the other.

They finished their prayer and said some nice things about the music. As we ate dinner, I almost put my fork in my eye a couple of times, but I managed to get through it. Brenda held on to me tightly as we weaved our way back to the Sunset

Marquis. I woke up the following morning and the vertigo had become noticeably better. It disappeared within three days. Coincidence? Who knows! My theological thoughts were in serious disarray, but leaning in a good direction! That's my story, but I'll leave you to your own conclusions. However, if I had doubted the presence of a higher power in the past, I knew I never would in the future.

Chapter 36

I want to give you an idea of the scope of the commercials I was asked to write and somehow, telling you "lots of 'em," doesn't paint an adequate picture. I had now created commercials for Schlitz (You Only Go Round one Time), Kentucky Fried Chicken (America Loves What the Colonel Cooks), the Nestlé Bunny (You Can't Drink it Slow if It's Quick), and V8 (It Sure Doesn't Taste Like Tomato Juice). I recorded spots for Dubonnet Wine, Annie Greensprings, Coors Silver Bullet, Hyatt Hotels, Peter Pan, Chicago Sun Times, McDonalds, Burger King, and Kellogg's. We added Wheaties with Walter Payton, the award-winning "Can't Read Can't Write Blues" for an anti-illiteracy campaign, Pabst Blue Ribbon Beer, Lowenbrau, Old Style, Heineken Beer, Corona, Budweiser, Miller beer, 7-Up the Uncola, Nestea, Orange Crush, Gravy Train Dog food, (the background singers barked like dogs), Don't Do Crack (an anti-drug commercial), The Olympics, the TV show Kids Are Us, network promos, and a theme for a huge Jesse Jackson banquet we called "Yesterday, Today, and Tomorrow."

To add to the list, I also did spots for Hoover,

RCA, three shampoos, four deodorants, Amana, four hair spray products, Standard Oil, car dealerships, Ford, Chevy, Oldsmobile, Cadillac, Honda, Alberto Culver, Dial Soap, Hires Root Beer, Sprite, Gatorade, Mountain Dew, Carnival Cruises, State of Illinois, AT&T, Hallmark, Colorado tourism, Ultra Sheen, Afro Sheen, Chicago Tribune, Tide, Screaming Yellow Zonkers, Jays Potato Chips, Taco Bell, Sears, JCPenney, Target, Carsons, Fiddle Faddle, Eggo Waffles (Leggo my Eggo), Beatrice foods (You've known us all along), Kraft, Kraft Macaroni and Cheese, Butter, The Egg Board, Kibbles and Bits, Pepsi, Sheridan Hotels; and these are just the ones I remember off the top of my head. There were hundreds more!

I became one of the go-to-guys for classically orchestrated assignments, based on my London work. Not bad for a guy who got kicked out of the Conservatory. So, I put together a demo tape filled with symphonic music and visited a producer at one of the ad agencies.

He listened through the tape and said, "You know what you need to do? You need to put together a tape with a lot of zingy music on it so it gets my attention."

Really? "If I put that spiffy tape together and got your attention, what kind of music would you hire me to write?"

He thought for a moment then replied, "Well,

your symphonic stuff is really powerful so I'd probably hire you to score an orchestral job."

I looked at him in amazement and said, "So, I take the time to bring you a hip tape to get your attention, and you say you'll hire me for what's on the tape I brought you today. You realize that is about the dumbest f****** thing anyone has ever said to me since I've been in the advertising business."

I shook my head and walked out, talking to myself.

I arranged and produced all the tracks for the "Coors to You" campaign, with Lee Greenwood singing the lead. I had to fly wherever Lee was performing at the time to have him record the vocals. It wasn't always easy to find a competent studio in some of those small towns. Yes, there *is* a decent studio in Des Moines, Iowa, but I had to search like the dickens to find it.

Sessions with Lee were a breeze, and it was the first time I recorded a singer who told me he could sing it better when I was already thrilled with what he'd already done. He was right! Every time he'd re-sing the commercial, it became better than I could have imagined.

Lee, a consummate pro and a trained musician, made it seem easy, and our sessions suffered few hiccups. The best commercial we did in that campaign was a Christmas spot recorded in Nashville with a full chorus and orchestra; that ended up as a gorgeous holiday classic the client played for years.

I had an interesting proposition for Lee. I knew a marketing group that discovered how to use the fledgling medium of late night cable television, to sell products and promotions. They developed "You Make the Call." The viewer would attempt to "call" a baseball play shown at the beginning of a commercial, and at the end they'd tell him if he got it right. They cut these together from some old baseball footage they purchased, licensed them, and made a fortune. The other successful promotion they put on the air, "Richard Simmons deal a meal," consisted of a Richard Simmons diet where you dealt out cards that told you what food to eat. Sold like crazy!

They offered me $100,000 to cover the cost of traveling to London and recording a Christmas album, featuring Lee singing with the London Symphony and my London background singers. They felt supremely confident that they could successfully market the album on late night cable TV.

I went to Lee's manager with the deal. Lee wasn't signed to a record label at the time, so we would own the master record for perpetuity. Lee's manager felt that advertising on cable TV was not for Lee based on what he had seen of it, and he nixed the deal. He was afraid it might demean

Lee's image, a concern that I understood. It wasn't unusual for some people to look ahead, while other people felt safer staying with the tried and the true. No right, no wrong, just different opinions!

I talked till I was talked out, to no avail. I cannot even imagine how much money that record would have made. The album would have been sold for the next 30 years. Cable was an exciting new advertising platform, inexpensive and surprisingly far-reaching. The value of cable advertising seemed obvious to me, but it took a while for the industry to see the potential and decide it was a worthwhile idea.

I fought tooth and nail to keep using live musicians, but many of my competitors were adding synthesizers to their arsenals of musical options. This enabled them to use fewer players, and keep down the cost of all their demo presentation tracks. I reluctantly jumped on the bandwagon and learned how to incorporate synthesizers into my sessions. I was used to being ahead of the curve, not behind it.

The new synthesizers were versatile, and the possibilities really fascinated me. We slowly incorporated synthesizer sounds into our music, but not when I could hire a live musician. Northwestern University started an electronic music department, and I figured that in a few years, they'd be popping out a group of cookie-cutter musicians who could do an entire orchestra on a piano-driven synthesizer. This did happen in the late 80's, and almost destroyed the business. More on that later, and I'll try to explain synthesizers to you in better detail.

Chapter 37

Brenda and I were butting heads. We'd both been working long hours and the stress was getting to us.

Mistake #1: I figured I had the solution.

Mistake #2: I'd surprise her.

Mistake #3: She'd love to go to Nassau for four days, where we could lie in the sun and unwind. Hopefully, we could rekindle a flame, or two.

As W.C. Fields said, "Anything worth doing is worth overdoing." So I brainstormed and hatched a plan. I even found an actor!

Mistake #4: He would dress up like Big Bird, sing a song I wrote for Brenda, and present her with the tickets.

Gigantic, humongous mistake #5: Wendy thought it was a terrific idea, and offered to pack for Mom.

So the night before the big event, I hinted that I had a surprise for Brenda, and this announcement was not greeted with enthusiasm. I should have canceled then and there.

The doorbell chimed at four in the morning, and the guy in the yellow-feathered Big Bird suit, entered the house, ramped up and ready to put on the performance of his life.

Mistake #6: I let him in!

Brenda stumbled down the stairs in her flannel robe, startled by the motley yellow apparition and grumbled, "What the hell is this?"

The bird started to dance, flapping his tiny wings, and slapping the carpet with his big floppy feet. He sang lustily and endlessly, like he was performing his eulogy, the last song he'd ever sing.

It damn near was! This constituted his big chance, and no one was going to turn down his volume, or stop him. I tried to shut him up when I saw the thunder clouds forming over Brenda's head. I made imaginary knife cuts across my throat, waved my arms, squirmed in my chair, and threw him pleading looks, but he had arisen at three a.m., fought his way into a stupid stifling bird suit, and he was there to perform. By Gawd he was gonna' perform!

I slumped lower and lower in my seat. Lightning bolts flashed from Brenda's eyes. Impending doom hovered in the air. When Big Bird *finally* finished, no place on earth remained where I could safely hide. It was worse than the Bobby Vinton concert.

Big Bird flew down my driveway about two seconds before I grabbed a shotgun and blasted his twitching yellow-feathered ass with birdshot. Silence permeated the room. In a desperate voice,

I told Brenda we were going to Nassau, we'd have a really good time, and then I said, "And Wendy packed for you."

As I looked at the murderous look on Brenda's face, the only thing that ran through my mind was a quote from Wendy when she tried to eat her peas with her knife.

"Ooooh, shit!"

Brenda glanced in the suitcase that Wendy handed her, gave me a look that melted my expensive new Ray-Bans, and stormed back upstairs to throw on some clothes.

I had inadvertently ignored the fact that Wendy, who knew what all the cool clothes were for a 14-year-old, would not have had a cotton-picking clue as to what was stylish for her mother. Crop tops and cheeky short-shorts were non-starters Oh boy! We were going to freaking Nassau!

I immediately started to gather up books to take as I figured there wasn't going to be much conversation on this trip. The only words she uttered between Chicago and Nassau were, "I'll have a double."

We arrived at the hotel, she dumped her suitcase out on the bed, picked a few things up, threw them down, gave me a withering look, (another one) then she uttered eight more words. "I'm going out to buy a new wardrobe!"

She returned a few hours later, laden down

with shopping bags filled with designer outfits and shapeless, button to the neck, flannel pajamas. She slipped on a bathing suit, grabbed a beach towel, and stormed off to the surf without looking at me.

I grabbed three or four books, and trudged after her. I read five books in two days and by the end of the second day she was finally speaking to me—in monosyllables.

"Yes! No! Whatever! Fine!"

I made reservations at a trendy restaurant, and she actually told me what she wanted to order. I think we were up to 35 words.

Things got a little better on the third day, and I (not so brilliantly) thought it might be fun to rent one of those pitiful little putt-putt scooters and go sightseeing. This seemed to be going well, until I spun around a corner, hit a patch of sand, and put the moped down on the gravel and tar roadway, scraping *all* the skin off my thigh. We found a grocery store that sold peroxide, gauze, and tape. After I got done screaming from the peroxide that she was taking delight in pouring on my leg, she bandaged me up with a whole box of giant gauze pads and two rolls of adhesive tape.

I don't remember the last day, as I was in so much pain. Second-degree sunburn would have been an improvement.

The flight home was excruciating. It's hard to wear pants when you have no skin on your leg.We survived the trip... just barely. I read 11 books. On the airplane, she extracted a solemn oath from me that there would be no more surprises, unless they involved jewelry.

"Oh yeah! Oh, hell yeah! I promise!"

We gradually returned to the quiet comfort that we shared almost all the time, on our own. I hope you guys learn something from this. I certainly did! Surprises can really bite the big one! Maybe she won't read this chapter.

Richard Wold and I finished up a round of songs that I thought were commercially viable. I decided it was time to take him to LA, and scout around for someone who liked our music enough to promote it. "Go West!" they said.

Chapter 38

Armed with an impressive array of new songs, Richard and I checked into the Sunset Marquis, ready to forge a path through the LA jungle. I hoped to attract the attention of someone who could help us place them with recording artists. We landed a handful of favorable meetings, but no one waved a contract in our direction.

We sat in a face-to-face conference with Russ Regan at Universal Records. Russ, a seasoned pro, instinctively recognized a spark of commerciality in our tunes. He paved our way toward Jay Landers, a young entrepreneur and an emerging force in the music industry. He felt confident that Jay would be interested in working with us, and Jay exceeded everything Russ told us about him. Though most importantly, he exhibited a positive vibe as he enthusiastically screened our songs.

Jay managed the LA office for The Entertainment Company, the new venture that Charles Koppelman operated on the West Coast. Charles, a legendary publisher/producer sat at the top of the Publishing world. I met with him in the 60's, at 1650 Broadway in New York, when he owned Koppelman-Rubin, one of the most successful operations of that decade.

Jay entered the industry with an impressive entertainment business background. Hal Landers, his father, produced all the Charles Bronson *Death Wish* movies, among others, so Jay grew up in the company of show business aristocracy. Since then, he had developed formidable professional relationships with many new contacts on his own.

Jay knew the importance of meeting as many music industry people as possible. The business encompassed legions of artists and their managers, and they all had a say in creative decisions. Having access to these folks is vital when trying to pitch a song. I told Jay I dropped off tapes at a record company. After a couple of days, I was going to call the label to see if they heard the material.

Jay said, "Wait a couple of months. If a producer hears a song he likes and wants to reach you, he will find you in the middle of Lake Michigan."

Little did I know! We left our catalogue of material with Jay and flew back to Chicago, feeling we finally had a shot at taking a chip out of that impenetrable rock known as the record business.

Wouldn't you know it! While fishing out in the middle of Lake Michigan, the marine radio crackled and the coast guard informed me an important call was waiting. They patched it into the communications channel.

Jay's voice cut through the static. "Rex Smith is going to record your song, 'Remember the Love Songs'".

I chuckled over that middle-of-the-lake thing and wondered who the hell Rex Smith was. Jay informed us that Rex starred in Grease on Broadway in 1978, and his song, "You Take My Breath Away," achieved hit record status. Not too bad!

"Remember the Love Songs" told the story of a fellow remembering the good times he and his love shared in the past. Snippets from vintage old vocal group love songs, brilliantly arranged by my friend Robert Bowker, wove in and out of the music track.

You can find the song if you perform a Google search for "Rex Smith 'Remember the Love Songs.'"

It did not become a big hit, but we had broken the ice.

I was in the middle of trying to finish a song titled, "When the Lovin' Goes Out of the Lovin'." Richard Wold dropped by to say hello. I'd finished the verses, then encountered writer's block. I played the incomplete song for Richard and asked him if he could contribute any thoughts, or help me finish it. He sat down at the piano and played a masterfully melodic bridge, which fell right into place. Perfect! We loved it, and so did several other people.

Jay managed to place the song with Barbra Streisand, Johnny Mathis, Ray Goodman and Brown, the legendary Walter Jackson, Nana Mouskouri (in Europe), and Rachael Dennison; Dolly Parton's sister.

I'm going to include a lyric here and there, so you get a sense of how we attempted to write stories that cut through the clutter with a tender theme.

Here are the lyrics for "When the Lovin' Goes Out of the Lovin'," written by Richard Wold and me.

When the lovin' goes out of the lovin'
And there isn't a thing you can do
But reminisce of yesterdays
Second-guess her changing ways
And fill your time with people just like you

When the lovin' goes out of the lovin'
And there isn't a thing that you can say
You bite your tongue and wonder why
And then you watch your life flash by
Hopin' things will turn around your way

Bridge:

There isn't a lovin' thing I can say
There isn't a lovin' thing I can do

*There isn't a lovin' way in this world...I can
reach you*
How can I walk away and be free
When lovin' you means my whole life to me
*There isn't a lovin' way I could ever leave and
be free*

When the lovin' goes out of the lovin'
And there's no easy way to pretend
That anything could ever be
As good a thing as you and me
It's hard to understand this is the end

(Repeat bridge)

Google "Barbra Streisand: 'When the Lovin'
Goes Out of the Lovin'" to hear the song.

I managed to stir up some activity back in
Chicago. I placed a song named "How do You Find
the Love You Lost," (When You Don't Know How
it Got Away) with one of my favorite Chess groups,
The Dells. Marvin Junior, their lead singer, one of
the finest soulful vocalists in the country, sang on
a slew of commercials for me. People were
universally impressed by his rich, gravelly, and
soulful baritone voice. Morris Jennings, my Chess
drummer, said "Marvin holds a note so long, you
got to turn the page."
Google "The Dells 'How Do You Find the
Love.'"

I had started to clean out my garage, and Richard appeared in the doorway with the start of an exciting new song with the working title "Coming In and Out of Your Life." We instantly knew this could be a career-making song for Richard, so I dropped my broom, we pulled out our pencils and yellow pads, and went to work. We called Jay and played him what we had written up to that point. He gave it a thumbs up, and we continuously consulted with him as the song unfolded.

We spent three frustrating days looking for one perfect line for the chorus. Perseverance paid off and we finally hit it. The resulting line, "I don't need to touch you to feel you," could have been a song all by itself.

Finally, we completed our musical quest, and knew we had a winner. I booked the studio to record Richard. We added three more of our songs to the session that we hoped might help launch his career as an artist. Every tune ended up a jewel, but "Coming In and Out of Your Life" turned out to be the crown jewel.

We overnighted the final mix to Jay and waited anxiously for his reaction. The day went by with no response. Richard trudged over to his nightly gig singing at Don's Fish Market, a trendy Rush Street food and beverage dispenser. A couple of hours passed, then Brenda and I walked into Don's carrying a bottle of Dom Perignon Champagne.

Richard took an immediate break, came over to the table. "What's up?"

We told him we had good news and bad news. He asked for the bad news first.

I told him, "I heard from Jay. You're not going to be an artist."

His face fell.

"But the good news is that Barbra Streisand is going to record 'Coming In and Out of Your Life' as soon as possible."

Jay sent the tape to Charles Koppelman, who screened it and immediately called Jon Peters, Streisand's manager at the time. Charles told him about the song and Jon requested a copy immediately. Charles met with him and played him the song. Jon immediately said, "We want it."

We toasted Jay and waited for the next step.

Streisand was in England recording "Memory" with Andrew Lloyd Weber, and Charles decided he'd let Andrew arrange our song. The day of the recording session, Richard and I were asked to stay close to a phone, in case Barbra needed to reach us with any questions.

We fielded a couple of international calls, resolved the issues they asked about, and anxiously waited for a copy of the record. Jay overnighted us a pre-release version, told us to guard it with our lives, and make sure no radio stations heard it before the actual record was released. We loved it! Andrew Lloyd, an incredibly successful producer, waved his magic baton and we sincerely believed the song had the makings of a huge hit.

"Coming In and Out of Your Life" soared up to the top of the Adult Contemporary charts, and we were awarded our first platinum record. I don't have the exact sales figures, but I heard someone say "Over 11 million."

I'd like to share the lyrics with you.

COMIN' IN AND OUT OF YOUR LIFE
Written by: Bobby Whiteside/Richard Wold

I still can remember the last time I cried
I was holding you, and loving you
Knowing it would end
I never felt so good, or felt so bad.
You're the one I love, and what makes it sad
Is you don't belong... to me

And I can remember, the last time I lied
I was holding you and telling you
We could still be friends
Tried to let you go, but I can't you know
And even though I'm not with you
I need you so
But you don't belong to me

CHORUS:

Comin' in... and out of your life...isn't easy
When there's so many nights I can't hold you
And I've told you
These feelings are so hard to find
Comin' in...and out of your life
Will never free me
'Cause I don't need to touch you to feel you
It's so real with you
I can't get you out of my mind

And I can remember, the last time we tried
Each needing more that we could give
Yet knowing all the time
A stronger love just can't be found
Even though at times this crazy world
Is turning upside down
You'll always belong... to me

(Repeat chorus)
But I can remember...

You can hear the record by doing a Google search for "Barbra Streisand 'Coming In and Out of Your Life.'"

After our success, I assumed the publicity generated from the record would lift my jingle business through the roof. It is dangerous to *assume*, as nothing *ever* turns out exactly like you think it will. My business actually fell off. I finally figured it out. Many clients thought producing jingles would be boring to me after having a Streisand hit record.

I had to perform some quick footwork, do an inordinate amount of advertising, and a plethora of expensive client entertaining, to reinforce my base. Fortunately, I contained the damage and convinced advertising folks that the jingle business never stopped being my priority, but it was touch and go for a while.

From that day on, I made it a point to stay very low key about my involvement in the record business. I answered questions directed my way by curious creative directors, but never repeated the mistake of talking about another business to a client who expected my undivided attention.

Chapter 39

I retained a small amount of publishing on "Coming In and Out of Your Life" and owned a percentage of all our other cuts. Jay and several prominent LA entertainment lawyers convinced me I needed to set up an international publishing coalition to collect my foreign royalties.

The industry held the convention for worldwide publishers in Greece that year. This gathering, a gold mine full of decision-makers from foreign publishing companies, enabled me to meet executives who could solidify deals. They were responsible for collecting royalties when the songs were released around the world. Next stop...Athens, Greece.

Brenda and I suffered through a long and arduous 14-hour plane ride and had no idea what to expect when we arrived. After sitting on that plane for what seemed like forever, we hobbled down the walkway, grumpy, stiff, brutally sore, and totally exhausted. I looked for a place to order a double-ouzo.

We checked into a hotel near the convention center. We split a bottle of Retsina wine, and sampled stuffed grape leaves and a baklava in a quiet sidewalk café. We retired early, anticipating a taxing day of lectures, meetings, and the inevitable cocktail parties.

At one of the opening day informative forums, the speakers introduced a groundbreaking new platform to present music: *the CD!* Talk about being on the ground floor of a development that would affect the entire music industry. We shared a pivotal moment in the world of songs. Many people thought it would never catch on, but history proved them wrong. The CD, one of the most exciting innovations that music business executives had seen in years, took the industry by storm.

We shook hands with strangers, wined and dined important people, and managed to line up some key movers and shakers for meetings to discuss their publishing services. We began to understand just how the international music community worked.

After evaluating all the possibilities, we decided to join a company headquartered in the USA. We started negotiations with Randall Wixen, from Wixen Music in Calabasas, California. The foreign wing of his company, a superb entity, encompassed a worldwide network of sub-publishers who monitored foreign sales, and my radio and television airplay. He agreed to be my administrator, collect my music royalties worldwide, and monitor all my publishing activities. Signing with Randall turned out to be the best decision I ever made in the music business.

I've been associated with Randall for 37 years, and he has done an unbelievable job of squeezing money out of a rock. When I looked over a statement and spotted a payment for 48 cents from Bolivia, I realized the far-reaching scope of his enormous organization. Wixen Music is the absolute *best*! Randall represented acts such as The Beach Boys, Neil Young, John Mayall, Journey, and hundreds of other leading artists. He not only collects my money, but he relentlessly negotiates any TV or movie song placements. Thanks for all the great years, Randall.

Brenda and I felt we had to take advantage of our one-time visit to Greece, so we set out to experience some Greek food, historical sights, and local culture. Athens reminded me of Brooklyn; a cluster of buildings stacked on top of one another. I will never forget seeing a tiny white church bridged by a skyscraper. The church refused to sell the property, so the builders surrounded it with the huge. ugly structures.

We shared many delicious and savory meals, but when we returned to Chicago, I didn't put feta cheese on anything for five years, as the Greeks slathered it in, or on, everything from scrambled eggs to steak. I winced when I spotted a container of feta cheese ice cream. Yuck!

We experienced one surprising peculiarity of the Greek culture; when we discovered that a certain percentage of Greeks refrained from the use of deodorant. When we climbed in a crowded elevator at our hotel, we tried to hold our breath for 14 floors.

Many of the main attractions in Athens, including the Acropolis and the Parthenon, were either closed due to acid rain damage or under reconstruction. We were extremely disappointed that we were unable to explore those famous historic sites.

We booked a relaxing four-day cruise around the Greek Islands. I had never been on a cruise, so I didn't know what to expect. We boarded the boat. As we settled into our cabin the alarm sounded, signaling a drill to locate our lifeboat in the unlikely event of an emergency. Bedlam broke out. We had no idea where to go. I stopped a ship steward, and asked him to point us toward our emergency station.

"Oh, don't worry about it. The drill is over and everyone is returning to their assigned cabins," he replied.

Great! I hoped there were no icebergs in the Greek Islands.

We consumed a typical cruise-ship dinner buffet and returned to our room to turn in. I chose the top bunk and pulled it down from its recessed storage compartment in the wall. There were belts wrapped around the bed, so I climbed into bed and strapped myself in. I thought, "What the hell kind of weather are we expecting?"

Brenda came out of the small washroom, took one look at me and almost choked to death from laughing. "Honey, the belts are used to secure the blankets to the beds so they don't fall off when you put your bunks up."

Thank God she didn't have an iPhone, or I would have gone viral! This story haunted me for years.

The ship pulled into the harbor at the island of Mykonos. Beautiful beaches, trendy nightclubs, and travel brochure reviews of a very lively cosmopolitan social scene, piqued our interest. However, we wanted to see some of the countryside, so we hired a cab for the day to randomly drive us around. The driver, a stocky balding Greek man of small stature, spoke passable English. We toured soaring 16th century windmills, quaint little fishing villages, several small museums full of precious historic items, some stunning churches, and snapped pictures of a very famous militant pelican that guarded the waterfront.

As we were motoring from place to place, our driver seemed a bit despondent. He informed us they celebrated May Day, a major family holiday in Greece, and his kinfolk were hosting a huge picnic not far from where we were. He graciously invited us to join them, and we accepted his invitation.

We arrived, captivated by the sight of his extended clan frolicking on a lush green hillside. A host of children played games, the men gathered together drinking ouzo and Greek wine, while the women prepared an assortment of mouth-watering food.

Then our eyes landed on one of the most beautiful women we had ever seen, which said a lot as we worked with gorgeous models all the time. She looked *stunning*! You couldn't help but notice her sensuous red lips and the long black silky hair flowing over her shoulders. Not only had she been blessed with a beautiful face and unusually seductive eyes, but we couldn't help noticing her abundant bosom, framed by a low-cut canary yellow peasant blouse.

She held court on a hand woven rainbow-colored blanket. Little children brought her flowers, and young men performed acrobatics to attract her attention. We assumed we were in the presence of the token "Greek goddess" of the family.

We met many of our driver's relatives who warmly thanked us for allowing him to put in an appearance. We filled our plates with food we didn't recognize, but wouldn't soon forget. Each dish, a new flavorful discovery, had Brenda asking about the recipes, and I sensed some delectable Greek food on our horizon after we returned to the states.

All of a sudden Brenda nudged me and whispered, "Look."

I followed her gaze over to the beauty queen in time to see her inhale a whole chicken. She went at it the same way a kid slobbers over buttered corn on the cob. She had grease in her hair, small bones and gristle on her clothes, a random piece of a drumstick lodged between her breasts, and she licked grease off her arms and fingers like a porn star.

Brenda looked at me, and I looked at her. No words were needed as we witnessed the fall of Athena from her tower. We finished a lovely day and returned to our temporary floating home.

We bid a fond farewell to Mykonos and moved on to several other islands, each unique in its own right.

The ship pulled into Santorini, the most beautiful island of them all, and we prepared for another day of sightseeing. The towering mountains looked like gorgeous white marble pyramids. Doll-like houses carved into the mountainsides and tiny intimate cafes dotting the cliffs, created a gorgeous picture. We looked forward to sharing a bottle of smooth Greek wine and a romantic view of a serene sunset from one of the tiny Bistros overlooking the Aegean Sea...a perfect way to end the day.

Unfortunately, there were hundreds of steps to climb to get to the top. I wasn't that nuts. The alternative: a ride up to the top on a donkey led by a longhaired kid dressed in provincial white.

Being an experienced rider, I opted for the donkey. The steep ascent was a bit bumpy, but it sure beat climbing a thousand stairs.

We dismounted, and lazily roamed through beautiful churches and tiny shops crowded with cheap plastic statues of Greek heroes, and gazed at marble sculptures of historical figures located in a small village.

As dusk approached, we ambled into one of the small cafés to sip wine and nibble on anything other than feta cheese. Refreshed, we prepared to descend from the mountain. I opted for the donkey again. They didn't tell us those little pajama clad, bridle-holding sons-of-bitches *ran* the donkeys down the steps! I bounced around like a tenderfoot on a runaway jackass.

It wasn't until after we thundered down the mountain in a rolling cloud of dust that I realized I had a barnburner of a blister on my butt. The rest of the trip—excruciating! I learned more ways to lie on my side than you can find in *The Kama Sutra*. Then, we had a 12-hour delay at the airport and I found it hard to sleep on that long flight home.

Thank God for the anesthetic effects of that

Greek wine we were taking back to the states. I thought for sure I'd end up ambulatory. I had managed to get the only blister in the history of burro stampedes that left enough scar tissue to scratch a match on.

Chapter 40

We returned to reality and, after the jet lag wore off, we re-focused on our business. Royalties and residual payments from our commercials consistently arrived in the mail and the company neared solvency.

Then, I opened a letter from an attorney. Some young aspiring songwriter sued us, saying she wrote "Coming In and Out of Your Life." I called Jay who laughed and told me what to do.

I reached the attorney to talk to him about the lawsuit. I asked him about the girl that filed the complaint. As I expected, she was a "wannabe" songwriter. She swore she wrote it, played it for us, and we stole it. I never met her and didn't know anything about her. I asked her attorney if he was experienced in entertainment law.

He said, "Not really."

I explained to him about Jay Landers, his stature in the industry, and how he had been on the phone with Richard and me every step of the way, while we were writing the song. If this girl persisted with her lawsuit she would never have a career after we exposed her in the trade papers. Also, since Streisand and Charles owned part of the publishing, there would be a monster countersuit.

I suggested he stick to the kind of law he practiced regularly, or at least do a better job of pre-screening his clients. We never heard back from them. It seems there is always some lowlife waiting to crawl out of the bushes to try to profit from someone else's work.

We were under constant pressure to entertain the current ad people I worked with, and host client lunches to try to attract new ones. I invited a group to join me at a Szechuan restaurant, a new experience for me. The waiters served bounteous appetizers that tasted delicious, even though I had no idea what they were. I ordered Szechuan beef as my main course. The red string beans were a surprise, but everything else had been tasty, so I popped one into my mouth and started chewing.

All of a sudden, my world exploded in a burst of pain as my mouth caught fire! Smoldering lava filled my nasal passages, my eyes streamed tears, and the top of my head blew off. I couldn't breathe. I almost choked to death. I desperately spit the "string bean" into a napkin, but the barn door was wide open. I drank every liquid on the table: water, beer, Jack Daniels, martinis, Coke, wine, pink umbrella drinks, and Lord only knows what else.

The waiters rushed over with a silver pitcher

of ice water. I grabbed it with both hands and started to drink from the spout. My life passed in front of my eyes for 15 minutes, but I finally caught a breath and they cancelled the ambulance.

The waiters were impressed. It seems no one ever tried to eat a whole cayenne pepper before. We left the restaurant to a standing ovation from the waiters, busboys, the kitchen staff, and the snickering patrons. The smart-ass bartender scribbled a "9" on a bar napkin that he smugly held up as I made my rather embarrassing exit from the restaurant. I stopped exploring new restaurants for a while, and I never ate another red string bean.

Hosting my clients on Lake Michigan fishing excursions filled up my weekends. They arrived at the lake house Friday night and we'd be on the water at dawn. I had never been a coffee drinker, but one of my prospective fishing partners needed his coffee every morning. In his eyes, a cup of coffee started his motor and warmed him up on a chilly day.

Um...I didn't know how to make coffee. How hard could it be? After the weary ad guy hit the sack, I took a can of coffee off the shelf and put a pan on the stove filled with water. He stumbled into the kitchen at five a.m. dragging a bit, in desperate need of his caffeine injection.

I boiled the water. Next I put a couple of

scoops of coffee grounds in the pan, and let it set for a few minutes. *Voila*! I poured it into a big mug. It looked kind of funny. I'd never seen little specks floating around in a cup of coffee before, but I handed him my mud-brown concoction. He sniffed the wafting aroma and took a big sip!

Did I forget to mention that he had a walrus mustache? He made a funny face. I wondered what those brown things were that were stuck in his mustache.

"I can honestly say that this is the shittiest cup of coffee I ever had," he stated.

We cleaned him up, using Brenda's hair-styling brush to remove the coffee grounds from his 'stache. On the drive over to the marina, we stopped at an all-night gas station, and bought a Thermos full of real coffee. We ended up having a rewarding day of fishing out on the lake.

I was afraid I'd never work for him again, but he hired me for a job with the caveat that I would stay at least ten feet away from the coffee pot. The following weekend, I bought a new electric coffee maker and read the instructions.

The Brand X, my 32-foot Carver cabin cruiser, became a control center for some intensive fishing. I studied angling techniques and prepared for trips on the lake the same way General Patton planned a battle. I plotted and schemed to find fish, but then I had to catch them. I tried to sway the odds in my favor by using fish finders, depth readers, and any other piece of electronic fishing gear that I could find.

One day while trolling a great distance from land, an unexpected dense fog rolled in. My boat, the only one equipped with a radio direction finder, became the guardian of the fleet. You couldn't see beyond 50 feet. I found 14 boats lost in the moist cloud, by tracking their radio signals, and we caravanned back to port in a very tight group.

I had to be extremely cautious when I fished on the lake, as the weather could change in minutes. I learned this the hard way, when I ended up trying to navigate through six-foot waves that blew up from a sudden squall. While I tried to enter the harbor, one of my two motors quit, and the Brand X missed crashing on a rock break wall by six feet. I think I still had at least two of my nine lives remaining, but my narrowly averted shipwreck definitely canceled one out!

I took a friend named Keith fishing one sunny weekday afternoon. The lake was devoid of weekend traffic and calm as a millpond. I was only allowed to fish two fishing rods for each fisherman, but I figured there were no other boats on the horizon, and I could throw a couple of extra lines in the water. Keith steered the boat from the flying bridge, and I told him to keep an eye out for the game warden. We fished for a while and all of a sudden I turned around to see...the game warden pulling up beside me.

We exchanged pleasantries and I looked up to see my "lookout" sound asleep at the wheel. I tried to convince the warden that another fisherman slept down in the cabin, but he laughed and wrote me an expensive ticket. Keith was off my Christmas card list for quite a while.

My older boys pestered me to take a group of their friends fishing. So one Friday night, they trooped up to the lake house. I woke them up and we climbed aboard the boat at 5:30 Saturday morning. They brought several bottles of Bloody Marys (they were afraid of my coffee) and, as I set lines in the water, they proceeded to imbibe spicy tomato beverages in the cabin. By 6:30 a.m., I realized I had nine intoxicated weekend sailors on board and stupidly thought, "What can possibly go wrong?"

Kenny, my fishing partner, raised one eyebrow, shot me a skeptical look, and turned back to steering. I had 16 fishing lines in the water when we motored through a school of Coho salmon. Every single pole popped up in the air with a fish on it.

My wobbly crew stampeded out on the deck and grabbed random fishing rods to reel in the fish. The boys were hauling fish on board, smacking each other in the head with the slimy creatures, and tripping over the writhing whoppers flopping on the deck. They also managed to create tangles and knots on every line that I had rigged up. I climbed up the ladder to the flying bridge to get out of the way and wait for the end of the carnage, which fortunately didn't take too long.

I shooed them back into the cabin and started trying to untangle the mess they made. It took me 45 minutes to cut off all the lures, restring all the poles, pick up the fish from the decks, and get them iced down in the bulging cooler. I finally placed a few lines back in the water and; fortunately, a majority of my totally smashed crewmates were sound asleep.

Kenny was a die-hard country music fan. My son brought along a screaming distorted rock and roll Whitesnake music tape. He popped it into the stereo, turned the volume all the way up, and wandered out on the deck to relax in a lawn chair and groove to the cacophonous music. The first song played for about two minutes and abruptly stopped. The sliding glass door opened and a muscular arm tossed something in the water.

"What the hell was that?"

My son had a bewildered look on his face.

"I think it was your Whitesnake tape. I forgot to tell you that Kenny hates rock and roll."

Common sense overrode alcohol-laced bravado, and he wisely decided it would be a fruitless effort to pick an argument with the hulking Kenny. So we finished the rest of the morning immersed in the dulcet tones of Waylon, Willie, and George Jones. We landed a few more Coho salmon. The boys swallowed double doses of Alka-Seltzer and returned to the lake house sunburned and hung over. I carried home a huge bag of plump fillets, destined for the grill later that evening. It had been a day to remember; another relaxing outing with the children.

Then, Charles Koppelman contacted me, and my career jumped into yet another gear.

Chapter 41

I landed in LA early in the morning, and felt like I'd been transported to a climate-controlled world, far away from the sporadic Chicago weather. During the drive from the airport to Hollywood, I cruised up Alta Loma, past the long rows of constantly changing specialty boutiques and restaurants. At Sunset Boulevard, I took a left and drove through the posh acreage of gated, imposing mansions belonging to the stars. The palm trees swayed in a gentle breeze, the exotic plants in the sculptured Japanese gardens, and the lush manicured landscaping made me wish I could live there. But alas! I was but a lowly jingle producer and had never been written about in The Hollywood Reporter, or had my face splashed on the cover of The Enquirer.

I finished my motorized California therapy session, and headed over to the Entertainment Company to meet with Charles Koppelman. Charles heard some of the tracks I'd recorded in England. He informed me that Barbra Streisand intended to record two more Whiteside/Wold songs, and asked me if I'd be interested in arranging and conducting the recording session.

"Yes!"

She intended to record live with the orchestra as she cut "I Need More," and her own version of our most recorded song, "When the Lovin' Goes out of the Lovin'." Richard and I were over the moon.

We settled on a date and I booked the session at Capitol Records' Studio in Hollywood. I'd never recorded there before, but heard many positive comments about the facility. I compiled a list of all the musicians in the orchestra to give to the engineer, John Aries, so he could set up microphones and chairs for the musicians, who would soon fill the immense tracking room. He set up a booth for Streisand where she could sing live as we recorded the music.

Charles informed me I would have to write each arrangement in three keys, the one she preferred, another a half- step higher, and the third a half-step lower. This enabled her to record vocals on the track that best suited her voice on the day of the recording. Six charts for two songs! Interesting!

I decided to take a handful of my favorite Chicago musicians and singers with me. I felt I owed them the opportunity; as their loyalty had been a huge contributing factor to my success. Playing on a Streisand session was a credit that would help expand their resumes.

I took Ed Tossing (my piano player), Bruce

Gaitch (now a sought after, internationally known guitar player), Bob Lisik on bass (touring with Brian Wilson of the Beach Boys), and Tommy Radtke, my rock-solid drummer.

I also assembled a powerhouse vocal group with Bonnie Herman, Don Shelton, Bob Bowker, (from Chicago) Edie Lehman, Patti Austin and James Ingram's brother.

I started on the arrangements. My copyist and my keyboard player checked and rechecked the scores for mistakes. Jeff Sturgis, a wonderful LA arranger and copyist, worked beside me transcribing the individual parts for the orchestra. I wrote a *lot* of music.

John Aries called me the morning of the session and informed me that the microphones for the orchestra had taken up all but one input. Damnation! No way could I do drums on a Streisand session with one input. I needed at least six to be able to balance the sound.

Tommy contacted Roger Linn, the electronic genius who developed drum machines. He built Tommy a portable sub-mixer board on the spot, so he could mike and mix his own drums, and feed them to John's one input. They sounded terrific.

Ed and I drove over to Streisand's house to rehearse the lead vocals and double check the arrangements. A member of her staff buzzed us through the gate and we entered her beautiful house, elegantly decorated in a tastefully sophisticated manner. We were escorted to a comfortable, but functional music room. The rehearsal proceeded smoothly and we returned to the hotel. I looked forward to hearing that gorgeous voice singing my music.

We booked the recording session for six hours, plus an extra hour if we needed it. When she entered the studio, we knew we were in the presence of show business royalty. She radiated power. We sensed we were working for an icon, a woman who had earned the right to be called a *superstar*.

She arrived with an impressive entourage: her friend Richard Baskin, her manager Jon Peters, the famous husband and wife writing team Alan and Marilyn Bergman, Johnny Mandel (the composer), and the legendary Quincy Jones. She also carried a container of wonderfully aromatic chicken soup. I faced an intimidating audience, but quickly started the ball rolling.

We dispensed with the obligatory greetings. Streisand walked through the studio and entered the vocal booth next to where I was conducting. We could clearly see each other through the glass and communicate if necessary. She selected the track she wanted to use on "Best I Could" and the orchestra ran it down.

She performed flawlessly. I made a few small

changes in the arrangement, and she sang until she recorded a version she liked. A consummate pro, she demanded the best from herself, and definitely knew when she achieved perfection.

We moved on to, "When the Lovin' Goes Out of the Lovin'," and here's where things started to unravel. She sang it through and at the end of the take she seemed unusually quiet. I waited, and she finally said, "It takes too long to get to the end and it doesn't last long enough when you get there."

I thought about the hundreds of recording sessions I'd produced, plagued with countless seemingly insurmountable problems. I needed to rectify the situation. I felt that was one of the reasons Charles hired me. I thought about Streisand's concerns, and figured out a solution.

"Okay! I'll fix it."

I focused on the chart to see what changes I needed to make to come up with a smooth piece of music that addressed her concerns. I cut two bars of music, rewrote notes on all the parts, and told each player what to play to accommodate the changes.

It took about ten minutes.

"I've shortened the track and when you get to the end I'll sustain the orchestra on the last chord. When you've held the note as long as you want, slowly lower your head and I will lower the orchestra at the same time," I stated.

We ran through the song. Flawless! She held

the note beautifully and we ended the track together, a perfect fix. I sensed that for some reason I had fallen out of favor. In retrospect I realized I had taken it upon myself to fix the problem, without any input from the artist. Never a good thing!

She held a conference with Charles and he stated that the chart needed to be a little more modern.

I'd been under the impression that Charles expected orchestral tracks comparable to the ones I recorded in England. If anyone mentioned "modern," I would have added two more synthesizer players and Skunk Baxter. So we removed most of the horns, lowered the level of the choir, and recorded the tracks with a smaller sound. Finally, they said I could leave. I asked them about mixing the songs and they told me they had it covered.

So we went back to the Sunset Marquis; Richard, Brenda and I shared a lovely dinner. John Aries was nice enough to make me cassettes of all the tracks and they were absolutely gorgeous.

The vocals were beautiful as is every Streisand performance. Barbra Streisand is one of the most amazing singers of all time, Charles is a brilliant producer, and I will always be grateful for the experience, and the opportunity, to have worked with them. "Best I Could" ended up on the *Emotion* album and "Lovin" ended up in a boxed set. There are Streisand versions of "When the Lovin' Goes Out of the Lovin'," and "Best I Could" on YouTube, if you would like to hear them.

Here are the lyrics to "Best I Could," written by Richard Wold and me.

I can't apologize...for the way I feel
Cause I've always been honest with you
I've loved you the best I could... in the only way
I knew
And if that's not enough, I've got nothing to say
And I'm not even sure that I would
Some days it was bad.... some days good,
But I loved you the best I could.

CHORUS:

I need more... I need someone to hold me tonight
Someone there when I turn out the light
Just to be here with me
I need more... I need more of you somehow
I need more than your time will allow
I want you in my life
Why can't you be here now?

You say you'd need me, then you'd be gone
The times I needed you
Then you'd hold me and say you're sorry
But what else could you do
Yet I know you really love me

So it's hard to let go like I should
Let's forget the past...remember the good
'Cause you loved me the best you could
(Repeat chorus)

Brenda and I started attending the Grammy Awards, and decided to partake in some of LA's eclectic social life. We had met a multi-talented singer/songwriter named Carol Connors. Carol was hilariously unpredictable, but as sweet as she could be. She composed the lyrics for Rocky, and one of my all-time favorite songs, "With You I'm Born Again."

Carol had been one of the original members of the group, The Teddy Bears, in the "60s." Their song, "To Know Him is to Love Him," soared up the charts. Phil Spector belonged to the group before he turned into a mega Hollywood record producer. She also penned "Hey, Little Cobra" for the Rip Chords, and songs for movies and TV shows including *Lifestyles of the Rich and Famous*.

Carol, a "fashionista," a beautiful tiny time bomb in a designer outfit, became one of our favorite people in LA. Sharing time with this joyously free spirit with an unshackled sense of humor, led to some fun times. She had dated Elvis, Robert Culp (*I Spy*), David Jansen (*The Fugitive*) and a host of other Hollywood A-listers. She shared lunches in trendy restaurants located on the exclusive Rodeo Drive; and power-shopped with Barbi Benton (Hugh Hefner's main squeeze), Zsa Zsa Gabor, Priscilla Presley, Dianne Cannon, and a zillion other stars and fashion designers.

Richard and I were invited to her glitzy housewarming party, a star-studded event, when she bought a dazzlingly beautiful home in the Hollywood Hills that she referred to as, "the house that *Rocky* built." Every time she ran out of liquor, she sent someone to the store for one more bottle, making him a very busy guy!

She owned a quirky Abyssinian cat named Songbird that acted like a dog; a perfect fit for Carol! She represented the rare part of the Hollywood elite that I thoroughly enjoyed.

One morning, after Brenda and I attended the Grammys, a friend of mine called saying he had a leftover limo and offered us its use for the day. I'd attended a dinner with him in the past, and his credit card declined. In a moment of mental instability, I loaned him mine. He owed me 400 bucks that I figured I'd never see, so we accepted his offer of a day in the limo.

Our chauffeur drove up into the mountains where we picked up Carol and wandered around Beverly Hills. We drove by homes of many celebrities and laughed at the opulent display of wealth that seemed so important in the lives of the Hollywood elite.

All of a sudden, Carol told the driver to stop. She jumped out of the limo, ran across a manicured parkway, and clambered up over a tall decorative, but functional, iron fence. This is hard to do when wearing a chic tailored suit, and a particularly tough feat if the bottom half of the outfit is a miniskirt. After she scaled the abutment, she stole some fragrant jumbo oranges. We moved on to a sprawling farmers' market and feasted on enticing food samples, purloined fresh fruit, and bubbly Champagne from the crystal glasses stocked in the back of the limo! It wasn't often that we were able to have a relaxing day off, so we enjoyed every minute of it.

On another one of my LA trips, Carol called me to say she needed a dinner partner for a benefit. I scrounged up a jacket and showed up at the Beverly Hills Hotel ballroom. She forgot to mention one small detail. It was a black tie affair!

She remarked that we'd be sitting with "just" some friends. Right! At the table sat Donna Mills from *Knots Landing*, Tony Geary and Genie Francis from *General Hospital*, Kyle Martin from *Hill Street Blues*, and so on. Much to my surprise, I spotted Rick Monday at a table down by the stage with some of the LA sports people, so I visited with him for a few minutes.

I don't know how many of you have seen acts by Gallagher, the comedian, but for the finale of his act he smashes watermelons with a huge wooden sledgehammer. People sitting in the front that are familiar with him, brought raincoats and ponchos. Obviously not too many of the Hollywood men and women, clad in their expensive designer dresses and custom tuxedos, had previously caught the act. I could never have imagined seeing so many ritzy outfits saturated with watermelon; and so many angry, excessively rich, people. It was worth the trip.

Today, Carol still runs at an amazing pace. She's involved in many charities, organizes large functions to benefit soldiers, and continues to be impressively creative. Our friendship with Carol lasted for a long time and was definately memorable, to say the least.

Chapter 42

Brenda and I decided to go on another European trip to another international music business convention.

This excursion entailed spending three days in London and three days in Paris, for fun. Then, we'd fly to Cannes, home of the *Cannes Film Festival,* for the business part of the trip.

We had become friends with several top Hollywood entertainment attorneys: Jay Cooper, who administered, "We Are the World;" John Branca, Michael Jackson's skilled attorney who helped me solidify my international deal; and Alan Leonard who worked with a plethora of movie stars and recording artists. We all agreed to meet in Paris.

Visiting our favorite city, London, never seemed to get old. We renewed acquaintances, ate pub food, shopped on Carnaby Street, visited the nightspots, and spent a afternoon gazing at the magnificent art at the London Museum. Our three days passed way too quickly, but it was time to move on to Paris.

Tired and bedraggled, we arrived in the exotic city of Paris in the middle of the afternoon. The people at the airport were rude, as was our cab driver. Most of the French seemed to harbor an obvious disdain for Americans.

The restaurants were closed until supper, making it difficult to get something decent to eat, and we were famished. We stepped into a lovely little Parisian cafe to get out of the rain for a moment. The chairs sat upside down on red-checkered tablecloths.

A tiny, grandmotherly woman came bustling out of the kitchen impatiently waving us back out saying, "Closed! Closed!"

Then she took a long look and saw two tired, wet, weary, and very hungry, travelers. She threw up her hands, gave us a sympathetic look, and pointed to a table.

We set the chairs back on the ground and gratefully sat down. She disappeared into the kitchen and reappeared with two steaming bowls of the best soup/stew I had ever tasted, a loaf of French bread, and a bottle of French red wine. Finding a compassionate and caring person was a welcome change, after the rudeness we'd experienced in the short time we'd been there. After we sated our hunger, we thanked her profusely, overpaid the bill, and left to search for our hotel.

We checked in to our *auberge* and made plans to meet our attorney friends for dinner. They chose an eclectic gourmet restaurant and we shared an epicurean, but very expensive meal. Those lawyers had it to spend!

Brenda and I set out on our usual round of exploration. We eagerly gourmandized a tasteful European lunch, topped it off with a glass of fine, white French wine in a charming sidewalk cafe on the Left Bank (that didn't break the bank). We wandered around enjoying the sights of Paris: the Eiffel tower, the architecture in general, and many of the obvious tourist attractions.

At dusk, we strolled down a narrow alley wondering what to do for dinner. We paused in front of a small café/bar named Hot Box. The sight of a mouth-watering steak sizzling on the wood-burning grill located in the window sealed the deal for me. I threw Brenda a quizzical glance.

She shrugged. "Why not!"

We entered to see a tiny intimate candlelit alehouse that sat about eight people at the bar. The bartender informed us there were three picnic tables located in the loft, so up we climbed.

Our very petit, elegant, raven-haired Parisian waitress wore a colorful embroidered dress, and long turquoise Gypsy earrings framed her china doll face. We quizzed this sweet girl about the limited menu and what she recommended. She advised us to order a butterfly sirloin steak cooked on the wood-burning grill, served rare. Sounded like a plan!

She delivered our meal. The perfectly cooked,

juicy, prime cut sat on the crest of a mountain of crispy shoestring French fries. We could cut it with a fork. Our food, served on a colorful china antique platter, sizzled with an aroma that hinted at the taste of the feast we were about to share. She followed up with a loaf of freshly baked French bread, a bowl of soft butter, and a bottle of smooth Beaujolais. Best of all, when our server presented the bill to us, it totaled the measly sum of $32! We tipped her generously. After spending $180 for dinner with the attorneys, we felt we'd fallen into a four-leaf clover patch.

Our wealthy friends told us not to miss Tour D' Argent, one of the top three restaurants in the world.

"You must go for the presentation of the food," they said.

You only live once, right? So, I made reservations. The restaurant, located in a stately historical building, sat on the bank of the Seine River. In a perfect world, we'd have a dreamy romantic dinner by candlelight in a top-shelf elegant eating establishment, and luxuriate in the soft reflection of the moon on the water. In a perfect world!

We arrived at Tour d' Argent to be ushered into a lovely wood-paneled sitting room crammed full of antiques. They served us a dainty before-dinner drink as we sat on a red crushed velvet loveseat. After a relaxing 15 minutes, the maître d' escorted us up to the opulent dining room, in a creaky wooden elevator. The elegantly tuxedoed head waiter guided us toward a table for two that offered a splendid view of Paris and the river.

The romantic part deteriorated quickly due to the six extremely loud, drunken and profane conventioneers dining at the next table. They apologized for being such obnoxious jackasses. In retrospect, I wish they had bought us a drink instead!

Our head waiter handed us oversized engraved menus. Mine had the prices listed on it, but Brenda's did not. We ordered another drink. Brenda decided to try a bowl of squash soup. She finished it, licked her lips, and I asked her how she liked it.

"Delicious," she replied.

I was delighted because it cost $42.

We decided to order the gourmet duck, the special meal the critics raved about. After we consumed a small, but tasty salad, two waiters appeared holding covered sterling silver dishes. One stood behind me, and one hovered behind Brenda.

They looked at each other, smiled, and said "*Voila*," which I think means, "Here it is."

Uncovering the food with a flourish, they placed our plates in front of us in a perfectly synchronized delivery.

I raised an eyebrow and looked at Brenda. She

smiled and said, "I think we just had the presentation of the food."

There was an infinitesimal quarter of a duck sitting in the middle of the large opulent plate. We ordered green beans and the paltry portion we were served came wrapped in a silk string, topped with three tiny almond slivers. I thought it was an inadequate amount of food to be served for the price of a small car. We ate our tiny piece of quackling and it reaffirmed my belief that no one makes duck better than Brenda.

We were thinking, "What the hell did we come here for," when Frick and Frack, our waiters, reappeared with two more sterling silver dishes.

They chorused another "*Voila*," and executed a second precision delivery of two more silver plates. They returned to their stations after taking a dignified bow. This seemed to be the other piece of our allocated half of the teeny weenie duck prepared an entirely different way. Close, but no cigar!

Underwhelmed by the food, and riding on my last nerve due to the crude conduct of the conventioneers, I walked over to their table and expressed my displeasure. They quieted down slightly for almost five minutes, then alcohol overwhelmed class and they started up again. We finished off duck version two, split a dessert, and sipped an after dinner brandy.

Then we got the check. WTF? Six hundred and

forty-eight dollars! Brenda and I made a pact to stop listening to those damned lawyers. They obviously lived on a different planet than we did.

We left Paris the following day and traveled over to Cannes. The monstrous convention center stood across the street from the French Riviera, on the Mediterranean Sea. The water glimmered with a rich aqua hue, but rough grey stones covered the beach which were not conducive to lying on a towel, getting a suntan, or walking in your bare feet. However, we were at the French Riviera, and everybody who was anybody sipped fine champagne, and sunbathed on someone's extravagant yacht.

If we found Paris to be expensive, we were in for more culture shock. A weak Bloody Mary and a scone cost $28. Breakfast? Forty to fifty dollars! If we ordered a Chicago size-martini it would have cost $60. We drank beer and wine.

We quickly learned that if you traveled beyond a three-block radius of the convention center, you could purchase a bottle of vodka for $15, and procure inexpensive munchies from a tiny grocery store to take back to our hotel room. The restaurants were also reasonably priced in that area. Valuable information to know!

The convention center, set up to handle enormous crowds, boasted 40 urinals on one wall of the men's room. We took a break from our meeting, I walked in and it was standing room only. The urinals were all in use when a cleaning lady walked into the bathroom. The Europeans ignored her and kept on doing their business, but the Americans immediately wet their pants, and there were a number of severe zipper injuries. Tourists simply had to learn to conform to the European culture. Europeans had very few reservations about how, and where, they went to the bathroom, as this upcoming story will explain.

The convention went well; we acquired copious amounts of knowledge and networked with people from all over the world.

We ventured on a side trip to Monaco, a mesmerizing place. We were amazed that so many elegant yachts, filled with beautiful people, could be docked in one town. The royal castle resonated wealth, and the towers of the Byzantine Cathedral de Monaco, soared toward the heavens. We stared at the breathtaking architecture, and shared a relaxing glass of wine at a waterfront café. We entered a casino, and it became apparent they didn't like women, or casually dressed Americans in their gambling joints. They kicked us out and I assumed we'd violated another dress code.

We decided to take a leisurely drive up the coast to spend the afternoon in Italy. We took the low road by the water, but when we reached the border we faced a four-hour wait to get in. We stepped out of the car and walked ten feet into Italy, so we could say we were there, after which we turned around and drove back inland on the high road. We wanted to tour some of the picturesque French countryside, and view the buildings, sculptures, and fountains that the small towns were famous for.

We reached a town named Vance, a haven for famous artists and writers. It overflowed with stonework, and arbors draped with fragrant, flowered vines. In the center of town sat "The most beautiful bubbling fountain I've ever seen," commented Brenda.

I took a picture of her romantically gazing at this marvelous bubbling piece of art.

Just as I lowered my camera, a guy walked up to the fountain, unzipped his pants and, um... made water. I quickly snapped a picture of Brenda looking at the offending urinator, with an incredulous look on her face. Before and after: a classic set of pictures.

We said our last goodbyes to our attorney friends and vowed to go our own way on the next trip. Chicago called, with a new challenge on the horizon.

Chapter 43

Again suffering from jet lag, I dove into my next project. A client requested an anti-smoking campaign featuring name singers. Minnie Riperton did a beautiful job on one of them, and they wanted Billy Preston and Syreeta (Stevie Wonder's ex-wife), to sing a duet. Billy and Syreeta sang the beautiful Carol Connors song titled, "With You I'm Born Again."

We nailed down all the contracts with the artists' managers, but the logistics were complex. Syreeta wouldn't leave LA, and Billy couldn't leave Tahoe for several weeks. As usual, the client needed it yesterday.

I recorded a beautiful string orchestra track in Chicago, and hired Bonnie Herman to ghost Syreeta's part. Robert Bowker sang a mock Billy Preston part. Bonnie and Robert performed their vocals on separate tracks, so Billy could sing with Bonnie, and replace Robert's part. Then, I'd fly to LA and Syreeta could sing a duet with the part that Billy recorded in Tahoe. Confused yet?

I packed up the tape, and an assortment of clothes for two seasons. Brenda and I flew to the airport in Reno, and rented a car to drive up to

Lake Tahoe. The sun shined brightly and the skies were clear. The man at the car rental place handed me a set of chains and said, "You're gonna need 'em."

He offered to put them on, but I brushed him off and threw them in the back seat. He smiled knowingly when I climbed into the car.

Chains? Hah! I looked forward to a scenic drive on this beautiful day. The weather went from gorgeous to blizzard in about fifteen minutes. It took me half an hour to put those frigging chains on, but I finally got it done.

When you come up over the mountain and have your first view of Lake Tahoe, it is breathtaking. We went directly to the casino where Billy was performing. We arrived in the middle of his show so Brenda and I waited backstage. All of a sudden, we heard a high-pitched voice when Sammy Davis Jr. looked at Brenda and asked, "Hey, girlie! Do you know how to play dominoes?" She replied that she didn't.

He took her hand. "C'mon, I'll teach you." That worked out well! I watched Billy's show while Sammy Davis taught Brenda how to play dominoes.

Billy finished the set and met me in his dressing room to talk. The whole project almost went off the rails when Billy frowned. "You know I've been thinking. I can't do this. I smoke!"

I reminded Billy we had a contract and we

went round and round for 45 minutes. I finally asked Billy, "Do you think smoking is a good thing?"

Billy thought about it. "No."

"Do you realize how many kids these commercials might reach, to help them rethink smoking?"

He placed his fingers on his lips for a minute and said, "I guess you have a point. All right, I'll do it."

I breathed a sigh of relief. We made arrangements to pick him up in the morning, and he promised to turn in early so he'd be ready to sing with a clear voice.

Brenda and I headed to our hotel. I'd created commercials for Hyatt hotels and, as part of my compensation, they guaranteed me lodging for three separate stays anywhere in the continental USA. Brenda and I were escorted to our room. Room? We entered a four-bedroom suite big enough to hold a party for two hundred of our closest friends. The oversized picture window framed the snow covered mountain slopes surrounding the hotel. After we recovered from the shock of the sight of our gargantuan abode, we decided to wander around to the other side of the lake to gamble, have dinner, and catch a show at the Playboy Club.

As usual, I lost, Brenda won. Dinner was exorbitant, but flavorful, and the show: a typical

Vegas-style review. There were lots of feathers and topless ladies on stage, but Brenda noticed me continually glancing up at the balcony. She gave me a sly look, nudged me, and said, "Hey, you're missing the show."

"Those are just boobs, but that guy up there playing with the band in the balcony is the greatest guitar player I've ever heard." Priorities!

We exited the club at one a.m., to encounter several feet of snow that had fallen during our entertainment spree. It took us a while to get back to the Hyatt, but we parked the car next to a drift, crunched our way through piles of the white stuff, and eased into our massive accommodations. We woke up early and called for the limo to pick us up. We went to retrieve Billy.

We waited. No Billy. Then, we waited some more!

Finally, his manager showed up and said, "Billy's sick. A bunch of his friends showed up last night and they drank shots until five a.m. He doesn't feel good."

I restrained my anger, and politely told his manager to get Billy's drunken ass out of bed and carry him to the limo, or there would be financial consequences. He could sleep all the way to the studio. His handlers took me seriously because about 20 minutes later, two beefy security guys came out carrying Billy and unceremoniously dumped him in the back seat.

Billy wheezed and snored the entire way to our workplace, which took at least 45 minutes. The studio, an impressive compound located on a picture-perfect property, sat in the heart of the mountains. We dragged Billy inside and started to force feed him coffee. While we waited for him to come back to life, I noticed a sign that said, "Don't play with the kitty." I asked the studio owner about the cat.

He led us into a small room where we beheld a large jungle-filled enclosure on the other side of a thick glass wall. We were eye-to-eye with a 120-pound cougar, and I don't mean an older woman. The owner took a beach ball and stepped through the steel door into the cage. I shuddered and covered my eyes. That ferocious cat ran at him, jumped on his back, started to lick his face and chewed on his ear. They romped like two six-year-old brothers playing in the mud. Then, the cat rolled over on his back to get his stomach scratched.

Now I'd seen everything. (No Brenda! You can't have one!)

Someone knocked on the door. "Billy's alive!"

It seems they came up with some Jack Daniels, spiked Billy's coffee, and that did the trick. I ran into the studio, propped him up and started to teach him his part. It took a while, but he finally replaced Robert's guide vocal, and we were able to pour him into the back of the limo to take his body back to the hotel.

Tapes in hand, we checked out and headed for LA. We finally arrived at the studio to record Syreeta. She showed up carrying her baby, accompanied by 12 people from her religious group. It seemed she wanted all of them in the studio with her while she recorded. Once we convinced the mob they couldn't talk while she sang and got the baby to stop crying, we completed her track. There weren't many dull days on this project.

We flew back to Chicago, mixed all the tracks, and the commercial won a cluster of awards.

Fortunately, we weren't faced with a lot of assignments that were quite as complex as this one. No one ever said that the music business would be easy, but I wouldn't have traded my life for anything.

Chapter 44

One of the perks of living in the Windy City pertained to the fact that it was central to all the cities I traveled to regularly. I could reach LA in four hours. I jetted to Nashville on a one and a half-hour short hop south, and made it to New York, after a leisurely two and a half-hour flight to the east. It seems we did nothing but travel, though that's not exactly true. I did most of the traveling, but tried to include Brenda on projects that were important, at a unique destination, or just plain fun.

During the years we ran the business out of the house, we were always there for the kids. When I moved our office downtown, Brenda came into the city after the children went to school, then returned home to make dinner, help with homework, and deliver the boys to their respective Little League games. In addition to being an awesome mom, a phenomenal cook, and a marvelous partner in life, Brenda kept the business running smoothly. I don't know how she ever managed to accomplish everything she did.

We made it a tradition to take an annual

vacation as a family. (Bet you never thought you'd hear the "V" word come out of my mouth.)We climbed on a plane to sunny Acapulco, Mexico the day after Christmas, and returned to a dismal freezing Chicago the day after New Year's. Business normally tended to be slow around the holidays, so it seemed a good time to escape the hustle and stress, and head out for a week of relaxation.

The kids loved those trips south of the border. When the boys were a little older, we let them leave a couple of days early. They booked a flight, grabbed a ride to the airport, and sat at the gate patiently until the airlines announced the flight was overbooked, which always seemed to happen at that time of year. Our fledgling entrepreneurs took the five hundred bucks the airline offered them to give up their seats, and accepted a complimentary seat on the next flight out. Good deal! Free tickets and spending money! They rented a room at a cheap motel in Acapulco, then joined us at the Hyatt when we arrived.

One year our sons were doing God knows what on their usual pre-vacation. The phone rang and they asked if they could check into the Hyatt one day early, as they had been kicked out of their motel. I didn't ask why, I just told them okay. I later heard a rumor about someone jumping off a third floor balcony into the swimming pool.

Brenda, Wendy, her girlfriend Jamie, and I

arrived at the Hyatt. Our boys met us, full of enthusiasm and bottled-up energy, or bottles of Dos Equis beer.

I checked in, and after I signed the register the hotel clerk pulled out a sheet of paper and said, "Do you want me to add this to your bill, or would you like to settle it now?"

I stared at that piece of paper not wanting to believe my eyes. It was a bar bill for $2,800. I raised one quizzical eyebrow and looked at the clerk for an explanation.

"Oh, yes! Your oldest son got drunk and bought the pool a drink."

I sighed and handed him my credit card... again! I wondered if this was how my father occasionally felt when I was growing up. Had I known everything our boys were doing, I probably would have had some second thoughts about the whole thing, but my dad always used to say, "Ignorance is bliss." He would know!

So, that's the way *that* vacation started.

At that time, Acapulco topped the list of perfect travel destinations. The cartels hadn't started to terrorize Mexico yet. We found it reasonably safe to take a normal everyday drive, and roam from place to place without worrying about someone receiving a ransom note!

We met for breakfast every morning at an outside table, in a cafe nestled in a lush tropical garden on the hotel grounds. My oldest son, the bighearted pool-party cocktail provider, was somewhat of a Romeo. We made bets as to which direction he'd come to breakfast from. We were rarely right. I guess he met more playful women than we thought. Occasionally, there were times we needed scorecards for all of the boys.

We enjoyed the usual activities like scuba diving, parasailing, boating, and deep-sea fishing. I cooled off in the luxurious pool (which obviously had a bar in it). We spent long afternoons in the stifling heat, perusing the contents of the colorful booths, and inhaling the appetizing aroma of the street food down at the flea market. Brenda spent hours haggling with the vendors over different objects: a rainbow-colored beach wrap, a granite chess set, and dozens of hand-carved teak dishes shaped like animals. Me? I bought a Cuervo t-shirt.

We rented two boats and headed to a remote restaurant, reachable only by water. Brenda and I settled in one boat with Peter and Joyce, a couple we'd met on the beach. Peter's son, their daughter, our kids, and Wendy's friend, were in the first boat to leave the dock. The little rascals cut in front of our boat and stopped dead in the water. I thought something might be wrong. When would I stop being a slow learner? As we drifted closer to their boat, they stood up and mooned us. I guess they were all *really* good friends.

Peter, a jolly chap from Britain, shook his head and said, "Gotdam, I got a love-hate relationship with *me* kids. I hate lovin' 'em."

Our favorite restaurants in Acapulco served tickle-your-tastebuds meals: grilled whole red snappers drenched with garlic butter, pounds of shrimp, lobsters, and every kind of fresh-caught seafood imaginable. It was possible to also find eating spots featuring American or international cuisines, so we could choose from menus of luscious food for every taste.

We became regulars at Paradise, an open-air restaurant located on the water. We immersed ourselves in wonderful feasts, to the soothing sound of waves rolling up on the sandy beaches.

Paradise served pink umbrella drinks and appetizers at a long tiki bar, located at one end of the spacious room. The walls oozed velvet pictures of matadors, dazzling serapes, black velvet sombreros, and brightly colored paintings of the Mexican culture. Whirling ceiling fans added to a gentle breeze blowing from the bay, and the family enjoyed the view as we dove into our meals, fighting off the seagulls that were trying to steal the dinner rolls off the table.

We left the kids at the hotel, after limiting the amount that they could add to my charge card. Accompanied by another couple, we caught a cab and rode for quite a while before we arrived at a secluded restaurant deep in the hills. We devoured an outstanding home cooked Mexican meal in the beautiful rustic hillside café, stayed too long, and when we tried to call a cab to go back, the owners informed us the drivers were done for the day.

Stranded! What did we do? We started to walk! There was little to no traffic on the mountain road, and as the sun began to sink below the horizon, waves of apprehension gnawed at our sensibilities. After 45 minutes of a foot-burning walk down a rocky mountain road in sandals, an old Mexican farmer driving a dilapidated truck, ground to a halt to see if he could help us. We offered to pay him to take us down the mountain into town.

With a quiver of his bushy black mustache, he smiled, held up five fingers, and we had to fork over fifty bucks for the ride. The ladies hoisted themselves into the cab of the truck, and my friend and I climbed in the back—with the pigs. I don't think I need to describe that ride, but I didn't eat pork for a couple of years after that. Thank God they weren't feral.

It was a tradition for the family to ring in the New Year at the same restaurant. I made a simple contribution to the celebration. I drank shots of tequila and played with a Mexican rock and roll band, the highlight of my trip every year. All the Mexicans were trying to figure out where this intoxicated gringo with the ugly shirt came from, and why he played "Johnny B. Goode" and not "Feliz Navidad." We rocked the place! As soon as I walked in, the guitar player waved, unstrapped his guitar, and handed it to me. Then, he went off to drink his own celebratory margaritas.

Parasailing was mandatory the following day. Nothing beat sailing over scenic Acapulco Bay, 150 feet up in the air, to get rid of a hangover. I noticed that if I didn't tip the guys who were catching me, when I came down, they let me crash into a pile of driftwood next to the landing platform. A few pesos guaranteed me a safe landing.

At the end of the trip, we fought our way through the over-crowded airport, braved the long lines, and headed back to the reality of deep wet snow and the arctic, Chicago winters. The memories the kids stored up from those trips... made it all worth it.

On the rare occasions when Brenda and I found a little time for ourselves, we booked two seats on Mexicali Airlines and jetted off for long overdue mini-vacations at Las Brisas in Acapulco. Las Brisas, a romantic resort, consisted of little pink casitas that honeycombed the side of a mountain. Each casita had its own pool, surrounded by a huge privacy hedge with a maze-like entrance. Every morning when we woke up and looked outside the door, we found flowers floating in our tiny turquoise water hole, and hot coffee and scones on the patio. We rented a pink Jeep to go shopping, or travel wherever the road led us, our own version of a small side trip.

The sprawling resort featured a plush, private entertainment center, where we hid from the heat and drank chilled beverages. This one-story adobe style building, comfortably cool, and tastefully decorated, became our oasis. We relaxed on the couches, played backgammon at the game tables, and the mixologist whipped us up colorful cocktails. When we drove down the steep road leading toward the bay, we crossed the highway and weaved our way through beautiful gardens and large haciendas—also rentals. At the very bottom sat a gourmet restaurant, a bar, and a saltwater swimming pool screened off from the ocean to keep the sharks out. The resort served as therapy to a couple of burnt-out music people.

Brenda and I took our pink Jeep for a ride in the mountains, which would certainly get you into trouble if you did it today. I navigated around a hairpin turn in the road and ended up in a camp of armed rebels carrying AK-47's. I don't know who was more surprised. I burned rubber in reverse and that ended our mountain explorations. We rarely left the resort after that.

Another afternoon, we stopped by the

entertainment center for a drink and met an affable couple, Buhl and Char. Buhl's denim shirt, torn shorts and unshaven face, made him look like a scruffy Ernest Hemmingway wannabe. Char was his "babe." They taught us how to play backgammon, and we ran into them a few more times during our stay. We agreed to meet for dinner at the gourmet restaurant our last night there.

Seated at an outdoor table in the midst of fragrant flowers, the sound of a bubbling fountain helped set a tranquil mood. Thousands of stars painted the sky with a tapestry of soft twinkling flashes. Buhl asked if we minded if he ordered the wine; his treat. Since Brenda and I knew very little about wine, we acquiesced, with the caveat that we would split the cost. The wine arrived, Buhl poured us a glass; it tasted smooth and rich.

We hadn't talked about anything personal up to this point in the trip, as we were casually enjoying each other's company. I told Buhl I possessed a meager antique gun collection. He said he also had a collection, but his divorce settlement required him to sell it. I asked him to tell me about it.

"I only got a million and a half for it. I had Wyatt Earp's gun, Buffalo Bill's gun," and so forth.

We asked Char what she did. "Well, I used to be a waitress, but the manager of the club gave me a hard time, so Buhl bought it for me."

The alarm bells hadn't started to go off yet, but something nagged at me. Then our server arrived with the check. At Las Brisas, you didn't pay cash for anything during your stay. Everything ended up on your credit card at the end of the trip, so I had quite a bit of cash stashed away in my wallet, and this restaurant definitely took cash.

I pulled out three hundred-dollar bills.

Brenda nudged me and whispered, "Not enough,"

I kept pulling out hundreds and she kept nudging me. Finally, I was holding $800 and that seemed to be enough. I asked Buhl if I could see the check, and much to my chagrin, he'd ordered a $1,000 bottle of wine. We said our goodnights and started walking back to our miniature casita. I had become extremely quiet.

Brenda said, "What are you thinking right now?"

I thought about it for a minute. "If I had known the wine was that expensive I would have had another f****** glass."It turned out that Buhl was Buhl Ford III, one of the heirs to the Ford fortune.

From that day forward, if we were at a restaurant and someone asked us if we minded if they ordered the wine, we responded in unison with a vehement *yes*, and ordered the house wine.

One last humorous recollection! One year, we received several thousand dollars in royalty checks as we were walking out the door to catch our plane to taco-land. Brenda said she'd hide them. She did! They re-appeared two years later, wrapped in a plastic baggie, when she defrosted the freezer. We were relieved that they hadn't become "liquid assets."

Chapter 45

Our arrival back in Chicago coincided with a challenge that required a quick turnaround. An advertising agency in Australia was about to lose the beer account that reportedly made up half of their total business. So, they contacted all their other branches around the world to see if someone could create a winning campaign, and save the account. I spent hours on my idea, and when I submitted my campaign to the agency, they jumped all over it. I ended up with bragging rights for winning an international competition against some formidable participants.

I sent in my bill, they paid my fee, and shipped the demo track off to be produced in Australia. I'd shoved the project to the back of my mind, until I received a frantic phone call.

One of my producer friends asked, "How soon can you get to Australia?"

It seems they were having a difficult time duplicating my track, and wanted me to sneak into Australia to produce it. Americans weren't allowed to work without a visa, so they asked me to come to Sydney and unofficially "consult."

Brenda and I climbed on another plane. After

a brief stopover in Hawaii, followed by a long, brutal flight to New Zealand, we ended the trip with a short-hop over to Sydney. A very nice chap from the agency met us at the airport and delivered us to our hotel in the center of downtown Sydney. Our room boasted a picture window with a panoramic view of the entire harbor and, the architectural marvel, the Sydney Opera House. An early chill filled the air as we walked down to the waterfront and toured old historical buildings, the antiquated Long Bay prison, and some unique exclusive little shops.

We took a shabby, worn-out water taxi over to Doyle's, a famous eating establishment built on a dock where we devoured a delicious meal. The seagulls must have been related to the Acapulco gulls, as they kept landing on the table, trying to snatch anything I couldn't protect with two hands and a napkin.

We found last-minute tickets to an ominous classical music performance at the Opera House. Music...not so good! Acoustics and sound...WOW!

The following morning, I met with the agency and the Australian musician they delegated to officially run the session. I understood why they were having trouble as this guy seemed clueless.

They flew a programmer in from Perth to program the Roland DX7 keyboard, which was so simple that Wendy could have figured it out when she was five. If you wanted a piano sound, you pushed the button marked "piano."

I met the rest of the musicians and looked at Brenda in despair. These guys were totally inept. At best, they were a bunch of rag-tag players who gigged in pubs and never listened to Motown Records. At least the studio was great. Thank you, Jesus!

We worked for hours trying to duplicate my track. I hated spending this much time with those bumbling musicians to duplicate a track I had originally completed in just 40 minutes, back in Chicago. It was like comparing a lawnmower to a Ferrari. We finally completed a barely acceptable track after two whole days. I began to doubt my ability as a producer.

We moved on to the Australian Amateur Hour, the string section. These dowdy ladies looked like they arrived by horse and carriage, straight from a quilting bee. They wore an assortment of old-fashioned house dresses that looked like kitchen curtains. Is it politically correct to say "frumpy"? Either I had fallen into a hobby day at a retirement home, or I'd been transported to a flamboyant Amish community in Kentucky.

The sound was awful! The Australian dude flailed his arms around like a madman, trying to conduct the strings, but his movements had nothing to do with the tempo of the music. I began to think he got the gig because he was someone's cousin; not for his conducting skills. I accosted him in the hall, and told him he better figure out how to direct this vapid mess, and get them playing at some semblance of the correct speed. That isn't quite how I said it, but you get the idea.

Subdued, he returned to the studio and made an effort, albeit a feeble one. Another day shot, and we ended up with another less-than-average track. Oh, boy! What next?

The choir! I faced a group of ten classically trained singers who never listened to Patti Austin, or Aretha Franklin. No self-respecting Baptist Church would have let them in the door. We rehearsed, and rehearsed, as I fruitlessly tried to inject some soul into those pompous pearl-shaped voices.

You can't un-teach classical training as Mr. Stroop, my old theory teacher, pointed out. It was like casting a goat to play a horse. Again, we got a less than stellar performance.

Tony Burrows, the recording artist from England, sang lead and did a fabulous job. I might as well have booked Celine Dion to sing with a kazoo band. We slaved away in the studio for six wasted days. We cut my original track, mixed with vocals, in three hours back in the Windy City.

The account executive took the tracks back to the agency and Brenda and I spent two days traversing a small part of Australia. We explored the outback for a short time, but had no way to tour anywhere else. We were hoping to charter a boat and go around to the Barrier Reef. The trip failed due to the incompetence of the musicians and singers. I didn't get to throw a boomerang, or see one damned kangaroo! What a waste of time. I felt like I'd accomplished nothing as we climbed on the airplane to leave Australia.

Two weeks later, the agency in Chicago called me in for another panicked meeting. The Australian tracks weren't cutting it (big surprise), and they wanted to figure out a way to use my original demo tracks in Australia. I gave them everybody's name that played and sang on the commercials, and returned to my office.

The agency kept the account, so I assume someone figured out the Aussie angle. I still have nightmares about working with that "talent." It certainly was "down under."

A gentleman from Los Angeles reached me. He wanted to fly me to California in order to evaluate a 13-year-old singer he was interested in producing. I flew into LAX, and he picked me up in his Rolls Royce. Posh! He drove me to the Sunset Marquis. I checked in and we took off to hear his singer at the Palomino, the big Hollywood country bar at that time. This tiny redhead sang in a way that belied her age. She received standing ovations from all those LA "cowboys" in their shiny boots, Rodeo Drive plaid shirts, and $600 monogrammed jeans.

Then, we followed her and her family down to a large country bar in Anaheim, and she received the same enthusiastic reaction. Interesting! Her mentor wanted to record her in Nashville and that seemed like the best path forward.

I flew back to Chicago and placed calls to some Nashville publishers, to forage for some top-shelf songs for her to sing. They responded by sending me exceptional material, and I started to cull the tunes down to select the four songs for her session.

Once I picked the tunes, I flew back to LA to rehearse the midget Loretta Lynn. When I felt she had a handle on the material, I jetted back to Chicago to set up the recording session in Tennessee. We met at Bradley's Barn, a landmark studio outside of Nashville. I had booked a great band: Ron Oates (piano), Wayne Moss (guitar), Norbert Putnam (bass), Kenny Buttrey (drums), Vip Vipperman (rhythm guitar), and Charlie McCoy (on harmonica.)

The finished music tracks were perfect and we started on the vocals. After a slow start, she rose to the occasion and performed professional sounding vocals. Pretty amazing for a (by then) 14-year-old!

I sent the mixed tracks back to the West Coast and her manager began to present them to record companies. We couldn't land the deal we wanted, and my friend asked me to move to LA to be part of her musical team, and handle her on the road. I couldn't just up and leave Chicago, so I politely refused the offer, and he continued to shop her songs.

She met Mae Axton, the Queen Mother of Nashville (who wrote "Heartbreak Hotel"), and Mae took her under her wing. Then, she signed with a well-known producer named George Tobin, out of New York.

Driving in my car one afternoon, I heard her hit, the redo of The Beatles' song, "I Saw Her Standing There," on the radio. The little girl named "Tiffany," became famous for playing her songs in shopping malls for hordes of screaming teenagers. I have a picture with Tiffany, and I'm wearing my "Hit Records Done Cheap" t-shirt. If only! Even though I left the project early, I enjoyed participating in the development of a promising young star.

We were unusually busy doing jingles for different Chicago ad agencies. I worked on my fourth national network Kentucky Fried Chicken campaign. We recorded the commercials in locations all over the country, and the client spent a fortune on their ads. Sales were lagging, so they asked the agency to develop a clever promotional campaign.

One of my clients handed me a script.

I read it, then read it again. "You have to be

kidding."

After all that expensive music, and memorable campaign songs, I couldn't believe they would go for a lyric like this!

"The 99-center...The 99-center,

Two finger-lickin'-good pieces of chicken...a roll and coleslaw."

I wrote an upbeat catchy melody to his lyric, and we recorded with an outstanding group of fun-loving musicians and singers. This goes to show how unpredictable the advertising business could really be. After spending millions on the previous national campaigns, this silly little piece of music became one of the most successful KFC promotions in history. Go figure!

While I'm talking about crazy assignments, one of my favorite clients called me to do some commercials for Agree Shampoo. The campaign line: "Escape the Greasies with Agree."

I just composed a song about a "99 center" so I figured I could tackle the "Greasies." I flew to LA for a huge production meeting. The conference room, filled with film people and ad executives, buzzed with ideas and opinions. After I listened to their creative plans, my client asked me what kind of music I had in mind.

"Disco!"

You could have heard a pin drop. After some throat cleaning, dubious looks, and deliberation by all concerned; they questioned my decision, and possibly my sanity.

We all knew that disco had gone the way of Travolta, but I had a secret weapon in mind: my New York band, Stuff. I realized my clients were taking a giant leap of faith, but I knew I could deliver. I'd completed successful work for almost everybody in that room, so after a lot of, "What do you think's," they reluctantly agreed.

I believe that some of them thought they were giving me enough rope to hang myself. Fat chance!

I flew to New York, produced a track with Stuff; and my powerful singers, Linda November, Leslie Miller, Stephanie Fuller, and Patti Austin. I had Richard Wold to sing some ad-lib parts to balance out the girls. The agency loved it. Final filming began, and I returned to Media Sound to record final tracks in different lengths.

The agency did a marvelous job on the commercial. The dynamic footage, enhanced by exceptional graphics and the accompanying pulsating disco track, cut through the competition when it played on the air. The campaign ran for a several years and people were drawn into the music and the film, to the point where the word "greasies" kind of slid by.

If you have an unfettered desire to see this commercial, Google "YouTube Agree shampoo escape the greasies." Then, you will be a witness to the fact that disco wasn't quite dead, yet.

Chapter 46

Brenda and I became best friends with our New York singer, the incomparable Stephanie Fuller. She invited us to share her lovely apartment in Manhattan on some of our trips east.

Unbeknownst to us, she started dating one of my main competitors, Tom Anthony, a formidable New York music producer. Tommy studied music at the renowned Crane School of Music in Potsdam, New York. Already a professional piano and trumpet player, he learned to play every other instrument in the orchestra. He excelled in writing and composition, and became proficient at conducting. He taught music for a year, then went into the army where he was assigned to special services at West Point, where he ended up director and conductor of the 1st army band.

He went back into teaching when he left the army. He ended up in New York where he worked for Mitch Lee, the biggest jingle producer at the time. He started in sales, learned the business, and opened his own company in 1967. The rest was history. Tom produced thousands of commercials; won so many Clio Awards that he used one as a door knocker. He rose to the top of the jingle business as a writer, producer, brilliant arranger, and conductor.

Stephanie worried that dating Tom might be a conflict of interest, but Brenda and I didn't care as long as she was happy. She couldn't wait for us to meet him.

In the middle of a session at Universal a five-foot eight, skinny guy with long, flowing blond hair down to his shoulders, looking like a smaller version of General Custer, walked into the studio. He said (with a New Yawk accent), "Which one of you chubby guys is Bobby Whiteside?"

"I am."

He still laughs when he remembers the startled look on my face.

He walked up to me, stuck out his hand and said, "I'm Tom Anthony."

He and Stephanie were passing through Chicago, and he figured it would be as good a time as any to meet me...typical Tom! The four of us went out for sushi and we've been friends ever since.

Tom and Steph tied the knot at their beach house on Fire Island. I flew in on a seaplane for the wedding. I devoured some aromatic seafood soup, and my throat started to swell up from a delayed anaphylactic reaction. I took four Benadryls and stayed up all night, waiting to see if we were going to have to call the medevac helicopter to take me to the hospital. I survived; and managed to feel somewhat like a living, breathing human being in the morning.

They held the wedding ceremony down by the ocean. The dress code: black tie and bare feet. Tom and Steph hired a tuxedoed string quartet, and placed a beautiful arbor entwined with scented cream-colored flowers close to the rippling waves. White folding chairs dotted the beach. They could not have asked for a better day. The sun smiled, and a gentle breeze whispered good wishes. Steph looked like an angel; Tom looked like the maestro he is.

An hour before the ceremony, Tommy plopped his Nikon camera into my hands and gave me twenty-five rolls of film. "The photographer is tied up and can't make it till later. You're it!"

So I photographed my first wedding. My pictures turned out to be excellent, and the real photographer showed up in time to shoot the reception at the beach house. I picked out my favorite photo, a close-up of Tom's dad who fell asleep during the wedding.

We shared unforgettable times with Tom and Steph on Fire Island. Their retreat was located on the bay, and the ocean sat 50 yards behind them.

Brenda and Tom pulled on waders and walked into the shallow water of the bay. They looked like they were doing the twist, but in reality they were stirring up the sandy bottom, driving the clams up where they could grab them. They managed to gather a bucketful for dinner. Early in the morning Tom could be found down in the ocean, surf fishing for sea bass. We had our getaway Michigan house and they had their own nirvana on Fire Island.

No cars were allowed on Fire Island; so boats, bicycles and flip-flops were the only means of transportation. When Tom and Steph headed to the island, they parked their auto on the mainland and took a ferry to the house. All the serious shopping had to be done on the mainland, so it was possible to rack up some hefty water-taxi fees if you didn't have your own boat. Any food, liquor, household items, supplies, and construction materials had to be delivered by ferry, or on a small barge. It took some intense planning to consolidate everything needed into a minimal number of water deliveries.

In the fall, after all the summer people and their dogs returned to the city, the deer emerged from the thickets into the yard and ate apples out of our hands. They climbed up a short flight of steps to the deck, and bumped their wet noses on the sliding glass doors to remind Stephanie to come out and feed them.

Tommy's business kept him writing day and night. The beach house was a place to unwind after his 70-hour work weeks.

Stephanie found the island to be conducive to

creativity. She stayed busy painting beautiful seascapes, mixing natural earth elements into her murals. She came up with her own version of Jamaican art, and worked on a series of line drawings of elegant ladies called *Demoiselles*. Her work can be found on the Web, or occasionally exhibited in art galleries in New York. As an artist she generated works that were unique, stunning, and impressive. It's very hard to do her creations justice, even with a lengthly detailed description.

When I moved to Nashville in the early "90's" Tom and I started a New York/Nashville company called, The Cumberland River Gang, that you'll hear more about later.

Chapter 47

I loved recording in LA. While taking a long drive through Laurel Canyon over the Hollywood Hills, into the San Fernando Valley, I came upon Devonshire Studios. I stopped to check it out and met an amazing couple, Dee and Dave Mancini, the owners. The tracking rooms were state-of–the-art and the entire studio radiated with a cheerful, but acutely professional, vibe. A cozy carpeted lounge contained comfortable couches and a well-worn pool table. An exceptional staff of creative engineers convinced me to start working there. Devonshire's location placed it near many prime restaurants that served food of every cuisine. The musicians enjoyed the relaxed atmosphere, and the terrific sound that emerged from the speakers every time we recorded.

Dave and Dee invited me to stay on the Mancini's 85-foot yacht, the Mauritania, instead of bunking at a hotel. The view of dazzling sunrises and sunsets, added to the ambience of staying at the Marina Del Rey Harbor.

The Mauritania's living quarters left little to be desired: three giant staterooms with king-size beds, a spacious luxurious lounge exquisitely decorated with peaches-and-cream-colored couches and chairs, and a dining room with an opulent crystal chandelier centrally located over an antique banquet-sized table. At the rear of the ship awaited two spacious sun decks, filled with random fluffy lounge chairs carefully positioned to welcome sun-worshippers. I could see my reflection in the polished teakwood, and the entire boat had been well maintained. I felt like I'd hit the jackpot and landed on one of those extravagantly elegant yachts in Monte Carlo.

The Mancinis surrounded themselves with a diverse group of friends. One of them owned a plane, another purchased a ski chalet, one of them inherited a spacious estate in Palm Springs, and their friend Tommy lived on a ranch at the top of a cliff in Calabasas.

An ill-tempered llama greeted us when we visited Tommy's rustic abode. He advised Brenda to use caution when we approached the beast, as the chauvinistic animal had been known to spit foul green liquid at females. Tommy owned seven German Shepherds, a couple of goats, several gorgeous Palo Peso palomino horses, and a menagerie of different animals that had free run of the place. He never closed the doors to the house, so we might find a goat on the table, or a horse in the living room. It was fun...different.

He constructed an unparalleled koi pond and many of his prized fish were worth upwards of

$15,000. The week before our first visit, he removed an $18,000 koi from the pond to show to a friend. It slipped out of his hands and flopped to the sparkling fish lagoon in the sky. Tommy's gold mines in South Africa were prosperous, so I guessed that waxing one or two fish wouldn't dent his bank account. The pond fed into a rainbow colored waterfall that dropped 80 feet down the mountain, then recycled back up to the top. Breathtaking!

At the end of the day we shared a drink, immersed in the marble hot tub on the back deck, and found ourselves mesmerized as we watched his pack of German Shepherds chase wolves through the trees on the mountain next to his land.

When night fell, we entered the house, shagged a pig off the couch, and enjoyed the unique décor of his countrified homestead. His living room showcased two enormous aquariums, one filled with a prismatic array of rare tropical fish, the other containing two vicious piranhas. We took a pass on watching him feed live mice to the piranhas. Spending time at Tommy's was like visiting the Woodstock version of *Animal Planet*.

The Mancinis thoroughly enjoyed their wide circle of friends. Every weekend they assembled as a group and used one of the individual assets. The buddy that owned the plane flew them to Vegas, or they motored to Palm Springs, or traveled to the ski resort in Vail. Great way to live! However; despite their opulent life, I found them to be two of the nicest, most unpretentious people I'd ever met.

One year, Brenda and I flew to LA for a Christmas party on the Mauritania. We ran into Skunk Baxter on the dock, carrying the biggest rifle I'd ever seen. He wished us a happy holiday and headed for the ocean to shoot sharks. I guess everyone celebrates Christmas in their own way.

We were glad we came out for the party. We partook in a gourmet buffet, caught up with dozens of music people, and old friends who luxuriated in extravagant Hollywood events. As the evening wore down, a little boy scampered around the yacht. Someone asked whose kid he was. Someone else said, "Stephen#####, (a recording artist).

Then someone said, "Stephen went home a couple of hours ago."

Then, a fourth person chimed in. "Call Stephen and tell him he forgot his kid!"

And that was Christmas in LA!

I recorded two vintage jazz tracks for the opening of the retired cruise ship, the *Queen Mary*, after investors converted it into a palatial hotel. The band featured the notable Shelly Manne on drums, jazz great Mundel Lowe on guitar, my old friend Mike Abene on piano, and the unparalleled

Ray Brown who played bass. Almost every legendary improvisational musician in LA showed up for that session. Dave Mancini commented that if someone threw a hand grenade into the studio, jazz would be dead in California.

A client asked me to create another anti-cigarette campaign directed toward teenagers, with the theme; "Do The Cigarette Mash." Dancers stamped out cigarettes while they danced "The Cigarette Mash." It gave me the perfect chance to produce another thumping rock and roll track.

I brought Wendy to LA to sing on the project at Devonshire. Her vocal quality had evolved into a commercially viable teen rock and roll sound. I teamed her up with three incomparable Hollywood singers, and we cut the track. The results were "smoking"! Our happy client was "dancin'"to the music."

The creative people did a superb job, and the commercial relayed the anti-smoking message clearly, with an overtone of whimsy. If you would like to see the spot, Google "YouTube cigarette mash 1985."

Once in a while, I had to record in other studios due to the fact that Devonshire was already booked. Three of those occasions led to interesting experiences.

I took a project to Evergreen Studios, a

favorite recording venue for many major music stars. While we were working, I heard the hint of a familiar voice coming out of one of the other studios in the complex. I listened to Neil Diamond recording, "Turn on Your Love Light." It appeared that his work had him preoccupied, as he didn't seem friendly, but I got a kick out of hearing that song being recorded.

One other time I ended up in a film studio on the Warner Brothers lot, to record a large orchestra. I found myself in awe of the monstrous room! The engineer set the podium directly in front of the horn section. I mentioned Jerry Hey earlier; the trumpet player that arranged those powerful Michael Jackson albums. He formed a horn section named Seawind, that performed with astounding percussive force. The shock wave from the punch of their notes rustled my hair, and shook the music score as I tried to conduct the orchestra. I actually had to move the podium over to one side. Working on a real film-scoring studio sound stage turned out to be an amazing experience. My mind was overloaded with a list of film music that had been recorded in that reverberant room through the years.

The third time, I booked Motown Studios in order to work with Bruce Swedein (Quincy Jones' and Michael Jackson's sound engineer). Bruce engineered some sessions for me in Chicago, before he moved West and hit the big time. A client of mine, Jim Glover, came up with an interesting idea for a McDonalds commercial. The soundtrack played a riff emulating a thumping Michael Jackson song. A Big Mac appeared in the sky like a spaceship from Star Wars, an ambitious, and well conceived, concept. The commercial turned out to be polished, exciting and cleverly produced, featuring some striking outer-space special effects.

I booked a fabulous band: Skunk Baxter and Elliott Randall on guitars, Nathan East on bass, James Newton Howard on keyboards, Boddicker on synthesizers, and Harvey Mason on drums. In addition, we added a section of percussive Hollywood strings. The track sounded like a major motion picture score, and the visuals were spectacular. Someone asked me how I managed to get musicians of that caliber to come in and do jingles at that time of the morning. It was simple. We were friends, but I had to take them out for sushi after the session.

I guess the arrangement snuck a little too close to an existing Michael Jackson song. We received a cease-and-desist letter from his attorney who wanted us to pull it off the air. We ignored it, the spot ran its cycle, and we heard nothing more from his attorney. Sometimes you get lucky.

My ad executive friend Tom Hall, the man who

hired me to write the first Oscar Meyer Weiner spots at the inception of my career, asked me to create a major campaign for Sears. Did I ever! The line was "Sears: your money's worth and a whole lot more."

I produced a gorgeous, fully orchestrated theme song that pleased both the agency and Sears. Almost more commercials than I could handle followed, but I relished challenges. We worked on the Sears account off and on, until I moved to Nashville. I'll get back to that in a little while.

Someone steered me to a sweet old Lithuanian lady named Carrie, who predicted the future. I never believed in fortune-tellers, but I made an appointment just for fun. She caught me off guard with the depth of her observations.

She told me there were two great ladies in my life, one who was personal, and one who helped my career. I interpreted that as the fact that she was referring to Brenda and Streisand. She said that there would be two more ladies who would contribute to my success. One turned out to be Mindy McCready, and my number one record with her. The other one? Hopefully I'll find her soon.

Then she said, "You have three sons and a daughter. One of your sons will have a terrible accident, but he will be alright." Then she paused, frowned, and said "Finally, there is something in your future that is too terrible for me to speak of right now."

I had never met this fascinating woman, but she knew facts about my life that were unbelievable. I walked away with a lot on my mind, with grave concerns for what was on the path ahead. I had a bad feeling.

A couple of years later, Brenda and I were in Michigan and the phone rang to inform us that Tarrey, our middle son, had been blown off a bridge while putting up a promotional banner for a triathlon. He fell 20 feet and landed on a concrete sidewalk, missing a parking meter by two feet.

Brenda and I rushed back to the hospital in Chicago. An excellent athlete in high school, he instinctively executed a slow flip and instead of smashing into the concrete, he slid in. The accident messed him up, but the doctors felt he would fully recover, probably with some problems from arthritis as he aged. It was a miracle he survived at all. I felt a chill as I thought of Carrie's words. I couldn't help but wonder what lurked in the future.

Chapter 48

The business changed rapidly. As I predicted, Northwestern University started cranking out cookie-cutter electronic music specialists, who could simulate an entire orchestra with one keyboard, by pulling from a library of different instrumental sounds. Always a proponent of live music I favored real musicians, many of whom were personal friends. They deserved to work, and the union deemed it illegal for a keyboard player to build tracks that made one guy sound like 20. It took income away from veteran musicians who had paid their dues and made their living by playing.

Here's where it began to get complicated. When a creative asked me to do a demo for a new campaign, he or she gave me $500 to produce it. I always ended up spending more money than that. I had to bring in enough musicians to demonstrate the idea, which certainly cost more than the demo budget.

I found myself competing with producers who spent nothing to get a fuller sound than mine, as they were artificially synthesizing their tracks. I'd submit a demo with guitar, bass, drums, and a singer. They'd submit one with an electronic string orchestra, and make mine sound like garbage.

I'd always been ahead of the curve and I sure didn't like being behind it. So, I bit the bullet and built my first in-house demo studio in one room of my office. I bought a synthesizer loaded with rock and orchestral sounds; into the fray I jumped. My cadre of musicians always boasted a wonderful keyboard player, so we were able to compete on an even keel with the electronics guys. I now had the capability to do full tracks with one musician when I found it necessary, in order to compete.

Let me take a minute and explain a synthesizer to any novices that might be wondering what I'm talking about. Simply, the early synthesizer was a long self-contained music box, with an attached piano keyboard. Above the keyboard sat a row of labeled buttons that designated the internal instrument sounds. When turned on, it played a piano sound. If the button labeled trumpet was pushed, it played a trumpet sound; and so on. The different musical instruments were electronically reproduced copies of live instruments; not great quality, but not bad either, and certainly adequate to enhance a demonstration music track. With the new system of multi tracking (unlimited empty tracks), a single musician could record the piano on track one, trumpet on track two, strings on track three, etc. Mix it all down and we'd end up with a one-man orchestra. *Capiche?*

Today, the modern synthesizer is a piano keyboard that starts with no sounds (hit a note...hear nothing). It reads whatever is fed into it from a sound library on a computer. A sound library can be compared to a player piano roll. If the roll is not in the piano, the piano won't play. When you insert the roll, it tells the keyboard the notes to play.

So, if the keyboard is given a piano part from an external library, it plays a beautiful piano. Feed it drums and it plays realistic drums. There are thousands of external sound libraries available now, from banjos to symphony orchestras, from a flute to a church choir, or an explosion to a Chinese gong. It's overwhelming. Plus, they are all played on the same controller piano keyboard (not at the same time, of course).

As the technology developed, the samples fed to the keyboards were actual sounds of a real player, who had been recorded live, after which his notes were transferred to a sound library. They did the same thing with entire orchestras, individual horns, and different groups of musical instruments. Nothing was off the plate, and a new software business exploded. It became harder to discern between a real player and the recording of a real player.

I recently finished my album, *Livin' the Golden Years*, where I played the piano, bass, violins, violas, cellos, trumpets, English horn, oboe, flute, and backing choir at home on my midi controller. All my sound libraries are now located on a giant Mac Pro computer, which is tied to my piano keyboard.

Universal Studios in Chicago changed ownership, so I moved my office over to CRC, the other best place to record in town. I rented warehouse space on the second floor of their four-story building and built a six-room suite consisting of three offices, a lounge, another small midi studio, and a bedroom. CRC filled the void left by the demise of Universal.

Decades ago, the building that contained CRC housed Hugh Hefner's first offices. My desk sat on the very spot where Playboy photographed the famous Marilyn Monroe centerfold. Frank, the ancient little soul man who worked there for years, took me upstairs and showed me what was left of Hefner's old apartment. It contained every electrical gizmo available at the time, and Hugh installed a two-way mirror into the bathroom (No editorial comment here).

I set up a two-burner hot plate in the copy room and started cooking up an old recipe of smoked pork hocks and black-eyed peas. The pot simmered while I was writing, and as the fragrant aroma of my soul food wafted through the building, Frank knocked on my back door.

I opened it. He sniffed the air to make sure he was in the right place. "What's cooking?"

When I told him, he grinned and made me promise to save him a dish. I filled up a Tupperware container with my tasty creation, and delivered it to his office in the basement. A few days later, I asked him how his wife liked my concoction. He told me he refused to take any home, as he wanted it all for himself. Then, he hit me with one of the funniest questions, ever. "Where did a chubby little white boy like you learn how to cook like my mama?"

My little studio helped me crank out sophisticated demos without breaking the bank. Directly outside my back door, the space next to the freight elevator functioned as a vocal booth. We stopped singing when someone used the lift but, for the most part, it worked out extremely well. We were feeling the pinch of all the new producers flowing into the business, so my simple studio became a fiscal lifesaver.

The overhead was killing us and the stress wore us down. The number of producers in the business doubled; clients were becoming hard to land, and even harder to keep. On a positive note, we were close to several trendy restaurants, and a candlelit late-night jazz club: Milt Trenier's Show Lounge. I could take a break from writing, run around the block, and sing a couple of songs. Of course, we were only an eight-block cab ride from Louie's.

Chapter 49

So now I'm 47 and celebrating my twentieth year in the commercial business. The good news is that I made it. The bad news is that now I'm one of the "older" guys whom I competed with when I started out. Screen, the Chicago advertising magazine, published a cover story on my 20 years in the business:

"Bobby Whiteside looks back on his 20 years in the commercial music business." The story portrayed a reasonably accurate picture of that time frame.

Laura Mazurra wrote the cover article:

Bobby likes to say that he's probably worked on everything over the course of his 20 years in the business. And unlike folks who might like to claim the same, the fact is, he probably has...

At any rate, the commercial business grew slowly, but surely for him, and it was the start of something big for the dude with the Nehru jacket, the long hair, and the sandals... The rebel routine may have mellowed over the years, but Whiteside is still highly regarded as an innovator by the people he works with.

As far as musicians who have worked with him

are concerned, Whiteside is both a skilled musician and a hell of a nice guy...Whiteside acknowledges the good times and attributes his success to the people around him. He says, "We have fun at our sessions...that philosophy has kept us healthy. In this kind of work you can't overlook the human element. You don't build a business like this one without people...I could be a lot of other places than here right now, but I'm more interested in making timeless, rather than timely, music."

Whiteside's company has chosen to stay a boutique company, with him being the only writer. He feels it is necessary to be involved in the whole process to try to give each campaign his personal touch and aim for unique.

People ran a number of ads thanking me for my creative endeavors, and made some introspective comments that let me feel that I'd achieved success, without losing my humanity.

My friend, the accomplished film director Bob Ebel, said, "Some men dream of worthy accomplishments, while others stay awake and do them."

Bonnie Herman, my warm-hearted singer, stated, "He'll be 90 and still be in touch with what's on the radio. His best quality is his care with people. He's never uptight, tells jokes, and puts you at ease. He is an all-around sweetheart."

Hal Kome, one of my first and favorite clients

added, "He was ever-friendly. He would call you up at two in the morning and hum a tune he was working on for you. He assumed everybody was up."

Tommy Radtke, my drummer commented, "He's a perpetual optimist and is very consistent. He gives freedom to his musicians; he has a great openness to try things. He is also very loyal to musicians and the people close to him."

Finally, Bob Watson, another one of my favorite clients and a friend, summed it up. "Bobby is more of a songwriter than a jingle man...he's also a great ad man. He is sensitive to advertising problems, client problems, and money problems. He's always come through for me!"

I took out a full-page ad to thank Brenda.

For twenty years you've handled it all. Sessions all night, re-bids, demos re-done, tune competitions, minor victories, major losses, sessions all day, agency politics, sessions all night, phone calls missed, demos loved, demos hated, musicians missing, musicians found, singers hoarse, sessions cancelled, being apart, children growing, dinners cold, and trips not taken...And still you smile and give me strength.

I learned a lot in twenty years: I learned to ride the crest, handle rejection, to never lose the desire to be the best, and how important people were to my life and my business.

I learned that I could never have made it without Brenda at the helm as she, non-judgmentally, let me be free to create, follow my dreams, and make a contribution to a lot of people's lives. My world was full of beautiful talented people, who only needed the chance to show their creativity. Thankfully, due to what Bonnie Herman whispered to me years before, I learned to listen to myself and tried to keep my dialogue on a positive course.

The rewards were immense, the satisfaction unprecedented, and my love for music flourished as each day brought a new challenge or another musical adventure. I learned that humor trumps up-tightness, and being receptive to input from my talent, enriched my world with the creative ideas of many other people. I knew I'd made the right decision when I followed the advice of my theory teacher and my college advisor when they said, "Just go out and do what you do."

Some days I just look up and say, "Thank you!"

I've lived a storybook life and loved every minute.

However, now it was time to move on and face the realities of everyday living, understanding that there were mountains to climb and rivers to cross, and all would not necessarily end up well.

Such is life!

While shoving furniture around and moving boxes in the office, I felt dizzy. I sat down and almost passed out. I felt like my heart jumped out of my chest. I knew of a wonderful cardiologist named Robin Mitra at Presbyterian St. Luke's Hospital, and he graciously agreed to see me. I climbed in a cab and hurried over to his office. He checked me over and my heart seemed to be stable. He asked me what I was doing when I had the attack and I told him. He had me pick up a small chair and walk up and down the hall.

Bingo! My heart went out of rhythm again. He wanted me to go straight into the hospital, but I had to go back to the office first. The only way he let me go was if I promised that I'd reappear in his office in two hours. Deal!

I turned off the coffee machine, stuffed a few necessary items into a small gym bag, and returned to the hospital. The following day they did an angiogram. I lay flat on my back watching a camera go up into my heart thinking, "Holy crap! I'm gonna die."

They found a slight murmur, but needed to look further. They wheeled me across the hall and I watched a snake go into my heart again. Robin started to shock it in various places until he kicked it out of rhythm. I had atrial fibrillation—irregular heartbeat. Just what I needed!

Fortunately, Robin was able to give me a drug that kept my heart in rhythm most of the time, but it was a precursor of things to come.

Another day, another speed bump, but there were much bigger bumps to come.

Chapter 50

I knew I'd been blessed with an exceptional family. I loved my kids and they made me proud. They certainly participated in their fair share of mischief, but never hurt anyone, needed to be bailed out of jail, embarrassed us, or left a stain on what I hoped remained of our good family name.

There were car accidents caused by hot coffee spilled in a lap, an icy day, reaching for something in the glove compartment, and several other bad breaks of the game. Some years later, Wendy told me she had only received *one* speeding ticket...um...for going 120 in a 60.

Brenda and I returned home from Michigan one Sunday night, to find a couple of rented erotic tapes under the couch. We threw them away. We figured the boys would have to come up with $120 to pay Blockbuster for lost tapes, so that would be punishment enough. We never said a word and neither did they!

Brenda found beer hidden in Torrey's bottom drawer. She convinced him it was out of date and spoiled, so he and all his friends threw their stash of beer away. I told you she was smart!

They learned about racism and intolerant people in a surprising way. We hosted a boisterous Hawaiian luau in the backyard for all our clients and Universal Studios musicians. All my Chess guys came as well. One of my sons answered the phone.

It was the neighbor who lived behind us, who angrily stated, "How dare you have Negroes in your yard, in this neighborhood?"

My son called me to the phone and told me what the man said.

I took the receiver. "Excuse me?"

He reiterated his question and I said, "Oh, you mean the guys who are driving the Mercedes and the Jaguars?"

Then I blew up. I ended my one-sided tirade when I called him a "racist asshole," and hung up. My kids had experienced their first brush with overt racism and later learned it usually came from unexpected sources.

Mo Jennings, my Chess drummer and one of the most articulate people I knew, overheard a bit of the conversation. He cracked that big smile of his and said, in a phony accent, "Mr. Bobby, I t'ink ahl drive mah Mercedes round the block, knocks on do's, and asks yo' neighbors how many times a weeks dey collects da garbage cause I'ze 'thinking 'bout movin' in here." We shared a big laugh.

Then, I went back out in the yard, flashed my neighbor the finger (God knows he was looking), before continuing to enjoy our Hawaiian feast and a number of pineapple cocktails.

Terry, my youngest son was turning out to be a terrific, personable, good-looking guy. As he grew up, we shared hours of fun, and talked a lot about his life and his friends. I loved it, and I loved him. He could be serious. He could be a riot. He researched things before he made decisions, and thought things through before he jumped to conclusions... good traits to have in this day and age. Brenda and I believed that Terry could do anything he set his mind to. He worked part time, studied hard, and excelled as an athlete. We spent hours of quality time in Michigan, a great place for a family to bond.

The boys dated amazing girls: no tattoos or piercings (that we could see). The little "angels" slid neatly into family activities. They all congregated at the lake house, sometimes when we didn't even know about it. No big surprise there! I wouldn't have wasted that place either, if I were a kid again.

Terry graduated from college and began easing his way into sales, a perfect choice, as he liked people and they liked him. An exuberant extrovert, he handled himself well in business circles. We believed his life was headed in a good direction.

We never had the desire to tell any of our kids

what to be. The fact that they were content with whatever careers they chose, made us happy. All in all, raising our boys seemed easy as they kept themselves busy playing sports, and filling up their time with school and over-active social lives. Thank goodness for that.

Today, Terry has a lovely family, consisting of his pretty wife Tammy (our talented, caring, wonderful daughter-in-law), and our energetic, personable, athletic grandsons; Landon and Justin. We love spending time with them. It's never enough, but the moments we *do* get to share are precious.

Wendy went through a wild-child period, giving us several heart attacks. She finally settled down, finished school, learned the nightclub business, and helped a group of investors set up a new venue. Gifted with a sparkling personality, she made people feel comfortable and I expected she'd never have a boring life. *Unpredictable* is the word that comes to mind as I fondly think back on the good old days.

Brenda went to the dry cleaners one day and picked up a huge armful of clothes, plus a $167 cleaning bill. It turned out that when Wendy had to make a clothing decision, she'd pull something off the rack in her closet and try it on. If it wasn't her "choice" for the day, instead of hanging it back up, she'd throw it down the laundry chute.

Needless to say...

A pretty face and a warm heart contributed to her persona, and she could be sweet when I least expected it. She is independent as hell, and a joy to be around. We love her to bits. She had a passion for the lake and anything to do with water; being on it, swimming in it, or just gazing at it. Everyone should be blessed with the wonderful glow I felt from raising a little girl who rescued kittens. Getting to watch her grow up to be a strong, caring woman, who will always have her own special place in my heart, was unrivaled. Family is important to her. Even though we live in Tennessee, and she lives in Chicago, we talk almost every day. She's still our baby girl. I'm glad I didn't put her into foster care!

Tarrey, my middle son exuded calm. Mr. Easy had a quiet strength about him, appeared to be totally unassuming, and many of his accomplishments seemed effortless, even though we knew he worked hard! His wry sense of humor made him easy to like. He excelled at sports, and school never seemed to get him down, or stress him out. He played defensive cornerback in high school football, and I complained to the coach that he didn't see much action. The coach laughed and said the other coaches didn't dare throw a pass in his direction, as they knew he'd be all over it.

At one point, we thought Tarrey might have

been overly shy... until the phone call. At three a.m., New Year's Day, the phone rang. I rolled over and picked it up. In a woozy voice I croaked, "Yeah?"

An irate voice said, "This is (blank's) father. Do you know what your son Tarrey did tonight?"

I groaned. "Enlighten me."

"He did a strip down to his underwear on my pool table."

I was quiet for a minute then I said, "Thanks for calling. I'm glad he's finally coming out of his shell."

Click!

After that we never worried about Tarrey being too laid back again.

He worked at a major Anheuser Busch distributorship, as an inventory control manager. He orchestrated the flow of beer to the city of Chicago, making sure they received enough to take them through every holiday weekend—a complex job. He continues to handle everything well, in his own quiet competent way.

He just moved to Tennessee from Phoenix, so we'll be able to see a lot of him and his lovely wife, the delightful and artistic Selena, his high school sweetheart. He enjoys fishing from our dock and kicking back at the house. We love having both of them here.

Chapter 51

Torrey's childhood mirrored that of his brothers. He excelled in sports, and worked his way back from a debilitating knee injury to play varsity football in his senior year. He was a sworn perpetual cheerleader; a self-professed overachiever. It seemed necessary for him to work harder than his brothers to excel in school, and he found himself extremely frustrated when he fell short of his goals. He brightened our lives with his buoyant personality, his sense of humor, and made significant contributions to the daily functions of our family.

He graduated from college, a sharp guy and a snappy dresser, who ran in high gear all the time. When he entered a room, you knew it. If he were stuck in a crowded elevator, he probably would have organized a sing-along. He exuded energy, and exhibited a drive to succeed that caused him to put too much pressure on himself. If he didn't accomplish what he attempted immediately, he became extremely frustrated. We equated slowing him down with trying to stop an avalanche.

Brenda and I worried about the fact that he

didn't know how to relax. We encouraged him to spend time in Michigan and use the ski boat, swim laps, or even sit on the deck overlooking the lake; hoping he'd catch his breath and chill out a bit.

Through a friend's recommendation, Torrey landed a job selling advertising for a radio station, a very lucrative job if you worked at it. He attacked that job with a vengeance. Before long, he became one of the company's top salesmen, no surprise to anyone. He also worked out, and maintained a hefty social schedule. We noticed a change in him. Along with his usual energy, we began to notice him acting hyper and jumpy at times.

And here my friends, is where the wheels started to come off the tracks. We were worried about him, but he brushed us off and claimed he simply found his job exhilarating.

While hanging around with a group of high-power jet-set folks, a DJ from one of his radio station clients convinced him he would be twice as productive if he did a little cocaine.

Cursed with an addictive personality, he became hooked the first time he tried the drug. He and Terry lived together, and one night Terry found his brother coming down from a drug induced high. Extremely upset doesn't begin to cover how Brenda and I felt.

We couldn't help but ask ourselves, "why", as most parents do in that kind of situation.

Then, a mantle of guilt engulfed me. I blamed myself, and asked the same agonizing questions, over and over. "What did I miss? What did I do wrong? What could I have changed that would have prevented this? Have I been gone too much? What did he need that I didn't give him? Did I do everything I could?"

Finally, I had to face the terrible reality that he is 30 years old, and it was not my fault. People keep telling you it's not your fault. And even though for a long, long time I tried to accept that, but I never really *did*. Then, the only relevant question left was, "How do we help him?"

His company noticed his performance falling off and confronted him. He told them the truth, and they sent him to rehab on the North side of Chicago. He'd show up at the meeting in his nice clothes, and look around at the people in various stages of addiction and dereliction. What does someone say to their son when he looks at them and sadly states, "I'm in a room with all these street people and drug addicts."

There's no easy answer!

Torrey came out of rehab, and for a while he seemed to be doing okay. Then he had one slip, then two, and before too long, he relapsed completely. Fortunately, he made a decent salary and tucked some of it away. As you can imagine, cocaine is not a cheap habit. We tried to be there for him, but he was headed down a one-way street going in the wrong direction. He found himself helpless, and he admitted it.

Finally, the situation deteriorated to the point that we had to intervene again. We told him we were sending him to Florida to relax. We quietly arranged for him to spend several weeks in a recovery facility in Florida that had reportedly achieved a decent record of successful recoveries. A formidable friend went with him to deliver him to rehab and make sure he entered the program. He fought it, but finally relented and entered that program. We waited, hoping against hope that he would come back with a new determination to fight this terrible disease. He returned to Chicago angry with us, but this abated over time and he seemed to be doing better. However, over a period of time his work deteriorated, his company could not afford to keep him, and they were forced to let him go.

Brenda heard about a program in Milwaukee, geared toward helping young executives with problems that exhibited an impressive rate of recoveries. We took the last shot available and he went to Milwaukee.

We couldn't see him for the first month. Brenda went up to meet with him and his counselors as soon as she could. True to form, he'd been elected president of his rehab class, and seemed to be doing as well as we hoped he would.

Then, Brenda had a disheartening meeting. This facility did in-depth tests and studied his physical and mental makeup. They confirmed the fact that Torrey was born with an addictive personality. Unfortunately, the percentage of people with his genes who achieved complete recovery, turned out to be unusually small.

We waited for him to get through the program, and hoped he had finally hit rock bottom.

He returned to Chicago and pursued marketing assignments out of our office. His daily outpatient rehab meetings were at Northwestern Hospital, six blocks from the office. He could easily walk over to see his group every day.

It was hard to tell how he was holding up. He and Brenda shared some heart-to-heart talks. He told her how discouraged and disappointed he had become with himself, and the guilt he harbored about letting his family down. We tried to stay strong and supportive to prop him up, but it became an overwhelming task. The stress was unbearable!

We suspected he'd started slipping again. We were devastated when we found out he used coke one night before a meeting. On the following day, he visited a dealer a block from the office, and did coke again to get up the nerve to tell his friends in rehab he relapsed. We were hanging on by a thread.

After a couple of months and many interviews, another radio station decided to take a chance on him. They gave him a job, but put him on probation. He seemed to be temporarily in charge of his life, but we were unquestionably nervous, as he would be returning back to his old circle of yuppie overachievers, where all of the trouble started. We hoped he might make it this time and that he was doing better.

The Friday before he was scheduled to start his new job, Brenda and I headed for the lake house to spend the weekend. Torrey agreed to drive up and join us after he ran a few errands. Brenda and I arrived at the lake house, shared a glass of wine, and waited for our son to show up to join us for dinner. It grew later and later. No Torrey!

Finally at midnight, we phoned some of his friends, but no one had seen or heard from him. We called the police. Of course, they said he had to be missing for 48 hours before they could list him as a missing person, but at that time, there were no accidents reported with the car's make or license number. So we waited... and waited. Nothing!

Monday morning, Torrey's new boss called and said he hadn't shown up for his first meeting. He was MIA. Then, the police called. They had found his car under a viaduct in the middle of Lake

Shore Drive. The door sat wide open and the keys were in the ignition. Torrey's briefcase and his wallet sat on the front sea, and his winter jacket lay on the floor.

They suspected he might have been involved in a car chase as his vehicle was heavily damaged. There were deep dents all over the fenders, filled with traces of paint that looked like the paint on the construction barrels under the overpass.

The police speculated that he exited the car, crossed Lake Shore Drive, walked behind the convention center, McCormick Place, and ended up in Lake Michigan.

We were crushed.

Then the waiting began. Ron Campo, our Darien Police detective, and his brother Mike were unbelievable. They put out a BOLO, called all the sheriffs' departments and police precincts around us, checked every missing person list, and worked the phones tirelessly.

This went on for weeks. Every Monday I checked missing persons hotlines and police stations in the area. At this point, a rumor surfaced that he might have been a victim of foul play. To this day we still hear an occasional murmur about that.

We did the best we could to hold the business and each other together, but we were losing the battle. Christmas without Torrey wasn't merry. The kids were filled with sadness, anger, and frustration from not knowing anything, and none of us understood why and how this cataclysmic tragedy happened.

January, the greyest month I'd ever seen, passed slowly. The dark clouds that filled the sky spilled down into my heart, and I wondered if the sun would ever shine again. Sometimes, you're holding on to hope so tightly that your mind fails to accept the truth, and you find yourself in a self-inflicted exile from a state of reality. Underneath it all we knew that nothing would ever be the same again.

Then, the phone rang. The police found our son. Lake Michigan currents carried him 120 miles across the lake, and he washed up on the shore in Muskegon, Michigan. They were able to identify him by the watch on his wrist, and our last little spark of hope blew out.

We held a closed casket funeral. I don't remember who was there, or anything about the service. We were all in shock. I felt like an empty shell, lost in a fog, and emotionally destroyed.

A small urn filled with his ashes was interred at the same Chicago cemetery where Brenda's parents lie at rest. There's a quiet bench next to his resting place where we can reminisce about the good days and how much we loved him.

I almost didn't put this chapter of our lives in this book, but there are so many people who have lived in the same nightmare that we did. We all relive the tragedy over and over again, and suffer from the horrible aftermath that follows a loss due to addiction. I want you to know, you are not alone. My most fervent wish is that somehow, somewhere, someday, someone will read our story about the crushing consequences and the family devastation that follows drug addiction. If I can help just one person say "No" to drugs, it will be worth the pain I went through writing this chapter.

Losing Torrey, and the circumstances that followed, led me to make some major decisions to help me get back on my emotional feet. There is never a happily ever after, once you have lived through something this horrible. There can be an "after," but it's hard to forget "before," and those wasted minutes, hours and years are gone forever.

Chapter 52

Business became a real struggle. The younger guys started to assert themselves, and some of my old clients began to look for newer, younger, "flavor of the month" music suppliers. Every totem pole has a top and a bottom. I started at the bottom and reached the top, but the time had come for me to slide back down. Brenda spent most of her time in Michigan, and I retreated into the insular space of my small apartment.

My dad's deteriorating health caused him to be in and out of the hospital, when he wasn't living at a nice assisted living facility in Evanston. He loved the King Home, had lots of friends, and participated in bridge tournaments and geriatric aerobics. My dad seemed as strong willed as ever. He had his hip replaced at 80 so he could play golf, and still successfully played the stock market at 90, yet I could sense him slipping. He had trouble swallowing his food and it made him miserable.

On one of his last stays in the hospital, I went to see him. He climbed out of bed and stood there with his little butt hanging out of his gown. I waited for five minutes then asked him, "Dad, do you want to go to the bathroom, or do you want to get back into bed?"

He didn't answer me immediately but then he turned to me, gave me a scathing look and said, "When I make up my damned mind, I'll let you know."

I felt he was still okay.

I picked up an assignment that required me to go to Nashville, so I climbed on a plane and headed south to do my session. In the middle of recording, the phone rang. I took a call from my sister, telling me dad passed away. The doctor went into his hospital room, examined him, and said he could be released to go back to the King Home. My dad looked at him and said, "Yup! Today's the day I go home!"

The doc left the room to sign Dad's discharge orders and realized he'd forgotten his pen. He walked back to the hospital room to find Dad had passed away sitting in his chair.

That's one of the things I always loved about my father. Right up to the end he still called the shots. He was sick of being sick, and tired of being tired. He'd lived without my mother for 30 years, and I think he simply decided it was time to go see her.

Double whammy! Things had become as bad as they could get. My nerves were shot, the overhead was killing me, and there was no end in sight.

Then, my friend Tom Hall called and gave me another package of Sears spots. Talk about a lifeline! I did Sears commercials till I saw "Sears" in my sleep. I finished the package, paid off the bills, and decided to wrap it up. I felt like all the air had gone out of my life and it was time to do something different.

I always wanted to be "just a songwriter." I turned down writing opportunities in New York and LA to stay in the stable confines of commercial production in Chicago. It enabled me to make a good living, raise our family, and pay the bills on a regular basis.

Now the business was shot, I had two too many people missing from my life, the kids had moved out, and "home" was knocked down to its foundation. I had to move on and start over. So, I told Brenda and the kids that I was moving to Nashville. Visions of Torrey haunted me and this little verse was embedded on my soul forever.

There's pain so deep, you never speak about it,
That no one else will ever get to see.
Someone you lost, a loved one gone forever,
Still lives on in your heart, and time will never set you free.

Chapter 53

I made several trips to Nashville to look for a place to live. If at all possible, I hoped to find a place on a body of water. I looked for houses on Old Hickory and Percy Priest, the two big lakes in the vicinity of Nashville. I found the lake homes for sale to be exorbitantly expensive, so I narrowed my search parameters to accommodate my economic constraints.

I began to look for a place on the Cumberland River, to no avail, and my frustration grew every day. Then, my luck changed. Following the path of the river, I drove through a cozy neighborhood in Madison, only seven miles north of town. I spotted a two-level brick home on an acre of land. Musty air assaulted my senses when the realtor let me in to view it.

It had obviously been empty for a while. I grimaced as I scrutinized the dingy fluorescent green shag carpeting in the living room, ugly black kitchen counters, foggy glass windows facing the river, and rooms covered with horrendous, antiquated flocked crimson and pink wallpaper. The house itself seemed perfect. It contained three bedrooms and a sizable living room. I was pleasantly surprised when I discovered an in-law apartment on the lower level that I could eventually convert into a studio. The place seemed to be in good shape in general. I smiled when I spotted a small dock gently bobbing up and down on the river.

Brenda flew down to check it out for me. She had become a successful real estate agent in Michigan, and developed a great eye for evaluating properties. She suggested I throw in a low-ball bid since the house had been on the market for two years. I did and after the owner finished laughing, he threw me back a counter offer that I could handle, providing I took the house "as is."

Brenda said, "Go for it!"

I took a leap of faith and became the owner of a house on the Cumberland River. The home inspection went smoothly. The inspector found one or two small issues, but nothing serious.

I traveled back to Chicago and gathered up my belongings. I took the furniture from the apartment, some items from the Darien house, and pulled all my family's antiques out of storage, including my parents' 150-year old mahogany dining room set. One of Brenda's construction crews drove the rental truck down to Nashville, as they were going to stay with me for several weeks to do some remodeling. (#1 priority... tear up fluorescent green carpeting.)

I owned a hideous, uncomfortable little red Mazda B2000 truck. I loaded the rest of my small possessions in a U-Haul and set off for the South. Driving my underpowered truck, sitting in seats harder than wooden church pews, I found it hard to reach 55 mph pulling that damn trailer.

Somewhere in Kentucky, I needed to pause for a bathroom break, so I pulled off at an exit to find myself on a parkway. The first highway sign I found told me I had to drive 22 miles to turn around. Due to the amount of traffic, I couldn't stop when I saw a convenient bush, so I had to suffer for 44 miles before I could stop squeezing my legs together. I thought I'd never be able to straighten my back again, and cussed everything from the truck, to the highways, to the whole state of Kentucky!

A month before I left, a doctor removed a cataract from my left eye. It hadn't completely healed. Consequently, I had a hard time reading the complex highway signs. I missed my exit to Madison and ended up downtown.

Let me explain the highway system in Nashville. The main highways run in a big circle around the heart of the city, and since the signs were blurry, I ended up circling Nashville three times. I finally passed one sign I could read, and headed in the right direction, back to Madison.

I ended up asking directions from two little old ladies who took one look at me and figured I was an idiot from the North. "Just follow us, sweetie. We'll lead you there." It was a wonderful first taste of that famous Southern hospitality, welcoming one grateful Yankee.

Donnie, my favorite carpenter, and his laconic pal Dick, the electrician, waited for me at the house. They nodded hello and continued to polish off their second case of beer. I made a martini in a soup bowl and joined them, and we were off on the first reconstruction phase.

In the morning I went out to take care of the most important thing that you need, to become an authentic *Nashvillian*. I needed to buy the mandatory pair of cowboy boots so I looked up "footwear" in the yellow pages. They listed a bulging boot corral at a major shopping center in the area, so I carefully navigated up the road until I reached the giant complex. I circled it twice, but didn't have a clue as to where to enter the mall.

I spied a surly-looking motorcycle cop, pulled up beside him, and asked if he could tell me the location of the Boot Corral. This churlish guy looked like he appeared straight from central casting for *Smokey and the Bandit*. He sweated bullets, looked at least 30 pounds overweight, wore big wrap-around blue reflective sunglasses, and gave me an arrogant look as he chewed on a toothpick.

He stared at me for a moment then said, "Y'all

go through that breezeway, take a right and go down a piece."

"Um...can I ask you a question?"

"Sure, boy."

"What's a breezeway, and how far is a piece?"

His face turned the color of a purple plum and he said (he really did), "Are you funnin' me boy?"

I could tell he was bent out of shape, so I hastily replied, "No, sir! I just moved here from Chicago and I don't know what a breezeway is. and I don't know how far a piece is."

He glowered at me over his toothpick. "That there arch over there is a breezeway and when you take a right and get to that there boot place, you'll know how far a piece is."

Then he turned his back on me, revved up his Harley, peeled out leaving a smoking strip of rubber on the asphalt, and blasted out of the parking lot in a cloud of blue smoke and bad attitude. I was relieved he didn't shoot me. Got some real nice boots, though!

Buddy Killen, a Nashville legend, started out as a bass player at the Grand Ole Opry. He paid an inordinate amount of dues, and ended up owning Tree Music, one of the biggest publishing companies in town. He sold it for a small fortune, built the Sound Shop recording studio, and began developing a massive enterprise that included new publishing and production companies.

I'd known Buddy for years, and we had discussed the possibility of starting a business together. His new publishing company boasted 14 staff songwriters, and each one of them wrote new songs every week. He tied up the Sound Shop to do all their demos, blocking out the many name artists who wanted to record there.

We talked about putting my little studio in his building. The overall plan: I'd screen the freshly written songs, and record rough demos in my compact studio. Then, we'd select the *best* songs in the batch, and take them into the Sound Shop for fully produced sessions one day a week. This opened up studio time for major acts to record their albums. We also discussed setting up a company to broker country stars to advertisers, a natural fit for me.

As many sensible plans do, this one fell apart right after I arrived in Nashville. Buddy left to go on a book-signing tour, and his wife decided to allocate the designated studio space for another purpose.

So, I installed it on the lower level of my house by converting the in-law apartment to an all-purpose control room. I partitioned off one side of the room with a soundproof picture window wall to create a separate vocal booth. The studio ended up somewhat unsophisticated, but effective and functional.

I began to "countrify" some of the pop songs I

recorded in Chicago by adding steel guitars and country singers, making my songs a bit more attractive to Nashville record producers. It bought me time to begin creating authentic country songs, with Nashville writers.

In my quest to expose myself to as much country music as possible, I discovered Douglas Corner, a nightclub that catered to songwriters. I started to hang out there four or five nights a week. Mervin Louque, the first friend I made in Nashville, owned the club.

A staple of the Nashville songwriters' community for a long time, Douglas Corner remained a favored music spot where many artists like Garth Brooks, Alan Jackson, Blake Shelton, and Tricia Yearwood performed at the inception of their careers. Mervin created a venue for artists to showcase their new material, debut their CDs, and participate in "writers-in-the-round." On those nights, four songwriters sat in a circle and traded songs for a couple of hours. There was also an "open mic" night that gave unknown songwriters a platform to perform their songs and gauge audience reactions. I found it to be a perfect place to network, and took advantage of that.

Over the years, Mervin attained a legendary status with musicians and artists. He excelled as a sound engineer, recording shows for all the networks and the record labels. He recorded music on tours for The Rolling Stones, Journey, The Beach Boys, Joe Cocker, David Bowie, Loretta Lynn, and too many more acts to mention. Mervin purchased the huge semi-trailer that contained the mobile studio and parked it behind the club. He wired it in, so he could record live shows, and shoot videos at the same time. Awesome setup!

A prolific songwriter, Mervin penned dozens of memorable tunes. He sang them in his club and strummed guitar like he'd been doing it for years, which he had.

In addition to being one of the most respected best liked music men in Nashville, Mervin handled his stature in the community with humility, and never lost the desire to lend a helping hand to young artists that simply needed to be heard. He introduced me to countless writers and musicians, and opened many doors for me.

Mervin and his wife, the lovely and spiritual actress Jennifer O'Neill, who starred in the tender coming of age movie, *The Summer of 42,* are treasured close friends. Jennifer continues to pursue acting roles when time permits, but her focus has been on her ministry named Hope and Healing at Hillenglade, that effectively helps veterans deal with their traumas through the process of equine therapy. She delivers passionate speeches to many pro-life organizations around the country, and her message resonates with both men and women. As a powerful voice for causes she believes in, her words of inspiration have touched the hearts of many.

The move to Nashville seemed to be a good fit for me. I loved the people, and found the South a friendly place to live. People said, "Thank you," were gracious enough to let you into a line of cars in crowded traffic, and smiled a lot. That special Southern hospitality "thang" was wonderful.

Chapter 54

So what is life without a few complications? Stephanie (Tom Anthony's wife) flew in to sing on a small project for one of my Chicago singers named Jeannie Filip. We were recording and I didn't feel well. I felt a pain in my side that became shattering. Jeannie and Steph loaded me into the car and drove me to a minor-league neighborhood hospital. Pain hit me in terrifying waves.

This hospital, a horrible excuse for a medical facility, refused to give me anything to abate the pain, so I lay in a fog of agony for five hours; while they ran around in circles trying to diagnose my problem. They finally administered a whopper of a pain pill and informed me they called in a surgeon.

He arrived disheveled, dressed in a shabby suit, scruffy as hell, and drunk as a skunk. His breath would have flamed a barbecue grill. He said, "We found a tumor as big as an iceberg in your left kidney, so I'll come in tomorrow and jerk that sucker out."

His reassuring smile was not!

Again, all I could think was, "Holy crap! I'm gonna' die."

I panicked for a minute and then the Lord turned on a light bulb. I called Linda, Buddy Killen's assistant. I figured someone of Buddy's stature had to go to the best doctors in town, and I was right! She calmed me down with her soothing Southern accent.

"Don't you worry, sweetie, I'll take care of everything."

Arriving in record time, an ambulance picked me up and took me downtown to Baptist Central, thankfully a major-league health facility. They scheduled me for surgery the following morning, with two brilliant doctors, Dr. Barnette and Dr. Mark Flora. Relief doesn't come close to how I felt!

I woke up to see Dr. Barnette staring at me over a clipboard. He said he had good news and bad news. The bad news: he removed a cancerous tumor the size of a baseball that had been festering in my left kidney. The good news: they were able to remove it completely and I wouldn't have to do any chemo. Mixed blessings!

After two days I could walk a few steps, and after five days they sent me home. Getting around was a bitch. I fought my way through the pain, determined to tough it out and survive.

Steph and Jeannie returned to their respective towns, but I made some wonderful new friends who came to stay with me. When people I didn't know heard a musician was in trouble, many of them called to offer help.

Then came the ice storm, the worst calamity to hit Tennessee in 50 years. The city predicted the power would be out for at least a week. The temperature dropped like a stone. The house came with an electric stove, so no heat there, and I couldn't get the gas fireplace to work. I racked my brain, trying to figure out how to stay warm; and how to keep my food from spoiling.

Thom Gillingham, my concerned next door neighbor, knocked on my door. "Bundle up. I'm taking you to Sam's Club."

This was not an easy chore for a wobbly guy who could barely take eight consecutive steps, but I popped a pain pill and Thom loaded me carefully into his van. He showed me his corporate membership card that allowed us admittance to the store one hour before it officially opened.

We both bought generators and several gas cans. We stopped, filled up the five-gallon red plastic containers; then Thom and another good neighbor hauled my heavy generator onto my front porch, poured fuel in it and started it up.

I had scads of extension cords left over from past Christmas light displays. My friends strung them all over the house, enabling me to run a small heater and several small appliances. They blanketed off the other rooms to preserve the small amount of warmth it generated, and I curled up under five or six woolen robes. The microwave functioned, enabling me to heat food. The hardest part turned out to be crawling downstairs to plug in the iceboxes. Ten hours later, I had to switch the power to the ones upstairs. The generator did not produce enough juice to run them both at the same time.

Let me tell you about trying to go down those stairs six days after surgery. Better yet, maybe not. Just think *excruciating*; walking five miles on a broken leg. A Good Samaritan came to the house every eight hours to gas up the generator, and Thom changed the oil every day. I knew if I could make it through this, I could make it through anything. If it had not been for my volunteer group, I would have been discovered in February, frozen stiff in my chair with a copy of *Guns and Ammo* in my lap.

Every tree in the neighborhood broke in half, power lines lay on the ground, and Nashville became a paralyzed horrendous mess. A half-inch sheet of ice covered everything. Winter wonderland, my ass! I could open the backdoor and hear the electrical transformers exploding. Finally, the power came back on after being out for the predicted week. I took a deep breath and thanked my lucky stars for the special people who came to save me, and the fact that the heat was finally working.

It took me a year to recover fully. Some days I felt okay, but on others, I couldn't move an inch. It put a crimp in my quest for a new career, but thankfully it didn't take much energy to write songs.

Back on my feet, I set metaphorical fire to the Mazda truck, and spent 5 hours negotiating with a "good ol' country boy" for a Ford Ranger. I was set: cowboy boots and a truck. Sounds like one of those boring country songs I refused to write! I geared up for my second assault on Music Row.

The quality of my writing partners improved, and I finally started to get the gist of formulating country music. We recorded extremely proficient, professional-sounding demos, and I felt ready to set up some meetings. I heeded the warning about Nashville. First meetings were easy to get, but second meetings depended on the success of the first one. I made it a point not to waste people's time with bad songs and frivolous conversation.

I met with Barry Beckett, one of the legendary Memphis session players, who needed songs for a Spanish artist. I thought I had a couple that might work for him. I sat with Barry and played him my two songs. He liked them, but they weren't right for his artist.

I said, "Okay, thanks for seeing me."

"Huh? You gonna leave? Everybody that comes in here wants to schmooze me and play me a lot of crap."

"That's all I have for your artist."

"Well, I'll be damned. Sit down and tell me

about yourself, and play me some more of your music."

We shared a cordial visit and he liked several of my songs. He told me I could call him anytime, an affirmation of the advice I'd been given, and a pattern I tried to follow most of the time.

As a producer, I experienced my own meetings with writers who kept saying, "Oh, wait. I want you to hear one more," after they flamed out on the first two. I hated everything else they were playing and didn't much like *them* either. So I could relate.

I started performing in nightclubs in some of the writer's rounds; Douglas Corner, the Bluebird, the Sutler, and many of the other landmark clubs that catered to songwriters. I loved performing and it brought back fond memories of the years I played in the folk clubs in Greenwich Village.

Tom Anthony and I formed a jingle company named The Cumberland River Gang. We called the studio "The Hideout." We offered to produce tracks with A-list musicians and singers from New York and Nashville, and found clients who loved the concept. We created a double-edged sword; we submitted demo tracks from both Nashville and New York and our clients could choose the track they liked the best, or both of them. I loved working with Tommy and the revenue helped me pay those pesky bills.

In addition, I did some composing and production for a man who started a custom jingle company that targeted small markets and local advertisers. He traveled to a mid-sized town, met with car dealers, stores, restaurants and so on; and sold them on the concept of doing an original radio commercial at a budget price. Then, he'd assign me four or five, and I'd create campaigns for these small businesses. I didn't make a lot of money, but doing several at a time made it worthwhile, and using my own studio to do the engineering cut down my overhead.

I couldn't get Brenda off my mind even though we lived 500 miles apart. We talked on the phone every day. Despite our trials and tribulations, I never stopped loving her. Occasionally, she came to Nashville to visit. One night, we engaged in a long, serious conversation over a glass of wine down by the river, and both of us admitted how much we missed each other. She agreed to move south for a year, to see if the sparks we felt could be fanned into a full flame again. Without her, life hadn't been the same, so I was bound and determined to get it right this time. To make a long story short, *we did*, and this year we'll celebrate over 50 years together.

She kept the Michigan house for a while, and we shared it with some of our new Nashville friends. We spent afternoons on the front patio writing songs, basking in the sun, and listening to the tranquilizing sounds of Lake Michigan. That beautiful home will always have a special place in my heart.

A charter boat captain brought my 32-foot cabin cruiser down from Chicago after navigating through a long chain of connecting rivers, and I rented a boat slip in Old Hickory, a marina near the house. The lake was treacherous with many dangerous shallow spots. If I ran aground, it damaged the propellers to the tune of $1,500. I hated to sell my gleaming fishing machine, but I traded it for an 80-foot houseboat, an old metal bucket that wouldn't hang up in shallow water. The first thing Brenda did? *Redecorate!* I named it *All Tied Up*. We only took it on one excursion, and an engine locked up. So it remained moored to the weather worn dock, our little cabin on the water.

We bought a sparkling blue 21-foot long Baja speedboat that we used to cruise around the lake. We camped out on the houseboat almost every weekend fishing, reading, and barbecuing on the back deck. Being in this peaceful environment, I often found the inspiration to create lyrics for eloquent songs. Our restful getaway waited for us only 15 minutes from the house, and we took full advantage of it.

Chapter 55

An amiable fellow from Houston reached out to me. His father, the founder of an unusually populous church, asked me to write an elegant theme song to use in inspirational films; and to enhance their promotional commercials. The church offered me a generous budget. He requested I use a full orchestra and choir on the tracks, and create a variety of instrumental versions.

Satisfied with my musical idea, he presented it to his dad and the church elders. They enthusiastically approved and we went into full production. He flew into town to supervise the sessions. We recorded a portion of the music at my studio and completed it at several major facilities downtown. He spent considerable time at the house, and Brenda and I thoroughly enjoyed his company. We felt the feeling was mutual.

He returned to Houston with the music, and his father and the church elders were deeply moved by the song. Not too long after that, his father suddenly passed away. The massive congregation lost its spiritual leader, and no guiding hand remained to take the wheel. Guest preachers stepped in, but that proved unsustainable.

One day he asked his mother, "Who is preaching tonight?"

"You are."

He objected profusely and told her that a media director did not equate to a preacher. His mother told him they had no other speaker for that night and God would show him the way. And Joel Osteen performed his first sermon that night. Today, Lakewood Church is now televised from a huge amphitheater filled with thousands of loyal worshippers.

I found Joel to be a humble man. Although I've never been a big fan of televangelists, I believe that Joel is a remarkable human being. Watching him develop into the relevant messenger he is today taught me to never underestimate a media director. Every time I listen to one of his sermons, I find myself yearning to be a better person.

I accomplished as much as I could with my small studio. My need for a better sounding studio convinced me to bite the bullet and construct a bigger, more sophisticated control room. I received substantial help from a couple of studio techs, and the new studio became a reality. We integrated a computer into the setup of the newly improved "Hideout" that enabled me to do more complex projects. The new equipment we installed ensured that the music would be better sonically, and I could produce a variety of polished tracks that ranged from country to orchestral. Our demos were on par with many of the bigger studios in town.

My friend Jimmy Nichols, a brilliant keyboard player, contacted me. While creating his signature keyboard tracks for a record producer, he met a new artist named Mindy McCready, who had recently arrived in town. Jimmy guaranteed me she possessed a commercially appealing country voice. He asked me if I had any work for her, a timely request, as I knew that several of my Chicago pop songs were in need of a country lead singer. I liked her sound and looked forward to working with her.

Mindy, an attractive blonde-haired country chanteuse, arrived at the studio, listened to the songs, and frowned. I asked her what the problem was, and it seemed she didn't care for the songs. Great start, huh? I questioned her as to why she didn't like the songs, and she said they weren't country. I reminded her that I hired her to help me change that, and the session went downhill from there.

She sang admirable vocals, but the whole afternoon remained uncomfortable. I figured that would probably be the last I'd ever see of Mindy McCready. Boy, was I wrong! We'll get to that in a minute.

Brenda slowly adapted to the South and loved the milder winter weather. I told her if she wanted to see chaos, wait until it snowed. Being from the North, it's incomprehensible that anyone doesn't know how to drive in inclement weather, but one day half an inch of the white stuff blanketed Nashville. On her bumper-to-bumper trip home from downtown, the traffic guy came on the radio and said, "Well, I hope you have some time 'cause I have 124 wrecks to report."

Then, our friends and neighbors cleaned out the grocery stores and the city closed the schools, all because of a miniscule amount of snow. We laughed about that for months, and Brenda added "wreck" to her expanding Southern vocabulary.

With Brenda's vast experience, she had no problem finding a position in an office, and I continued on my quest for another hit record.

Chapter 56

I'd been archiving song title lists for years. If I heard a great line in a movie, or read one in a book, I added it to a title list. Over a long span of time, I accumulated pages and pages of song titles. One of the biggest time-wasters at a writing session seemed to be figuring out what to write about. By perusing my lists, we could quickly settle on a subject to start with, and dive right into creating the song.

The titles and ideas came from everywhere. Before I left Chicago, I dropped into a dimly lit hotel bar around the corner from the studio, for a nightcap. The bartender, a free spirited blonde Scandinavian beauty, lamented her life.

"So I had a date with this gorgeous guy, took him back to my place, had my way with him, and kicked him out. Now all he does is call me, send me flowers and gifts, and all I wanted was a date. What's the matter with him? Guys do it all the time."

I borrowed a pen from the bar back, wrote that line down on a damp cocktail napkin, returned to my apartment, and transferred it to my "best song title" list. I sketched out a rough idea, then I put it aside to address at a later date.

Tom Long, the creative director at Balmer Music, suggested that I meet with a writer named Kim Tribble. Kim and I sat in Tom's office, listened to samples of each other's music and scheduled a date to write. Kim, a song machine, came up with a tune every time he picked up his guitar. We convened in a comfortable writer's room and started to search for something to write about. I pulled out my title list and "Guys Do It" jumped off the page.

Kim dove off the musical deep end and we had the framework for our project in nothing flat! We made a list of all the things guys do that aggravate women, and the song almost wrote itself. We recorded a demo and the final product exceeded everything we hoped for.

Five different people presented the song at the weekly A&R meeting (artist and repertoire) at RCA. Joe Galante, president of the company, believed it could be a smash hit... for *Mindy McCready*. Oh crap!

She didn't like the song, didn't want to record it, and probably *really* hated it when she found out I was one of the writers. RCA brought her in from her tour and insisted she do the song. She recorded under duress, and it turned out to be her only #1 record. That's why artists should heed the advice of their producers and label executives.

She didn't attend the #1 party, but Kim and I have a nice picture holding our ASCAP #1 certificate, standing by a life-size cardboard cut-out of Mindy.

A sad footnote to the story: Mindy, a troubled young woman, ended up taking her own life cutting short a fairy tale success story. Having that song on my resume helped my career immensely, and I owe her a debt of gratitude. I've seen too many artists' careers derailed by the immense pressures and stress of the industry, and I'm sorry she was one of them. Many people miss her. RIP Mindy.

Here are the lyrics to "Guys Do It All The Time," by Bobby Whiteside and Kim Tribble.

Got in this morning at 4 a.m.
You're as mad as you can be
Well, I was drinking and talking and you know
how that goes
Time just slipped away from me
By the time I knew what time it was
It was too late to call home
Stop carrying on, acting like a child
I wasn't doing anything wrong

Guys do it all the time
And you expect us to understand
When the shoe's on the other foot
You know that's when it hits the fan

Get over it, honey, life's a two way street
Or you won't be a man of mine
So I had some beers with the girls last night
Guys do it all the time

I know I left my clothes all over the place
And I took your twenty bucks
No, I didn't get the front yard cut
'Cause I had to wash my truck
Will you bring me a cold one, baby
Turn on the TV
We'll talk about this later
There's a ball game I wanna' see

Guys do it all the time
And you expect us to understand
When the shoe's on the other foot
You know that's when it hits the fan
Get over it, honey, life's a two way street
Or you won't be a man of mine
So I had some beers with the girls last night
Guys do it all the time

You look like you just took
A long look in the mirror
Tell me baby if things don't look
A whole lot clearer

Get over it, honey, life's a two way street
Or you won't be a man of mine

So I had some beers with the girls last night
Guys do it all the time

You can find the video on YouTube.

Kim and I tried to do some of our own promotion, but we also hired one of Garth Brooks' PR people, and she booked us for several radio station and magazine interviews. She wanted me to pose in drag, for a promo picture. That was not only a "No," it was a "HELL NO!" It seems no one figured out that two guys wrote this song. Bobby and Kim? Who would have thought?

Once we realized this, we ran with it. We conducted a radio interview in high soprano voices, answered questions, dispensed boyfriend advice, and finally at the end of the show announced that we were really guys. The phone lines lit up. So did record sales! Finally, after a laborious decade, I received another platinum record!

Kim and I also wrote a song called "Don't Ever Sell Your Saddle." Randy Travis recorded a tasteful version of our ballad and placed it on his *Inspirational Journey* CD. The song was also featured in an episode of the TV show, "Touched by An Angel."

In Nashville, I booked a writing appointment, wrote for several hours, then ran on to work with the next writer. At times I'd get excited about a song, but we'd run out of time and the next opportunity to write with that writer would be in three weeks. Of course, when we reconvened the vibe would be different, and I found it difficult to get back into the rhythm we were in at the original writing session. When I started writing a song, I wanted to finish it.

I sat down one day and took a comprehensive look at my production and writing log. I had thirty songs started, and my appointments to compete them were spread out over the next two months.

I listened to all the songs, kept ten of them, and made up my mind that I wouldn't write more than three times a week. In the past, when I'd found myself rushing to complete a song, I had never been happy with the finished product. In retrospect I thought, "If I'd only taken a little more time on that verse..."

Writers like Kim Tribble could write two or three great songs in a day. I just wasn't put together that way. I had no deadlines, and nowhere I had to be. So I started spending more hours on each song, taking however long it took to complete it to my satisfaction.

I kept my nose buried in technical manuals, trying to assimilate the thousands of pieces of information on new studio recording engineering techniques. The music computers available at the time were producing many new and improved programs of orchestral sounds that enhanced the tracks in surprising new ways.

The songwriting populace threw innumerable industry parties, and hung out at a few select watering holes. At the end of the day I'd stop by a restaurant/bar named Sammi B's, that was always jam-packed full of writers and artists. It became my Nashville Louie's. By that time, I'd become acquainted with many of the writers and publishers in town, so every time I dropped in I'd see a familiar face or two.

One afternoon, I sat at the bar next to an enigmatic older white-haired gentleman who had the unmistakable demeanor of country aristocracy. We exchanged pleasantries and ended up discussing life, music, and the state of the world, ad infinitum. He turned out to be Harlan Howard, one of the most famous songwriters in history. He wrote hundreds of songs over 6 decades, and had so many hit records they needed to buy a storage building for all his awards.

I shared many indelible thought-provoking conversations with Harlan. We talked about writing a song, but never got around to it which is one of my biggest regrets. Harlan was a philosopher, a historian, and one of the most intelligent, interesting men I had the pleasure of meeting in the business. I never knew whom I'd end up sitting next to at Sami B's.

I continued to perform occasionally at different clubs, and Brenda and I often went out to hear other writers and groups. Once in a while, I'd find a talented singer I could use on a demo, or a new writer I wanted to pair up with. Nashville moved at its own easy pace, a far cry from the chaotic pressure we faced during the Chicago years.

Chapter 57

Dr. Mark Flora, my surgeon, told me I needed to get a regular doctor. He recommended a young MD he thought I'd really like who was starting to build a new practice. He introduced me to Dr. Stephen May. As I went to see Steve for one issue or another, we realized we had a lot in common. He played drums, loved music, liked to shoot, and I got him hooked on sushi. It doesn't get any better than that. Brenda and I liked Beth, Steve's attractive wife, the first time we met her. She was funny, kind, and we felt like we'd known her for years. When she smiled she filled the room with joy, and they made a perfect couple.

It was the beginning of a remarkable friendship. Steve and Beth married young. He started as a respiratory therapist and she worked as a trained nurse. He enrolled in medical school and they were blessed with two exceptional children. They probably had some tough financial years, but it all worked out for the best.

We saw a lot of each other and Steve became the little brother I always wished I had. When I hit rough medical times, it was uplifting to have Steve at my side, both as my friend, and my doctor. This treasured friendship has lasted for years.

I found Steve to be a fantastic doctor and started recommending him to our friends, who recommended him to their friends, etc. Being such a capable, caring doctor he now has hordes of patients from the entertainment industry. We need to present him with his own gold record, for being the #1 "Doc" to a close-knit group of seasoned professionals, who all have great respect for *his* talent.

Brenda and I returned from a trip. She stood by the kitchen sink and said,

"Boy, that was weird."

I asked her what happened. She said everything she looked at was pixilated and chopped into little pieces, but it only lasted for a short period of time. Despite her objections, I called Steve. He advised me to take her to the emergency room. She vigorously protested and told me she would go to the eye doctor the following week, so I put her on the phone with Steve. He listened to her discourse then he said,

"Brenda, I'm your friend, but tonight I'm your doctor and I want you to go to the emergency room."

So, off we went to the emergency room, but she wasn't happy with me. We were in the ER till about three in the morning. Brenda shot me another scathing look as she left to go up for a final

CT scan.

She came back down from her test and anxiously waited to leave. The doctor poked his head in the door and said she had to stay. The CT scan showed some irregularities and they needed to do an MRI first thing in the morning.

After the MRI, Steve came in and informed Brenda that she had a meningioma brain tumor sitting on the veins that sent blood to her eyes. This type of tumor grows up the outside of the brain, then starts to dig in. It had been smoldering for a long time, but if she had waited another 6-months she could have been rendered blind.

We found a preeminent surgeon, named Dr. Carl Hamf, and quickly scheduled surgery for the following week. He told us how lucky we were to have a doctor who recognized the symptoms and insisted on the tests that found the tumor. I thanked my lucky stars that Steve May had become a part of our lives.

The surgery took a while, but the doctor felt it had been successful. There were a few difficulties, but she pulled through it and spent her recovery time at home. I had a hard time preventing her from doing too much, but after several months she finally started to feel like herself and returned to a semblance of a normal routine.

In a burst of newly found energy she decided the house lacked storage space, and the black counter tops in the kitchen had to go. Two storage units full of furnishings and assorted items needed to be brought to Nashville from Chicago.

Brenda always saved her expressive words for special occasions. This conversation between Brenda and I can only be told the way it happened. We were having a discourse about the house, and her frustration boiled over.

Brenda: You have too much s**t!"

Bobby: "You have more s**t than I do."

Brenda: "Yes, but my s**t is good s**t."

So, that is how we decided to add on to the house.

If a marriage survives a rehab or a remodeling, it is a strong marriage. This was our third one, so I figured we were veterans at this and what could possibly go wrong. Ha!

We consulted with an architect who presented us with carefully drawn up plans for the expansion of the house. We went to a highly recommended construction company who boasted a first-class project supervisor with an impressive resume. We signed contracts, and the workers started to tear our humble abode apart.

The head carpenter turned out to be a handful, not to mention a petulant argumentative jackass. We assumed the supervisor could control him. Everything was going as planned for about two weeks, then the carpenter got into a climactic violent argument with the supervisor, who told him to "shove it," and walked off the job. Uh oh! We had a long meeting with the carpenter and he assured us he was capable of finishing the job with no problems. (Big mistake! Should have pulled the plug.) We reluctantly agreed since we were already well into the tear down part, but we shared numerous reservations and wondered about the outcome of our decision.

We soon found out! It was a disaster.

Brenda knew five-times as much as I did about rehabbing houses, but she worked her day job, and left me with the animals, trying to make decisions that would have been easier for her. Either way, the chauvinistic males on the crew didn't want to take orders from a woman. Therefore, round and round we went.

My blood pressure pinged at 200.

The roof of the house remained open to the elements, but we had planned a two-day trip to Gatlinburg. Richard Wold, my writing buddy, and his wife Crissy were kind enough to house sit. When we returned, they told us how much fun they had watching the birds fly around the family room.

I won't bore you with the rest of the rehab nightmare, so I'll just skip to the morning that the carpenters didn't show up for work. They figured they owed me a lot more work than I owed them money, and they split for places unknown.

We initiated Plan B! Brenda jumped on the

phone and called her construction crew from Michigan. Dick, Donnie, and one of his sons, came down and lived with us for four months to finish the project. Her crew had to redo many things that the obnoxious Mr. "Know It All" carpenter screwed up, but it was a relief to be back living in a place that wasn't a construction zone. We sent for the contents of the rental units in Chicago, and Brenda's "good s**t" had a new home.

The house rehab almost destroyed two years of my life, screwed up my writing career, and threw everything off track; although I continued to network with publishers, producers, and other songwriters. At least I was able to get back into my studio so I could record some demos, and I could sit down and write a song without air hammers and power saws providing a background percussion track.

Unfortunately, the next ten years were full of medical landmines that I had to navigate, and these issues disrupted my life immensely.

Chapter 58

Brenda's company invited her to attend a meeting at their corporate headquarters in Atlanta, so we thought we'd take a few days and embark on a mini road trip. We planned on driving to Atlanta, then motoring over to South Carolina, coming back through Asheville, and taking the scenic route home through the lofty Smoky Mountains.

We spent a couple of enjoyable, but hectic, days in Atlanta cruised through the scenic Carolinas, and ended up in Asheville... on Halloween. Asheville is a beautiful town; very craft and artist oriented. Downtown is inhabited by a very close-knit group of free spirited talented people, quietly living in a community honeycombed with small Bohemian shops and art galleries. It reminded me of my old stomping grounds, Greenwich Village, when I was hanging out with all the hippie poets, artists, and musicians. This city seemed to be an intriguing quirky place. We were about to find out *how* quirky.

We wandered into a store that sold hand-made jewelry, having encountered an old man with a full white beard, wearing a flowing long robe, holding a Shepherd's staff. We commented to the salesgirl about his creative costume and she said,

"Oh no, that is Irving. He dresses like that all the time."

Well that was just the beginning!

We stumbled upon a delightful sidewalk restaurant, after being entertained by mimes, spray paint artists, tap dancers, and other street performers. We sat at an outside table so we could watch the people passing by. An affable middle-aged couple entered and settled in at the table next to us. We initiated a conversation, and it turned out she had been a schoolteacher in Michigan and now taught in Asheville. Brenda asked her if the kids dressed up for Halloween. A horrified look crossed her face and she exclaimed,

"Oh no, not in Asheville!"

We asked the reason, and she told us that the county was a hotbed for witchcraft, and the kids were not allowed to dress up. Great... and here we were... on Halloween. As we finished our flavorful dinner, we heard what sounded like tribal drums. We queried our dining companions as to what was going on. It seemed that on the day of witches and goblins, the "villagers" assembled in a concrete amphitheater that seated about 200, and had a jam session followed by a raucous celebration in the town square. They informed us that all the shopkeepers, artists, etc., played various percussion instruments. Our curiosity peaked and we decided we'd take a look. We walked toward the drums, and as we reached the celebration, all we could do was stare open-mouthed at the scene before us.

The amphitheater contained about 70 or 80 people dressed in tie dyed hippie garb and a myriad of wild costumes, playing an assortment of drums and innovative noisemakers. A father and his son were fighting an imaginary light-saber duel, wearing Darth Vader costumes. At the center of the free-spirited activities stood a dude dressed like a Russian Cossack (complete with a broadsword), who pounded on a massive drum with a beater that looked like the one used by the Energizer Bunny. A group of gay men were parading around dressed in drag, showing off their dogs costumed in matching flamboyant outfits. A tiny slip of a girl in a long flowing gown danced with her Basset hound, and an angelic looking young lady seemed in a trance, twirling a baby stroller in tight circles.

Then we spotted a woman arrayed in a blue velvet evening gown, lying in the middle of the concrete floor looking like a dead person. One bare leg was ticking straight up in the air, her stiletto heel pointed at the sky. Another young damsel was swaying back and forth with her eyes shut, a dreamy look on her face, and a garland of flowers in her hair. The rest of the celebrants were beating on their drums, following the groove set down by the Russian dude.

All I could think was, "Damn! Those must be some great drugs!"

The dead girl came to life, pulled herself up off the concrete slab, and walked through the crowd. She proudly told people that she was a performance artist. She asked us how we liked her performance. I started to say, "Lifeless," but Brenda gave me "the look."

Mesmerized, we continued to watch the scene playing out before our eyes. After observing the theatrics for an hour, we reluctantly left the bash and walked down the street to grab a nightcap in a small unpretentious bar, before we went back to the hotel. The proprietor told us she would be closing early, as things were about to get rough. As we left, we heard a rowdy crowd a few blocks away, and later found out they were fighting, turning over cars, setting fires, and breaking windows. We ended up on a seedy street with menacing men loitering in doorways, making me glad I carried my .32 magnum revolver. We made tracks back to the hotel and triple locked the door.

The following day turned out to be a day to remember. We headed for the Biltmore Estate. The imposing mansion, the centerpiece of a sprawling estate, sat in the middle of gardens and vineyards that seemed to go on for acres. We parked and wandered down a lengthy pathway to the entrance hall where we signed up for a tour. We walked from room to room and up staircase after staircase! I noticed that I was becoming increasingly short of breath, so I told Brenda we needed to return to the car. Fortunately, we were able to catch a ride in a passing golf cart, as I didn't feel like I could make the walk.

We ordered a light lunch at a small cafe, climbed back into the car, and headed back through the Smoky Mountains toward Nashville. I felt terrible.

I immediately went to see Dr. Steve. He took one look at me and rushed me to a cardiologist. After a battery of tests, she informed me that my mitral valve had broken loose, and my heart was no longer functioning as a pump. It was simply vibrating. I needed surgery, or I'd be leaving the planet within a few weeks.

My cardiologist attended the same medical school as Delos Cosgrove, head cardiac surgeon at the remarkable Cleveland Clinic (rated #1 in the nation). He had no openings for the next three months, but I managed to forge a telephone friendship with his assistant, who told me I'd be her first call if he had any cancellations. I received a last minute phone call from Cleveland. They wanted me to be there "tomorrow." Some guy decided to wait until after Christmas for his procedure, and cancelled. Cosgrove could perform the delicate surgery the following week.

Brenda and I threw some clothes into suitcases and set off for Cleveland, exceeding every speed limit on the way. We arrived at the mammoth campus that surrounded the Cleveland Clinic, and checked into the family/patient quarters.

I started an endless battery of tests at eight a.m. the next morning. In the middle of the afternoon the intercom speakers crackled and asked that Mr. Whiteside report to reception. There had been a change in plans. Cosgrove could operate on me the following day. My head was spinning.

The following morning, the nurses prepped me for surgery at 4 a.m., and we waited. Then we waited some more! At about four o'clock in the afternoon, they wheeled me off and rolled me into a prodigious operating room, filled with giant packing cases. I asked the nurse if they were setting up for a Kiss concert.

"No sweetie, this is all for you."

Terrific! I was glad I was sedated. Then, we waited... and waited again.

Finally, the anesthesiologist put some music on and said,

"Here we go!"

The procedure lasted for 14 hours, and when I woke up the nurse told me that Dr. Cosgrove had successfully performed microsurgery. He sewed my mitral valve back in place, and did some repairs on the tricuspid valve, as he didn't like the way it looked after he entered my heart. I found it hard to believe he performed it through a four-inch incision in my breastbone. Wow! No wonder he was the #1 surgeon in the country.

They called it a non-invasive procedure. Let me tell you, there isn't any such thing. I felt like I'd fallen off a cliff onto a pile of boulders. I remained in Cleveland Hospital for 6 days, then Brenda bundled me into the car to head back to Nashville... in a snowstorm. I painfully discovered that there were a lot of bumps in the road between Cleveland and Nashville, because every time we hit one I felt like I'd been knifed. If I hadn't fastened my seatbelt, I would have been hanging from the roof of the car.

Despite the blizzard and the treacherous highway, Brenda's skilled driving brought us home safely; and I started another long year of rehab. Some days were not so bad, some days I couldn't move. My heart surgeon may have been in Cleveland, but Steve, and my very skilled Nashville cardiologist, monitored my recovery. I felt a sense of calm knowing that my excellent support group was a simple phone call away.

Steve sent me to a Electrophysiologist (a doctor that specializes in heart rhythms) named

George Crossley. He was brilliant, and we hoped he could treat my irregular heartbeats. Over the years, George had to cardiovert (shock) me eleven times, to put my heart back into rhythm. It's scary when your heart is going 360 beats per minute.

Four ablations, and many miracle drugs later, I'm still here.

Dr. Crossley is a rock star.

In 2004, I scheduled a family reunion for my cousins and my sister. Two days before they were due to arrive in Nashville, I slipped on a plastic mat and broke a bone near my ankle. I ended up flat on my back under the carport, with a leg that I couldn't move thinking, "Now what?"

Brenda worked downtown, too far away to be any immediate help. Luckily I had my cell phone in my pocket and was able to reach my neighbor. He called an ambulance, and off I went to the hospital again.

Steve arranged for an orthopedic surgeon to put a plate in my leg, and the night after my surgery I wore out the morphine dispenser pumping it every ten minutes. How the hell could a broken bone hurt that much? I was thinking about the massive dose of morphine I had ingested through the night when the hospital doctor came in and said, "We're going to give you a really strong painkiller."

I flat-ass refused. They poo-pooed me and

firmly insisted that I take the dose, but noted in the chart that it had been administered despite an incredibly vigorous protest from me. So I knocked it down.

Brenda left for the airport to pick up my cousins. On her way back she called the hospital to check on me. The duty nurse told her she couldn't find me. Brenda called shortly after and got the same run-around, so she demanded to speak to a head nurse. After a lot of hemming and hawing, the nurse said, "I'm sorry but there has been an *incident,*" and she told Brenda she would have to talk to the doctor.

My boys always said, "You don't ever want to really piss mom off!"

Blisters flew off the phone and they rapidly located a doctor who told her I had a "code blue" (cardiac arrest). It seems that the nurse came in to take my vital signs, and I didn't have any. I had been overdosed, and was about five minutes away from staying dead. After a monumental reaction from the crash team, they furiously wheeled me up to the drug unit.

Brenda arrived at the hospital like a spinning tornado. When the staff saw the venomous look in her eyes, they tried to stay out of her way as she waited outside the ICU, where they were loading me up with Narcan and every other antidote they could think of. Seven hours later, I finally heard someone shouting at me from a distance, and I slowly regained consciousness. I couldn't believe it. I'd been *killed* having broken-leg surgery.

After taking four bad falls and shattering most of my ribs, the hospital took a full body bone scan. The nurse asked me if I had ever been hit by a car. It seems my ribs looked like a stained glass window.

Welcome to the "Golden Years!" A few of my nuggets have lost their luster, but my sense of humor remains intact, and I consider myself lucky to still be able to enjoy my loving family and some close friends.

Chapter 59

The day Don Pfrimmer died; December 7, 2015, I put my guitar down, and I haven't picked it up since. Part of my musical soul died with Don, and it will take a long time to recover. I think about him all the time. So does Brenda. How does a big tough teddy bear fill my heart and my world in so many ways, that I keep looking around to see if he's really gone? It's one of the bitter mysteries of life.

One day, in the middle of the 90's, my songwriting partner Richard Wold said, "Hey, Bobby! I got a guy you need to meet. His name is Don Pfrimmer. He's in his office. Let's go see him."

We walked over to Don's writing room, knocked on his door and heard an irritated voice snarl, "WHAT?"

Richard pushed open the door and I caught my first glimpse of Don Pfrimmer, an imposing man, despite the Ben Franklin glasses precariously balanced on his nose. We interrupted him in the middle of writing a song. He sat planted in a leather office chair, hunched over his desk, a stubby faded orange pencil in his hand, and a dog-eared yellow legal pad of paper on the table in front of him. The walls of his office were covered by an overwhelming display of gold records.

He glared at us over his glasses. "What the f*** do you want?"

Richard told him we had written three Streisand songs together, and that I'd penned a number one hit for Mindy McCready. He thought Don and I might be able to create some eloquent songs.

Pfrimmer launched an intimidating look in my direction. "Sit your dumb ass down and write something."

And there you have my introduction to Don Pfrimmer.

Years ago, Don established himself as a proven songwriting fixture in Nashville. However, before he arrived he lived a life filled with white-knuckled experiences he almost didn't survive. He grew up near the dense forests in the shadow of the towering peaks of the Rocky Mountains, in Montana. He trekked in the footsteps of his father, a professional guide, and learned to navigate the thick foliage to always find a path home through the endless acres of wooded land. While most kids get a BB gun to learn how to shoot, Don's father presented him with a full size deer rifle. He had just turned seven.

He roamed the mountain range, avoiding the yawning chasms and the towering steep cliffs, ever on the lookout for predators. He moved stealthily through the forest, never breaking a twig, as he hunted deer for food. He caught silver fish almost as big as him, in the glittering glacial lakes. He forged paths up and down the banks of rock-filled mountain streams checking his traps, and sold the harvested furs for spending money. Don developed a quiet strength and a resiliency as a boy that helped shape the man he became. Then somewhere along the line, he developed compassion and a warm heart, and that was the Don Pfrimmer that Brenda and I loved.

He attended school, but it wasn't a priority. He ducked the game warden for sport. He performed an unusual feat of delinquency as he fished with a bow and arrow, perched in a tree, much to the warden's chagrin.

A motorcycle jacket kind of guy, and a pernicious Golden Gloves champion boxer, he lived a rough and tumble life. Although, surprisingly, he warbled an occasional tune with a pleasing voice.

Seventeen, and bored out of his mind with algebra, he decided he wanted to see the world, so he fibbed about his age and joined the army. His sergeant, stunned when he saw how well Don shot a gun, immediately transferred him to the army's sharpshooting team.

Life ran smoothly, until he hurt his back in a surfing accident and the hospital disclosed his real age. The perennial crap hit the fan, and they offered him an honorable discharge, providing he returned to Montana to finish high school. He labored through his last two years and earned his diploma. For whatever reason, or due to some revelations about life in general, he decided to keep going.

Don graduated from the University of Montana in 1965 as an English major with an Art minor. Along the way, he discovered a unique proficiency for writing lyrics. He also developed a penchant for woodwork, something he did till the day he died. Now, when I say woodwork, I mean he built some of the finest crafted statues, lamps, tables, cribs, gates and anything else that could be created from wood. Don became a creative genius when he held lumber in his calloused, but steady, skilled hands. He covered an entire wall of his den with elegant glassed-in china cabinets and an entertainment center that looked like a $7,000 piece of furniture.

Sheepskin in hand, he moved to Kodiak Island, Alaska to teach English to the Eskimos. At times he utilized the skills and the knowledge that he learned as a youth in Montana and hired out as a guide. He survived many harrowing experiences in the wilderness, but secretly the adrenaline rush thrilled him. Plus, he always found that pathway back, as he did in real life, time after time. He thrived on his almost inadvertent misadventures while hosting hunting and salmon-fishing trips, and even worked on a commercial fishing boat in the stormy seas of Alaska before he returned to the lower 48 states. Talk about having an array of stories to pull ideas from!

Don shared a humorous memory. When he first arrived in Alaska, he met some wizened old fishermen, lounging in front of his apartment building drinking local Moose's Tooth beer. They engaged in a congenial conversation and one crusty fellow asked him if he liked halibut. He took that as a welcoming gesture and naturally said yes. He returned home the next night to find a 70-pound halibut leaning against his door. I laughed, and asked him what he did with a 70-pound halibut.

He said, "I filleted that son-of-a-bitch for four hours, froze some, and distributed 50 pounds of fish to indigenous Eskimo families."

Good sport... warm heart! Vintage Pfrimmer.

Finally answering the call of his artistic side, he moved to Nashville in 1970 to pursue songwriting. He never learned to write music, but became one of the best lyricists that ever hit the songwriting mecca of the USA. His efforts were fruitless at first, but in 1978 he composed a smash hit for Mickey Gilley called, "The Power of Positive Drinking," that launched his career.

Don wrote 11 number one records, 20 top twenties, and had over 200 songs recorded. Some of his most notable compositions included:

Front Porch Looking In – Lonestar
Meet in the Middle - Diamond Rio
Mr. Mom – Lonestar
All I Want is a Life - Tim McGraw
She Keeps the Home Fires Burning - Ronnie Milsap
She's Sure Taking it Well - Kevin Sharp
You Put the Beat in My Heart - Eddie Rabbit
You Should Have Been Gone by Now - Eddie Raven

Don also had songs recorded by Marty Robbins, Hank Snow, Barbara Mandrel, Tammy Wynette, Tanya Tucker, George Jones, Eddie Arnold, Wayne Newton, and a host of other true country artists.

Don didn't have it in him to write anything half-baked. He expected perfection from those he worked with, but he was hardest on himself. Don could say more with fewer words than anyone I'd ever met.

I thought I knew how to write a decent song. My successes included five platinum records, three Streisand cuts, and some other respectable credits. I felt confident about my writing abilities—until I met Pfrimmer. Don became my reality, the exposure of how little I really knew, and he laughingly took credit for pointing out the volumes of lessons I had yet to learn about communicating with lyrics.

Writing with him was an educational, mind-expanding experience. He knew every cliché, old title, and idea *not* to use. He taught me the importance of notable first lines of a song, and how I needed to engage people in the first 30 seconds of a record. He wrote openly, honestly, and with such a beautiful simplicity, that I continued to be amazed at how real the world became through Don Pfrimmer's lyrics.

He taught me there were unlimited ways to look at life and be realistic. I went to him with an idea I called "Give Her My Love."

He said, "Explain that idea to me."

I told him the story about a guy who shared a loving relationship with a girl, and lost her to his best friend due to his own selfishness and ignorance. As he stood outside the chapel where they were getting married, he whispered, "Give Her My Love." Nice idea, huh?

Pfrimmer said, "I'd hate that f****n' guy. What a wuss."

Dammit! I never thought about that. Obviously we didn't write it.

Don remained Nashville's true dinosaur, the only writer I knew who still wrote with a pencil and a yellow pad. He said computers stifled his thinking. He finally broke down and bought a smartphone with a recorder in it, much to everyone's surprise.

I'd compose a melody and match it to a title I thought would be appropriate, and he'd come out to the house and accept every new challenge. He'd grab the rough tape of my idea and meander out to the back porch, to mull the idea over while sitting in his favorite rocking chair. He loved the peace and quiet as he gazed at the placid Cumberland River, waiting for inspiration.

He never ceased to amaze me. I remember when Richard Wold and I spent three days searching for that one perfect line for our song "Coming In and Out of Your Life" for Streisand. Pfrimmer accomplished that with every line he wrote, and he did it in minutes.

I refused to write bouncy, meaningless up-tempo songs, so most of the songs Don and I collaborated on were ballad oriented. As 2010 arrived, I knew I would never achieve creative satisfaction by writing bubblegum cowboy rock, which seemed to permeate the airwaves. Country music started to sound like the disco records I produced in the 80's. I loved traditional country and wanted to write songs that could be listened to 20 years from now, not a song that would disappear after a 13 week run on the radio. I suppose I might have been nuts to jump off the bandwagon like that, but at that point in my life, I wanted better; to be better and to write better. Pfrimmer was a tough taskmaster.

Here is an example of a beautiful song we wrote. Don sculpted the lyrics, and in a simple way told a lovely sad story.

WRITTEN IN THE WIND
Pfrimmer-Whiteside

I'm not sorry...that I loved you
I'm just sorry ...it went wrong
Like a footprint...in the soft desert sand
We woke up and it was gone
(Chorus)It was just...what it was...
When all is not enough
Now we know...what we couldn't dream of
then
It's too late ...too bad
The love we had we thought would never end
Wasn't written in the stars
It was written in the wind

It's not our fault...we were honest
We're just victims... of goodbye
It's the mystery... of the thorn and the rose
It's the pain without the why

(Bridge:)
It should have been carved in an oak
Burned on our souls
Announced to the world... hammered in gold

But no...it was written in the wind

It was just...what it was... when all is not enough
Now we know... what we couldn't dream of then
It's too late... too bad
The love we had, we thought would never end
Wasn't written in the stars
It was written in the wind

It was amazing how a big, blustery guy like Pfrimmer possessed a profound understanding of life, coupled with a sensitivity that so few people ever attain. His unshackled sense of humor set him apart from many doomsday seekers, and he would be the first responder to help anyone with a problem.

Don Pfrimmer became one of the most respected and best loved guys in Nashville. He'd write a song with a name country music star, then turn around and work with a little girl from Nebraska who had come to Music City with stars in her eyes, hoping to be a writer. He wrote with Garth Brooks; and many other big acts when they were starting out. Many give him credit for helping them learn how to write.

He fixed my fence, built me an arboretum, designed half the shelves in the kitchen, supports for my speakers, a bookcase for my equipment, and constructed a ramp for me so I could go into the living room in my wheelchair when I broke my leg. He crafted two beautiful end tables out of a barn door to match an antique coffee table that Brenda and I purchased. There was no end to his giving. I can't look around any room in my house without seeing something that Pfrimmer built.

Don always said, "Songwriting is a job! Songwriting is a constant learning process." Some people are born with perfect pitch, some with perfect voices, many with natural musical talent, and others somehow manage to become songwriters. The obvious way to become a songwriter is... to start writing. Some individuals have a flair for words, but most have to start at the bottom, and let their ideas and vocabulary grow with their life experiences.

He advised songwriters: "Write for yourself. Tell your story. Focus on life, not things."

Chapter 60

For any prospective songwriters who read this, here are a few things to note. Always gather ideas from your day-to-day experiences. Keep a notebook of great lines, ideas, scenarios, and any random incidents that might trigger a song somewhere down the road.

Don't be afraid of new technology; just don't let it dictate how you write. Remember a song has a melody and a lyric. Yah Yahs, ee ees, huh huh huhs, and long brassy solos will never get you a record cut; much less a second meeting with an experienced record guy. Keep your demos simple, and avoid long intros and instrumental bridges. Producers are only interested in the song, not how well you play the guitar; although, a good signature guitar riff doesn't hurt if it helps the personality of the song. An A&R man's time is valuable and they hate having writers waste it. But you will learn that by trial and error.

Producers and record guys may smile a lot, but for the most part they really don't give a damn what you think. Your song must sell itself. If you find yourself sitting in a meeting explaining a song, go home and read this paragraph again. You may think you have written the next big Garth Brooks' hit, but the producer probably has ten like it in a pile on his desk. You have a better chance of earning a cut with a mid or up-tempo song. Historically, artists choose most of their ballads before you even know they are looking for material.

When you start to play in clubs with other songwriters, remember you are part of a group. Introduce your song, keep your comments brief, and forget those long intros and solos (unless you are Keith Urban or a top studio player). People go out to hear a variety of songs. After you've written two or three hits, your part of the program will become significantly more interesting.

When you start pitching your material, remember that if a producer likes one of your compositions, he will either take a copy on the spot or call you if he feels it's right for one of his artists. Don't climb on the phone and ask him if he's listened to your song yet. That is the kiss of death. He'll let you know. The wait is the hardest. If three or four months go by and you still believe in that song, submit it again.

Wise to the ways of the music world, Don always tried to advise writers against making obvious missteps that led to the derailing of their aspirations. It's a tough business and anything you can do to avoid mistakes that hurt your career should be underlined in your own book of rules. I filled mine up with *Pfrimmerisms!*

Pfrimmer, a rare artist, who needed nothing but his pencil, pad, and brain, never tuned the radio to a country station while he drove in his truck. He refused to listen to the country charts. He wanted to prevent another writer's catchy lines from ending up in his brain, subsequently interfering with his own creative stream of thoughts. When an original song concept came to him, he wanted to bring the ideas to life with an uncluttered mind, and this also prevented him from inadvertently stealing someone else's music.

The best story about a Pfrimmer song-writing appointment is a marvelous example of how songs appear right in front of you, if you keep your eyes open to life's endless array of notable events.

Don set aside a day to write with Frank Meyers and Richie McDonald, the lead singer of the group Lonestar, out on Richie's farm. When he arrived for his appointment, Richie's horses bolted from the corral. They spent hours catching mustangs and fixing the fence.

At dusk they climbed up on Richie's front porch to quaff a well-earned drink. Don glanced through the window and caught a glimpse of Richie's beautiful family sitting on the living room floor, and sat down and wrote, "Front Porch Looking In," with Richie and Frank. This song became a number one hit record and was the most played record on country radio in 2014.

Don, his wife Gail, and Brenda and I, shared amazing times together. We were family. Gail was the strong woman that every man needs behind him: his love, his conscience, his cheerleader, and his business manager. She made their house into a home for him. She became his confidante, the chairwoman of his life's board, and the hands on the reins that gently slowed the runaway pony that sometimes emerged from Don's constantly active mind. They were perfect for each other. They dated in high school, went their separate ways, and as in any grand love story with a happy ending, they married years later. He found his rock and he knew it. He loved her to pieces. Larry Henley, one of Don's songwriter friends, told Don that Gail inspired him to write "Wind Beneath My Wings."

In 2012, I noticed Don losing weight and his voice sounding raspy. I asked him about it and he continually brushed me off. Finally, one day when he was out at the house, I pinned him down. "What's going on with you? And you ain't leaving here till you tell me!"

He admitted he'd been seeing Dr. Steve, who had run all the tests he could, then referred him to a specialist, a well-known oncologist. He'd been diagnosed with esophageal cancer. I asked him why he'd kept it a secret. He replied he didn't want us to worry about him. Talk about a punch in the stomach. Giving Brenda the devastating news was one of the hardest things I ever had to do.

We were there for him if he needed us, but we respected his wishes to handle things his own way. The doctors subjected him to radiation, but the medical diagnosis pointed toward surgery. This entailed cutting out his esophagus and pulling his stomach up to make him a new one. The night before his operation, I called him to wish him luck and tell him all our thoughts and prayers would be with him. He responded with his favorite Pfrimmerism:

"Go f*** yourself!"

The surgery proved to be incredibly complicated and the rehab; horrible. Forced to suffer through chemo and radiation at the same time, he lost over 70 pounds! His stomach shrank to the size of a fist, and he could barely eat a cup of food at one sitting.

After a long recovery, some elements of the old Pfrimmer began to re-emerge and he started to write again. Occasionally, he made his way to our house for dinner, but his taste buds were shot and he couldn't tell if he was hungry or had ingested too much food. He became tired easily, but felt comfortable enough to fall asleep in the middle of a visit, which we were happy to see him do.

Best of all, he could laugh again, revel in the

reborn joy he found in his newly extended life, and live for the moment with his friends, his loving wife Gail, and his passion for songwriting.

Dr. Steve was over one Sunday afternoon doing some computer work at Brenda's desk. I was tinkering around with a new melody on my keyboard. As it fell into place, and the orchestral parts fit perfectly, it turned a noteworthy piece of music.

Steve looked over at me and said, "Why don't you do an album?"

It was 2015. Frustrated with the business, I thought about doing one last album as a singer, writer, artist, arranger and producer, but I'd make it age-appropriate. I'd been fraught with thoughts about getting old, and how life was changing for me. So I decided to do an album called *Living the Golden Years*.

So many times in the past, during the songwriting process I had to come up with a new line, because the original one made the artist sound too old. I asked Pfrimmer if he would help me rework some of our songs, and make the lyrics apply to life in the golden years. He jumped on it (He didn't pass away till later that year).

The first song, "Living the Golden Years," told the story about my father and the 30 lonely years he had to live without my mother. It set the tone for the album.

Cursed with bulging vertebrae in my neck, it hurt when I raised my head to look at something. So we wrote a song called "When I Look Down" about all the beautiful things you miss when you are looking up, and the whole new world that opens up when you have no choice, but to look down.

Then, we rewrote a song titled "I Want to be 29," about an older dad who wanted to relive the past. We followed that one with a song called "You Are my Anchor," dedicated to Brenda and Gail. We re-worked, "Today Was Not Enough." *Be there for me tomorrow, for today was not enough!*

We finished up with a song I'd started years before, called "This is The Last Song I'll Write For You."

Upon its completion, Pfrimmer looked at me and said, "You son-of-a-bitch! You just had me help you write your epitaph."

-

We sadly watched as Don grew weaker and lost more weight. He developed leukemia. He spent more and more time in bed, and became very reclusive. This guy, normally an ebullient extrovert, couldn't stand to have anyone remember him as sick. He said a few days before he passed away, "I don't want to see anybody. I don't want to cause any of my friends the pain they'll feel when they visit me."

Pfrimmer shared everything, but his pain. As

hard as it hurt not to visit him, we knew he wanted to spend the time he had left with the one person he loved more than life itself, his wife Gail. Some of the words we wrote in our song, "Today Was Not Enough," seem appropriate here.

I cannot believe we'll ever say goodbye
'Cause memories don't erase, and a spirit never dies
Whatever pain I feel is the one thing I won't share
'Cause I'll be part of every breath
You breathe when I'm not there
I'm not afraid to close my eyes. Baby it's okay
I swear to you I won't be more
Than one heartbeat away
Before I go, thank you for your love
Think of me tomorrow, 'cause today was not enough

The only thing that brings even a touch of a smile to my face is one of the last things he said to me.

"Go f*** yourself."

You find so few true treasures in life, especially a rare jewel like Pfrimmer. I knew we'd miss this big man, his big laugh, and the big heart that resided behind his gruff exterior. Don, a true poet, wrote lyrics that could bring tears to my eyes. He fixed my fence, loaned me his truck, and cussed me out the whole time he was doing it. That's how I knew he liked me! Incredibly ethical, he always chose the right path and continued to be a source of inspiration to all to his friends up until the end. Always protective and fiercely loyal, he became my shrink and my father, and his friendship was absolutely unconditional.

Mike Reid, a Hall of Fame Songwriter and a close friend of Don's, summed it up perfectly. "You don't ever get over losing someone like Pfrimmer. You go on, but you don't get over it. The world is just too different without him in it. "

It is only appropriate that I include these lyrics that Don and I wrote for anyone who has lost someone close to them.

HE'S NOT EXACTLY GONE
Bobby Whiteside/Don Pfrimmer

He can't call and he can't ever write
But he checks in on me every single night
We talk awhile and then I fall asleep
I can't keep him-but I can't let him leave me

(Chorus) He's not exactly gone, not exactly here
He's a soul that fills my soul, a voice that I still hear
If I ever really lost him, it would be harder to go on

569

So he's not exactly gone.

All our friends, ask me how I've been
Another year, and spring has come again
Memories of him get stronger everyday
Life may end... but love don't go away

(repeat chorus)

Now I don't care what's real
I only know-what I feel............

RIP, Pfrim! Brenda and I miss you!

Chapter 61

I know I've had to span some years in several of the preceding chapters, but some of the stories needed to be chronicled from beginning to end. So now we roll back the clock to May 2010, when the skies exploded in a burst of bad weather, and rain poured down like a waterfall. The deluge descended in sheets and ominous reports from the weather stations promised no relief in sight. So, it rained—and rained!

The Cumberland River poured four feet of water into the lower level of my house in the late 70's, after which the owner constructed a concrete block seawall around the perimeter of the inner back yard. Since I've lived in the house, the river overflowed its banks several times and crept up into the yard. I breathed sighs of relief when the water failed to rise high enough to breach the wall.

This day started differently. I didn't ever remember seeing deadly darkened skies like that; the rain came down at hypersonic velocity, and the usually predictable river level edged toward the house at an unprecedented rate.

The cataclysmic monsoon started on Friday,

and by Saturday morning I felt new heights of concern. Memphis, located southwest of us, accumulated a freakish 15 inches of rain, and the ferocious storm soon engulfed Nashville. The rain pooled down by the garage, and my straining sump pump couldn't eject the water fast enough to be effective.

The lower level of my house contained a spacious three-car garage, filled to the bursting point with three decades of involuntary suburban hoarding. The garage sat adjacent to a comfortable client lounge that housed a custom bar, a cushy white leather sofa, and a stately antique pool table lit by a stained glass Tiffany lamp.

My recording studio files and the only backup copies of all the music I'd written in the last 50 years were stored on that level. A closet stuffed with electronic gear and musical instruments sat on one side of a fully functional, well-stocked kitchen that we used to prepare food for outdoor lawn parties..

I knew my custom vocal booth, lined with shelves containing dozens of extra cables, small electronics, hundreds of classic LPs, and too many other items to mention would be a problem to empty. Seventy-five photo albums that archived our numerous trips and contained pictures of the children at various stages of their youth were carefully stored in a huge cabinet. The walls of the studio, papered with gold records, awards, photos of past recording sessions, and mementos of various artists I worked with chronicled the history of my career. I shuddered at the thought that all this would probably end up obliterated.

As my concern deepened, I called Brenda downstairs for a brief conversation. "I think we're in serious trouble."

She said, "Let's start picking things up off the floor."

I shook my head. "I don't know how to tell you this, but we'd better start carrying anything worth saving upstairs. I have a terrible premonition about this storm."

We started stripping the walls and carrying all the items upstairs. The rising river didn't threaten some of the neighbors, so they reached out to help those where flooding was inevitable

Several neighborhood men pulled the lawn equipment and power tools out of the garage. I filled Brenda's small convertible with personal items and backed it up the driveway, where another of the neighbors drove it to his house to keep it safe.

A frantic telephone search led us to an available family-owned moving company who assured us they were on their way. I drove to a truck rental place and procured the largest Budget truck I could, then headed to Lowes and bought more than 200 various-sized moving boxes and large quantities of packing materials. Our charitable helpers started to fill cartons and load them into the truck.

At one point there were 35 friends and neighbors working side by side, some of whom I had never met. As chaotic as it seemed, there was a surprising sense of order. Pack and load! Pack and load! Talk about the wonderful people of the South, a godsend and a testament to the good hearts and helping hands of the folks who lived in the neighborhood. Our movers arrived and began to carry the heavy furniture out the door.

The water relentlessly continued its climb toward the house. Mid-day on Saturday it reached the berm. I watched it build up,, and knew only a short time remained before it flowed over the seawall. The punishing work didn't slow our neighbors down, and they worked tirelessly and relentlessly throughout the day. Fifteen inches of rain fell in Nashville.

The Army Corps of Engineers held the responsibility for monitoring lake levels at the dam upstream from us. No one ever figured out what the hell they were doing to control the floodwaters, or in this case, not doing. When they finally showed up (or woke up) they realized if the lake rose another foot, it would pour into the dam and ruin all the hydroelectric machinery that generated power. Had they been diligently managing the floodgates, they could have opened them and initiated a controlled lake dump on Friday. They panicked when they realized what their negligence had contributed to and opened the lock, which let water pour freely from the lake. Due to the miles of river the water traveled between the dam and our location, I figured we had a few hours remaining before the tsunami reached the house. We frantically increased the intensity of our efforts.

Downstairs, our struggles continued to get worse. The septic tank backed up and raw sewage water bubbled out of the toilets and shower drains, causing us to work in the worst possible conditions. Sweat poured from my body and the moisture trashed my iPhone. Brenda dropped hers in the water, so we dispatched someone to Walgreens to pick up a burner phone. We needed a means of communicating. We knew the kids would panic if they couldn't reach us.

The studio, built with hundreds of permanent soldered wire connections, would be impossible to dismantle. I swooped up all the small electronic gear that I could carry, and returned time after time for anything else quickly accessible. I feared that my big recording consoles, all the keyboards, tape machines, computers, furniture, and electronics, were destined to be under water.

When I found myself forging through chest-high sewage, I had to abandon my last ditch efforts and see if I could salvage part of my office upstairs.

I silently thanked Dr. Steve for keeping me current on my tetanus shots. We had no idea of the magnitude of the disaster, or how high the water would ultimately rise.

The upper level of the house had a six-inch drop into the sunken living room and my office. The water rose four inches into that area. Fortunately, the movers and our helpers had removed the furniture from the living room, but my office and most of the equipment it contained, took a hit.

Outside, the river claimed the porch furniture after the legs of the chairs punched holes in our custom screens. The brand new freezer in the garage floated up to bump the ceiling. Dozens of cardboard storage boxes dissolved under water.

We feverishly continued to clean out the upstairs, but when the water level reached the exhaust pipes of the trucks in front of the house, we knew the time had come to evacuate.

Due to the torrent emerging from the open lock in the dam, the river level rose from 36 feet to a peak of 53 feet. It was normally 20 feet deep at that time of year. Our weary neighbors straggled outside. It was 11 p.m.

We pulled the trucks up the street to Carol and Richard McDonald's house, and parked them in their driveway. They generously asked us to stay with them for the night. We gratefully accepted.

As we rushed from the house, we grabbed a few items of clothing, and our pre-prepared emergency to-go bags containing medicine and other necessities. We were only a short distance from the house at Richard and Carol's; and safe from the floodwater.

The following morning we drove down to our home to assess the damage. Our ever-helpful neighbor across the street brought his Jon boat over and rowed us up to the front door.

We entered the house to survey the situation. Ten feet of muddy river water filled the lower level. The bedroom carpets seemed damp but weren't fully soaked. Surprisingly, the water did not invade the clothes closets. 1,400-square-feet of distinctive terrazzo tiles lifted from the sub floors, and most of the finished hardwood boards on the upper level, needed to be replaced due to the moisture that had accumulated in the lower level ceiling insulation. I glanced out the kitchen window to see that the water had risen to within two feet of the roof of my next-door neighbor's house.

By Monday, the river receded and we tried to comprehend the full extent of the disaster. The damage on the Cumberland Riverfront could be described in two words. "Catastrophic!" "Billions!"

The magnificent Opryland Hotel suffered tremendous losses. The hotel, a landmark tourist attraction, featured three cavernous arboretums filled with towering palm trees. The hotel showcased hundreds of colorful tropical plants, shaded walkways and bridges, a peaceful grotto, and two cascading waterfalls. Most of the plush rooms on the first floor, the tastefully decorated hotel restaurants, and dozens of meeting halls, turned into a lake. The adjoining Opry Mills super mall, housing over 200 retail stores, remained closed for almost a year as they rebuilt the massive enclosure.

Downtown Nashville had been hit hard. The recently completed state of the art concert hall suffered massive damage. Water flowed into three sub-floors filled with vintage instruments, and caused millions of dollars' worth of damage to the acoustically magnificent concert hall.

The river surged into a cartage warehouse located on the river, where many musicians stored musical gear. It destroyed dozens of studio drum sets, expensive amplifiers and sound systems, hundreds of beloved guitars, and a multitude of other musical instruments. The stores and clubs downtown were in the process of pumping murky river water onto the street, creating new flooding issues.

Entire neighborhoods up and down the river were wiped out. Some folks carried insurance, and others did not. We were fortunate. I purchased as much coverage as I could and it saved our financial life.

The destruction defied description. The flood took out our air conditioners, wiped out the enormous 220-amp electrical panel.

The studio was a total loss. The billiard room and kitchen were devastated. The smoked glass window wall in the vocal booth broke into shards and the soundproofing started to flake off. The furniture turned into a filthy mess, all the carpets were caked with sewage, and I found the destruction in the garage indescribable. My only back-up music tapes were history, and all of our precious photo albums were mush. Part of the studio ceiling had crashed down on all the equipment.

The ambulance-chasing cleanup companies, the after-a-disaster preying vultures, repeatedly appeared on our doorsteps. The neighbors that flooded were panicked by the threat of mold. So we were forced into quick decisions; instead of making choices after considerable thought and careful perusal of competing estimates.

Brenda and I realized the lower level needed to be torn down to the bare studs. This task had to be completed quickly before bacteria spread up into the house, so we ended up hiring a vulture.

There was nothing like a flood to make me realize how little I really need. A large crew began the cleanup. They shoveled out hundreds of wet piles of sludge. Donna Brooks, our wonderful neighbor, snapped hundreds of pictures of everything they dragged out; to document our losses for the insurance company.

Clearing out the garage turned into a major project. The crew hauled broken items to the refuse pile out by the street. Unbroken objects went into the back yard. Some things, like dishes, survived, even though the boxes dissolved.

The mound out front grew with the addition of discarded lawn paraphernalia, umbrellas, the freezer, the ice box, 4000 classic LP records, awards, framed records from the 60's, books, boxes, and everything else that is generally stored in a big garage.

The studio itself resembled the aftermath of a hand grenade attack. I looked at random stacks of ruined equipment, four-foot high piles of twisted wires and shredded electrical cords, and disintegrating recording tapes strewn all over the room. The custom equipment racks were splintered into jagged pieces. The weathered barn-wood paneling had to come down, and the mirrors imploded under the weight of the falling debris. My hard-shell guitar cases contained puddles of sewage. I could go on and on.

The back yard was a mess. The previously manicured landscaping was a complete loss, and my boat dock, stuck in a tree ten feet above the ground, provided an eerie reminder of the chaos that transpired.

The towering pile of ruined refuse by the street, ballooned to 100 feet long and ten feet high, and stretched across the entire span of our property.

We rented three of the largest climate-controlled storage spaces available and filled them to the top with the contents of the trucks. Our neighbors were always there to help and keep an eye on our possessions, to make sure they didn't disappear.

Our son Terry flew down from Chicago to see if he could help. I found him standing by the garage trying to process the surrounding destruction. He took stock of the giant mound of ruined possessions and the hundreds of pounds of water logged construction materials that had been unceremoniously ripped from the house. He wistfully gazed at remnants of his past, items we owned since he'd been a child that now lay in fragments. We looked at each other.

"Dad, you know you see this sort of thing on the news, but you can't comprehend the damage until you stand in the middle of the remnants of your life."

Reality is a cruel teacher for all of us. Terry had been an enormous help, and gave us a tremendous emotional boost. We hated to see him go back to Chicago.

The lower level became a vast black hole, stripped down to a skeleton of its previous life, an empty shell surrounded by lonely wooden studs. Twenty huge fans and eighteen dehumidifiers ran for a week to dry out the wood. There we were, left with half of a house, trying to figure out how to move on. It took two city trucks and two days, to haul away the pile of debris from the front.

Chapter 62

We knew we needed to find temporary living accommodations for the next six months. We thanked Richard and Carol for welcoming two bedraggled neighbors into the comfort of their home, and informed them that we were moving to an extended stay apartment hotel. They wouldn't hear of it and insisted we live with them for a while.

We ended up enjoying their gracious hospitality for over six months. Being with such wonderful friends helped temper some of our frustration, and dulled the feeling of loss that dogged us during the rebuilding period. I have never in my life met two such warm-hearted people, and we will be friends forever.

When the flood forced us to move out of the house, we left one old faux-leather couch, an antiquated projection TV, and my worn-out desk chair. I took another drive to Lowes, where I purchased an eight-foot long portable table that I set up in the dining room area. I added the couch, my desk chair, and my laptop; then hung long sheets of plastic from the ceiling to create a small, enclosed seating area. I bought a floor air conditioner and a baby refrigerator, and began to utilize my functional construction office, which was cooler than the 100-degree weather outside. With all that plastic hanging down surrounding me, it felt like I was working inside a carwash.

The electricians set up a temporary power box. I ordered Comcast to hook up the Internet and TV so I could use my laptop, or sit on the couch and watch TV if I felt like taking a break. You could find me in my chair by 6:30 a.m. every morning.

We were ready to rebuild the lower level of the house and we brought in a contractor, recommended by several of our neighbors. In retrospect, I never figured out what they saw in him, as he turned out to be a monumental flake.

I never knew if he was going to show up with five guys, or just a bottle of vodka and the girl who swept the floors. He began to shore up the ceiling joists, but I found his work to be sub-par. Then, there were days he didn't show up at all. I couldn't help but think, "Here we go again!"

Stuck in a serious quandary, and handcuffed by an untenable situation, I relayed my tale of woe to a friend of mine.

He came up with a solution. "You have to meet Lennie and Carlos."

They practically built his entire house and he

couldn't have been more complimentary toward them. Lennie and Carlos, two affable Hispanic brothers, appeared at the door. Lennie spoke English, Carlos... not so much. Lennie walked around to inspect what had been done to date. I heard him say, "Umm," several times.

I asked him what umm meant and he said, "No good!"

We hired them on the spot. The first day, a crew of nine men showed up and reworked everything that my first contractor messed up. Lennie's men functioned like a superbly trained professional sports team. Every worker knew his responsibilities, and managed to perform them seamlessly.

They installed new plywood to prepare for the installation of new hardwood. I drove to a lumberyard and picked up the heavy boxes of oak flooring. I pulled up in front of the house, my truck dragging the ground under the weight of the ponderous cartons. One of Lennie's pint-sized supermen was working outside. I pointed to the flooring and suggested that he get some help to unload it. He laughed at me, picked up a box under each arm, and ran them into the house, leaving me speechless.

The reconstruction lasted through October when we finally had a dry bedroom, the stove was hooked up and we could sit in my little plastic enclosure. Painting, tile, and a slew of other dust-creating finishing touches remained. The heat, air, and electric were functioning, so we moved back into our barren, but livable abode.

Looking back, I don't know how we ever finished that monumental project. I never want to live through anything like that again. In fact I don't think I *could* live through anything like that again.

It felt wonderful to write music in peace and quiet, despite the fact that the finishing touches continued until the end of the year. As our next-door neighbor rebuilt his home, he slept on a cold concrete floor, so we invited him to come and crash with us. He lived with us for six months, until his house was habitable, our way of paying it forward.

A marine construction company pulled my dock out of the tree, rebuilt it and hauled it back into the water. It seemed to be the seemingly endless little things that wore us out.

I've attempted to paint a vivid picture of the flood, the damages, and the rebuilding, but it's so hard to explain the emotional impact that results from a catastrophe like this. Victims of a crime feel violated. People hurt in accidents end up traumatized. However, when someone lives through something this serious, they experience many different emotions. We felt a sense of loss. Our family pictures, 50 years' worth of music, my livelihood, and so many of Brenda's and my precious possessions were gone forever. We felt a sense of displacement from being out of our house for six months, having to live somewhere else.

I considered myself lucky. I've always handled adversity well, and Brenda has a backbone made of steel. We were ripped from our previously impregnable island by a freak act of nature. Words from my father shaped our future: "Get over it!"

We couldn't afford to remain lost in the past and needed to focus on the future; the only path we could take in order to move on. We strove to make new memories. I constructed a new studio, and created new music. We felt incredibly blessed that we still had each other, and could rebuild and re-energize our lives together.

We spent the rest of that year setting the engine of our lives back on the track from which it had been so callously derailed. When the dust settled for good, I bought the biggest computer available, and filled it up with all the music software I could find. I created a compact studio control room. All the mixing boards, the space consuming hardware, and mounds of equipment that had previously filled a large space, were now located in an Apple computer tower as software. I packed the hard drive with libraries of drums, orchestras, voices, and every other program that I could find in the music section at the computer store.

Chapter 63

The learning curve for my new studio pointed straight up, and it took me most of the following year to learn how to write and produce sessions in an entirely different fashion. By the end of the year, I felt I'd acquired enough knowledge to be comfortable, recording in my small office on the *upper* level of the house. Never again would my music be jeopardized! I figured if we ever had another incident, I could grab my computer and run out of the house, and my music would be held safely under my arm.

Thousands of sounds, instruments, and voices had become available to me on my home computer. I could start a track at the house with library sounds, then take it to a major studio in Nashville and add live musicians. At that point, I could bring the computer file home and continue adding parts from my music programs and mix everything down on my Mac. It made it easy to slide back into the musical production world.

I focused on songwriting again. The business changed. The record labels were consolidating. When I first moved to Nashville, there had been at least 30 record labels to pitch songs to, but the number decreased significantly. There were fewer producers and A&R men to play country anthems for, as the companies cut their staffs with each corporate takeover. When I moved into town, there were 20,000 writers. Then, the number began to dwindle, and today there are less than 1,000 actually making a living at songwriting; without holding down a second job.

I was more than ever determined not to write songs about pickup trucks and beer, so I focused on writing songs that made me happy. I especially enjoyed creating music with my pal, the brilliantly prolific Pfrimmer, who was still with us at this time. I also composed some new material with another "song machine:" Tim Johnson.

Tim established himself as a hit writer by formulating a host of number one songs. He unselfishly dispensed his talent to the Nashville community, by writing lyrics and melodies that were recorded by many country artists. Tim possessed his own style, and a dramatically unique touch in his approach to musical concepts. We collaborated on many songs, including "Brinks Truck" that Randy Travis recorded.

Tim was a facetious character who was horrible about returning phone calls. However, when I finally tracked him down, the results were always stellar.

One late afternoon, Brenda and I were driving

home from downtown and my phone rang.

It was Tim. "Where the hell are you guys?"

I asked him what he was talking about. He sounded like he was in a snit. He said that we were supposed to be at his house for dinner. I didn't remember ever getting an invitation, but I looked at Brenda.

She said, "Whatever!"

I turned the car around, and drove 25 miles to Tim's farm. We arrived and he was laughing his ass off.

"Gotcha."

Vintage Tim! Despite his shameless antics, we enjoyed Tim and his lovely wife, Megan, and we spent many uproariously entertaining evenings together.

I noticed that Tim looked pale and sickly. He had been diagnosed with pancreatic cancer. We were stunned... he just turned 51. On October 21, 2012, he passed away; leaving a gigantic hole in the world of songwriting, and a painful time for his family, friends, Brenda, and me. I treasure many warm memories of Tim and he is forever present in the music we created.

When it came time to record my album, four of the songs were written with Tim. I tailored some of the lyrics to target old guys like me, but his music, his heart, and his distinctive style shine through in the music.

I never ceased to be impressed by the people I worked with. I'd been fortunate enough to record with many of the top professionals in the business, each with their own unique talents. Even after all these years in the business, it still amazes me that I continue meeting people who inspire me and fuel my desire to make music.

Moving to Nashville turned out to be one of the best decisions I ever made. The friendships run deep, the talent is immense, and it was a perfect place to land after such a bumpy ride.

The next couple of years were marred with some more heart issues that slowed me down, but I continued my quest to create intelligent and meaningful music. Life passed at a markedly slower pace and, after losing Tim, I realized how easily life could end abruptly. I became even more aware that time was becoming an increasingly valuable commodity, not to be frittered away.

Chapter 64

There were no pressing musical challenges on my immediate horizon, so I decided to take Steve May's advice and record my last album. I turned 74 and had the desire to leave something substantial behind that *my* generation could relate to. *Livin' the Golden Years* went into full writing mode. Fortunately, Don was still alive at that time, and we were able to rewrite the songs I told you about earlier. Then, I penned two songs by myself.

The idea for the first song, "You Don't Have to Get Up in The Morning," came from an old joke about a guy whose doctor informs him that he is going to pop off in the morning. His wife is less than sympathetic. I thought it was hilarious. My kids called and asked me if there was something I wasn't telling them.

When Brenda said, "That's jaded," I knew I had a winner.

Then, I came up with a song called, "The Playground." It flashed back to the time before cell phones and iPads became a way of life. Kids actually played together on playgrounds and communicated with each other by speaking instead of texting.

Then I reworked another song from my past, written with Chuck Leonard. "Old Hands," the story of a grandfather who felt no one needed his "old hands," ends like a Hallmark movie when he finds out that his grandson needs him.

Next I dove into Tim's songs. "So Little Time," and "I Will Know That I Was Loved," then I followed up with "You'll Never See a Brinks Truck Follow a Hearse," (cut by Randy Travis), and ended up with one of my favorite songs, "Live For The Love of Life."

After completing the lyric rewrites, I began the process for creating the album. I finished the title song, "Living the Golden Years," and I was off on a journey that would take me a better part of two years. I recorded basic layout piano tracks, then added bass, strings, oboe, horns, choirs and percussion. I performed these instrumental parts on my piano keyboard, hooked up to my computer. Not being the greatest piano player of all time, I spent weeks working into the wee hours of the morning, editing out and fixing mistakes I'd made, and the computer enabled me to write in new notes where necessary.

Finally, after months of recording and editing, I completed as much music as I could in my home studio, and it was time to move on.

My friend Jimmy Nichols, one of my favorite studio musicians, replaced six of my simplistic piano parts with flowing keyboard tracks at his own studio.

I went to Beard Recording Studios in Nashville where I added electric guitar, acoustic guitar and live drums.

Following my session at Beard, I took the tracks over to another studio owned by Kenny Mims, a genius electronics guy, and a master at recording vocals, where we put background vocals on all the tracks. Then I spent the next three weeks with Kenny singing the lead vocals. In the following weeks, I went to three terrific studios, where I worked side by side with Matt McClure, Bob Bullock, and Bob Bennett (three of the industry's foremost engineering wizards) to mix the tracks down for the final compilations for the master record.

Since the whole process had been recorded on computers there were no problems transferring the song files from studio to studio. Finally, the record was mastered. We pressed up some copies and I took the first one to Don. I was gratified that he was able to hear the finished songs before we lost him.

At the end of 2016, I hadn't quite recovered from the long sleepless nights I spent producing the album. Bobby Delich, my good friend, literary coach, and original drummer in the "60's," came to visit me.

"What are you working on?"

"Writing a song or two!"

We visited and reminisced about the good old times, and the humorous anecdotes were numerous.

He laughed and said, "You gotta write a book!"

So, here we are.

Chapter 65

A butterfly starts life in a cocoon, evolves into a caterpillar, and finally emerges as a butterfly. The butterfly is a magnificent creature that gracefully dances from flower to flower, sharing its kaleidoscopic beauty with the world. Then, it simply disappears.

This metamorphosis is very similar to a person's life. You start as an embryo, go through the learning years, after which you meander through adulthood, sharing your individual skills and unique talents with a multifaceted social order. Eventually, you reach the disappearing part. Unlike the butterfly, you are still alive during these last years, but you have disappeared from the eyes of mainstream society, and you feel like you exist in an altered state, often devoid of acknowledgement.

I am presently living in the Golden Years. In the old days when I was younger, confident, and on top of the world, people noticed me and nodded, and smiled. However, now that vibrant young guy from the past is an old man leaning on a walker, the smiles and nods have all but disappeared, and I am acutely aware of the fleeting, sympathetic looks that emulate from well-meaning people. I may have physical limitations and boundaries, but fortunately there are no impenetrable walls that exist to close off my thoughts. It's sad that only I know that.

I have a hard time accepting the fact that I am no longer bullet proof, and when I look in the mirror I see the chapters of life, deeply etched into my face by time. The mountains I have left to climb are but gentle hills, and the valleys are immeasurably deeper. On the other hand, in light of the fact that my world is shrinking, I've been compelled to discover myself.

My address book is filled with forgotten names of lost friends, and relatives I don't contact often enough. I spent years seeking happiness. Now I find myself seeking relevance. I know that time is not my friend and life's last reprieve, but ironically I have too much of it on my hands. In any event, I suppose that beats the alternative.

Living in the twilight of my life, every so often I find myself floating in the remains of my perceptions from the times I can remember. I may have limited mobility, but thankfully, my mind is undeniably free to wander.

I am so lucky that Brenda, my rock and my never-ending essence of encouragement and inspiration, is still in my life. I have never been more in love than now. My family is my strength, the fountainhead of the devoted, unselfish affection that keeps this old man going. I view the changing world with cynicism; sorry I'm not young enough to help make it better, but glad I'm the age I am, so I won't have to live in a society I take umbrage with. As grandparents often do, I can't help but worry about my grandchildren, and fervently hope that they will be able to navigate around the inevitable landmines buried along the pathway they must follow to grow up.

I'm not bitter about being old, but I feel a sense of frustration at times, when my body won't do what my mind tells it to. There's this involuntary tremor in my hands that makes my signature look like it belongs on a prescription, and my rascally little fingers keep typing extra letters on the computer that I don't authorize. Despite all that, the most significant directive I have in my living will is:

"When I lose my sense of humor, pull the plug."

When I turn the last page of the book, and there are no words left to write, the story ends. Recriminations dwindle with the passage of time, and I no longer feel remorse over erstwhile bad choices. Shoulda, coulda, woulda's are irrelevant, but being human, no matter how hard I try, I can't stop feeling a nagging touch of futility.

I live in my memories, cherish the people I treasure, and struggle to hold on to the friends who are now so few and far between. My daydreams leave me with beautiful thoughts, and I find myself at peace in the surreal world that surrounds me. I'll fight to live another day, but I realize that when it's over, it's over, and it is what it is.

I've had a blessed life and I hope it continues for a long time, despite my creaky bones and the gettin' around issues. Sometimes I find myself searching for a word that eludes me, and recalling a name takes an increasing amount of thought. Although, in the scheme of things, I guess that's not important. My mind is getting older, too.

If I was still able to drive I'm sure I'd lose the keys, and maybe my way, once in a while. My heart no longer beats like a metronome, but it still beats. Home is my haven, and the love and the warmth that flows from my family, will keep me content for whatever time remains in my life.

But is it time for the last song? Well, this is the last song on my album.

This is the last song I'll write for you
You've been my soul... you've been my inspiration
You've been in every note I played
And every tear...that ever filled my eyes
Here's to all the years
And here's to us and here's to you
As the ending nears

I still can hear the echo
Of the first time...you said, "I love you"

This is the last song I'll write for you
So listen now, in case you missed
Some of the words I wrote before
And then you'll know that it was you
Who filled my life with so much more
Than words could ever say

There's no tomorrow
There's only yesterday
And I can't borrow...any more
Of someone else's time
And so I'm leaving, not easily
Cause loving you the way I do, it's time to set you
free

This is the last song I'll write for you... and for me

So, is this it? Is this the last song?
Hmmm. Maybe I'll pick up my guitar again, and start writing a beautiful New Age album.

Maybe...

AVAILABLE
ON:
AMAZON
and
ITUNES

1. LIVING IN THE GOLDEN YEARS   (Bobby Whiteside)
2. OLD HANDS   (Chuck Leonard Bobby Whiteside)
3. YOU DON'T HAVE TO GET UP IN THE MORNING (Bobby Whiteside)
4. I WILL KNOW THAT I WAS LOVED (Bobby Whiteside, Tim Johnson)
5. LOVE OF LIFE (Don Pfrimmer, Tim Johnson, Bobby Whiteside)
6. WHEN I LOOK DOWN (Don Pfrimmer, Bobby Whiteside)
7. BRINKS TRUCK (Bobby Whiteside, Tim Johnson))
8. SO LITTLE TIME (Bobby Whiteside, Tim Johnson)
9. TWENTY NINE Don Pfrimmer, Bobby Whiteside)
10. PLAYGROUND   (Bobby Whiteside)
11. YOU ARE MY ANCHOR (Don Pfrimmer, Bobby Whiteside)
12. TODAY WAS NOT ENOUGH (Pfrimmer-Whiteside)
13. LAST SONG   (Don Pfrimmer, Bobby Whiteside)

PRODUCED AND ARRANGED BY BOBBY WHITESIDE
MUSICIANS: Bobby Whiteside, Jimmy Nichols, Eddie Bayers, Tommy Hardin, Dennis Holt, Pat Bergusen, Larry Beard
BACKGROUND SINGERS: Kim Keyes, Tabithe Fair, Vickie Carrico, Michael Black, Lala Deaton
CHOIR: Arranged by Robert Bowker; Singers: Robert Bowker, Jeff Morrow, Bonnie Herman, Judy Storey
RECORDING ENGINEERS: Jim Deblanc, Bobby whiteside, Kenny Mimms, Jimmy Nichols,
MIX ENGINEERS: Bob Bullock, Mat McClure, Bobby Bennet
COVER DESIGN: Susn Erwin

CPSIA information can be obtained
at www.ICGtesting.com
Printed in the USA
LVHW052012150222
711021LV00002B/2